1 BRIEF,
50 DESIGNERS,
50 SOLUTIONS

IN FASHION DESIGN

1 BRIEF, 50 DESIGNERS, 50 SOLUTIONS

IN FASHION DESIGN

ROCKPORT PUBLISHERS
BEVERLY MASSACHUSETTS

First published in 2011 in the United States of America by
Rockport Publishers, a member of Quayside Publishing Group
100 Cummings Center
Suite 406-L
Beverly, MA 01915-6101
Telephone: (978) 282-9590
Fax: (978) 283-2742
www.rockpub.com

ISBN-13: 978-1-59253-713-6
ISBN-10: 1-59253-713-8

10 9 8 7 6 5 4 3 2 1

Publisher: Paco Asensio
Editorial coordination: Anja Llorella Oriol
Editor and texts: Natalio Martín Arroyo
Art director: Emma Termes Parera
Layout: Esperanza Escudero
Cover image: Ferran Casanova /Blue Studio, for Juan Vidal
English translation: Cillero & de Motta

Editorial Project:
maomao publications
Via Laietana, 32 4th fl. of. 104
08003 Barcelona, España
Tel.: +34 93 268 80 88
Fax: +34 93 317 42 08
www.maomaopublications.com

Printed in China

Contents

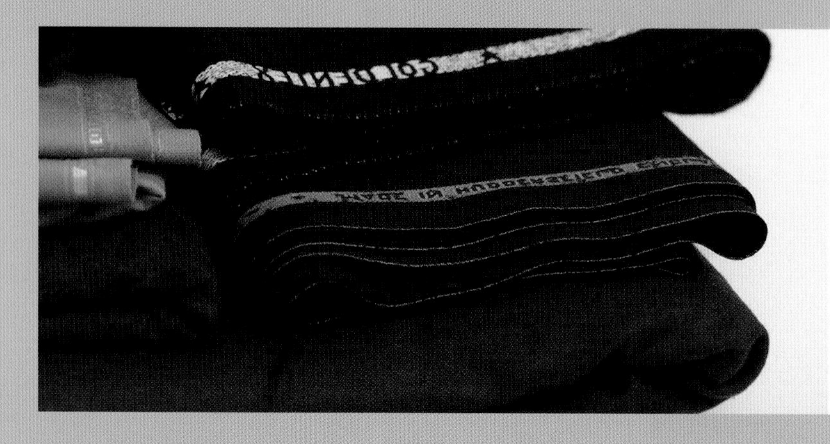

PASSION FOR FASHION

A book that includes the word "solutions" in its title brings to mind promises and a commitment to provide remedies to situations that we may have to face in the future. As it isn't my intention to disappoint you, I propose to offer solutions to situations that arise for this single purpose, thanks to the collaboration of 50 designers who want to share their experience and secrets in something as intimate as their creative process.

Many of you will recall the rebuke Andy Sachs (Anne Hathaway) earns in the film *The Devil Wears Prada* from her boss Miranda Priestly (Meryl Streep) about the route taken by cerulean from when Óscar de la Renta presented his first collection in that color until much later, when it appeared as the season's color in department stores all over the world, representing millions of dollars to the fashion industry. It's a vain discourse, but a truly admirable one because of the great amount of knowledge it conveys.

It isn't easy to know how the complex fashion industry operates. There are always new things to learn, details, and curious facts. What happens for a color no one has ever heard of to appear in all the international fashion magazines in a matter of months? Where do trends start? What cultural influences are in a collection? What software do computer-aided fashion design experts recommend?

This is a book for inquisitive people, for those keen to know all the ins and outs of fashion in a practical way. This is why, before seeing how each of the designers works, we give an overview of the creative process in fashion, backed by views from specialists. This is a base from which to understand the workings of an industry none of us are ever free from. So we can all be a little more Miranda Priestly, because, like her, you and I have a great passion for fashion.

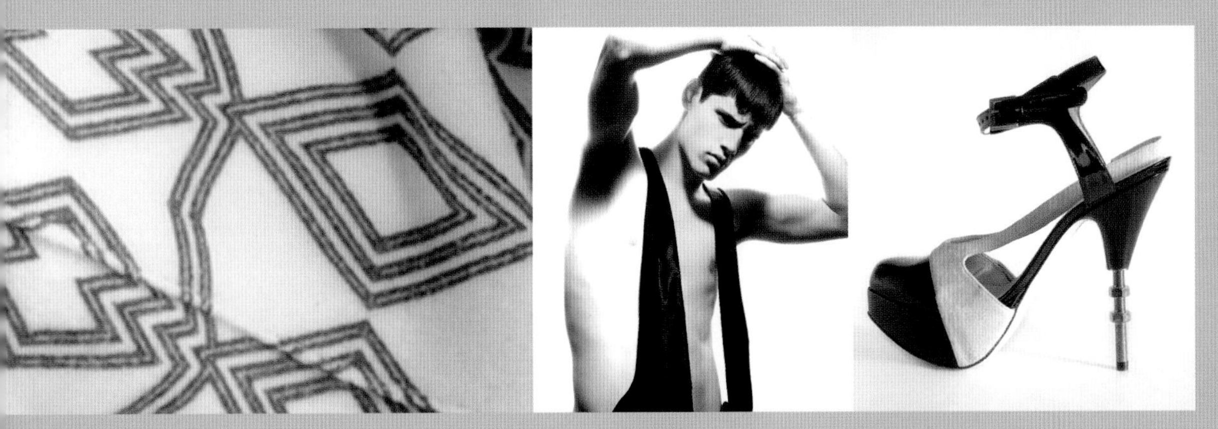

On the previous page, selection of fabrics from Mason Jung for his project Sleeping Suit and look by Taro Horiuchi. **Above**, printed fabric from Alexi Freeman's latest collection, Lucien Thomkins in a vest by FXDXV (photo by Rull&Ferrater), and shoes by Amaya Arzuaga, fall/winter 2010/11.

Knock knock... Come in!

It is wonderful to have 50 designers willing to open the doors to their ateliers and to show us how they work, how they develop an idea from start to finish, regardless of whether they are established designers with brilliant careers, young designers straight out of prestigious fashion schools, or multi-faceted artists who have found a new form of personal expression in fashion. In the time it has taken for this book to come together, I've had the pleasure of sharing a coffee or a moment's conversation with some of them, getting to know their personal stories. Each designer has a very different profile, and perhaps the most fascinating thing is discovering the human face behind each name, behind each label.

I underscore the word "human" because a garment, in the end, is designed by a person based on their particular taste, feelings, and inspiration, and it ends up being part of another's wardrobe, that of a person who identifies with the designer's style. This is why, when the challenge of setting out a briefing for 50 designers, I decided it should be related to people (person vs person), in this case with *It girls* and *It boys*.

If a designer could choose his or her *It girl* or *It boy*, would they have a name? What would be their modus vivendi? And above all, how would they dress? Under the heading "Dressing my It," the designers have the opportunity to give a subtle outline of their ideal, to tell us who they design for, who their inspiration is, and to show us their creative process.

Image from the ¿Por Qué Todo Ha de Ser de Color Rosa? (Why does everything have to be pink?) collection for fall/winter 2010/11 by Manuel Bolaño.

DRESSING MY IT

The term *It* was coined by the novelist and screenwriter Elinor Glyn, who used it to describe the actress Clara Bow as she appeared in the 1927 Hollywood silent movie *It*. According to Glyn, "*It* is the quality possessed by some which draws others with its magnetic force. With *It* you win all men if you are a woman – and all women if you are a man. *It* can be a quality of the mind as well as a physical attraction."

In recent decades the term has progressed, picking up different connotations depending on the moment. There was a time when it was used as a derogatory adjective associated with the exaggerated eccentricity of very pretty and stylish girls who did nothing else but worship their own beauty. However, in the present day, people look for much more than beauty, elegance, or friendliness in an *It girl* or in an *It boy*. They seek an exciting lifestyle, a unique profession, or a different way of thinking. The Internet has given us an evolved meaning, thanks to the fashion bloggers, who find in it the perfect means through which to tell the world what their favorite collection of the season is, or how they dressed for an event, or how many pairs of shoes they have in their closets. Fashion students, models, musicians, designers, actors, photographers, and stylists, among others, are the new stars of cyberspace who have managed to attract the attention of fashion designers and international magazines.

The terms *It girl* and *It boy* can be defined as people with great powers of attraction who know how to use them, who dress fashionably, are trendsetters, and who have a particular lifestyle that many people see as exciting.

Portrait of Prince Pe
by illustrator Jorge Herrera
(www.jh-neo.com)

INTERVIEW WITH THE QUINTESSENTIAL IT BOY

PRINCE PELAYO

His name is Pelayo Díaz Zapico, although many know him as "Prince Pe." He was born in Oviedo, Spain, in 1986. He lives in London, where he studies fashion design at the prestigious Central Saint Martins College of Art and Design. In 2007 he set up his blog Katelovesme in honor of his much-admired British fashion model Kate Moss. In three years Pelayo has become the most famous It boy, a true e-celebrity dandy, a symbol of the Me Generation, who enjoys talking about his flirting with the world of fashions and trends, turning up at the coolest parties in London, Milan, Barcelona, and New York, or a day out shopping with his also popular friend and It girl Gala González (am-lul.blogspot.com). We've seen him in magazines the world over, his name appears in hundreds of blogs and on websites, and he sits in the front row in shows such as those by Dsquared or Dolce & Gabbana in Milan and Neil Barrett in Paris. This can all be attributed to his personal style, his way of dressing, his overwhelming personality, and his honest way of expressing himself.

Where can you find him?
Blog: www.katelovesme.net

Social networking sites:
twitter.com/princepelayo
chictopia.com/katelovesme

Of interest:
We measured his media impact through his hits in Google. We googled "katelovesme": 75,000 results; we googled "Prince Pelayo": 80,600 results; we googled "Pelayo Díaz Zapico": 31,000 results (June 2010).

You started your blog Katelovesme on March 9, 2009. Your first post opened by saying: "Someone starting a blog knows they won't have many visits anytime soon because these things take time..." While you were writing it, did you ever think that in only two years you would come to have over two and a half million visits? Doesn't it take your breath away to think that 4,000 people are following your life every day?

It's true that when I started to write Katelovesme I already had a very small following, but I had been expressing myself on another platform where I was continuously being censored, until I decided not to go back there. I remember the first time I pressed the counter on my blog, almost a year later, and I was overwhelmed. I thought, "Wow! 4,000 people a day, this has definitely changed." But, despite what people think, nobody follows my life. Readers only follow the little part of it that I let them follow.

Soon they labeled you "It boy." According to Glyn, It is the quality possessed by some which draws others with its magnetic force. If this is so, what do you think there is in you that arouses that attraction?

I don't know if I have magnetic force to attract others, but it's probably my lifestyle and my way of saying things that keep people curious to know what I'm up to. I think everybody is special and everybody has a great way of looking at life. Maybe my way of looking at it is my magnetic side.

What do you like most and least about being a famous It boy?

What I like most is the number of people I've met. They're people I would have met sooner or later, but this means has made it easier for me. And least? The fact that there are people who believe they know me and have the wrong idea about me, but that's life...

Images posted on Katelovesme.
Bottom right, photo by Ricardo Hegenbart.

Your media impact does nothing but grow. You've done advertising campaigns and dozens of articles have been published about you in magazines like *Nylon*, *GQ*, *Vogue Korea*, *Vanidad*, *L'Officiel Hommes*, *H Magazine*, and *i-D*. What other benefits do you believe you've gained by making yourself known through Katelovesme?

It doesn't matter what you do in life. A little media impact is always good to make yourself known, for the world to hear about you. For me, this road is simply something that, by chance, has prepared me for when I graduate and decide to let people know what I do.

I recall an interview where you confessed that all of the "benefit" your blog brings you is pure coincidence and that you future is in the real world, in the things you don't tell people. Could you at least give us some clues as to what you'd like to be in the future and what values are behind your endeavor to achieve this?

In the future I'd like to have my own label, to live from it. I'd like to put my point of view into my own collections and have the women (and men) of the planet continue to read about me when they open a magazine or look at a blog. And values? Those I learned as a child: hard work, honesty, and perseverance.

Model, stylist, coolhunter, designer... You're multifaceted and fit in with any role you set for yourself in fashion. Perhaps the part we know least about you is that of a designer, which you are receiving excellent training to become. Are you afraid there will be too many expectations of your work as a designer?

Sometimes I wonder if everything I'm doing is enough... Then I wake up and realize that I simply never stop doing things. I don't care what people think while I have a reason to be a designer and there are people buying my clothes. And if I don't become a designer, there are thousands of different jobs in the fashion world that pay better and let you live with less stress.

Some of the magazines Pelayo Díaz has been featured recently. Photo by Saga Sig.

PELAYO DIAZ ZAPICO

FOTOGRAFÍA: PANTELIS

Diseñador de modas, modelo, stylist, escritor, lo que se proponga logra hacerlo con éxito y sobre todo con mucho estilo. "Pe" se ha convertido en el nuevo darling del mundo del ciberespacio, gracias a su blog - http://katelovesme.blogspot.com/ - en donde podemos seguir sus aventuras alrededor del mundo, siendo parte de las mejores fiestas y eventos de moda.

028 STATUS 029

Picture taken from an article on Pelayo published in *Status Magazine* in 2008. Photo by Pantelis.

Here's a game. We give you five words, five professions associated with fashion: assistant, designer, art director, model, and stylist. Could you tell us whom you would work for in this role and why?

Assistant: Anna Dello Russo. I know her and I am sure it would be so much fun arranging her trips and her wardrobe. I'd have a great time!
Designer: Balenciaga. Some day this label that was originally from Spain – more specifically from the north, like me – should return to Spanish hands.
Art director: Givenchy. I love Ricardo Tisci's way of seeing the Givenchy man, and it has a great deal in common with my ideas.
Model: Dsquared. I love the models they work with. I want to be one!
Stylist: For any photo session with Steven Klein.

We've seen you surrounded by great designers like Dsquared and David Delfín, working at Giles Deacon's studio, and dressed by new fashion talents like Katie Eary. Besides, you're always present on the international runway circuit and at countless parties and fashion events. Do you find that such an intense association with fashion as the one you have with it helps when it comes to designing or, on the contrary, does so much information overwhelm you? What inspires you?

The truth is that when I'm with Dean and Dan, or with David Delfín, the last thing we talk about is fashion. However, everything helps: the parties I've been to thanks to them, the places I've visited, the people I've met, the experiences I've lived, the clothes they lend me, the runway shows I see, and the trips I make – it all forms part of that self-sufficiency a designer or any creative person needs.

If you had to design a look for your beloved Kate Moss, what would it be? And how about one for you?

It would be a long dress (my speciality) with a leather jacket on top. And for me? It would have to be some torn jeans and the same leather jacket.

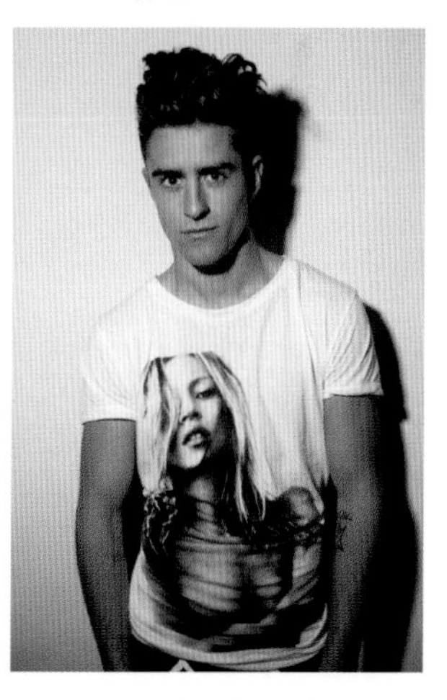

Photos posted on Katelovesme. **On the left**, Pelayo dressed by Katie Eary. Photo by Saga Sig. **On the right**, Pelayo dressed by David Delfín. Photo by Kiko Buxo. **Below**, Pelayo in a leather jacket. Photo by Zach Burns.

THE CREATIVE PROCESS IN FASHION

1 Briefing

"Creativity is the result of hard and systematic work." Peter Drucker

Briefing is a very common practice in the day-to-day operations of companies in different sectors, particularly in the advertising industry, although its use is increasingly gaining ground in others such as fashion. Generally, a brief is an accurate written description of the parameters a product must be based on in order to reach and satisfy the needs of demand as much as possible. Briefing is an important tool when designing a product. It helps to order and plan all of its possibilities, its market feasibility, and, at the same time, it sets the guidelines to support the creative process. In fashion, briefing comes at the start of any creative project that can be set for fashion designers or other professionals in the industry, like stylists or art directors. The brief will respond to questions such as: What product is going to be brought out? Who is it for? Why? How will it be made? A good example of how a fashion designer should respond to very different briefs are the collaborations that are often – and increasingly more so – carried out by prestigious designers with other fashion firms or with companies from other sectors. This is how Karl Lagerfeld came to design a bottle for Coca-Cola Light – the name given to Diet Coke in Europe – with his personal hallmark; Gwen Stefani designed the uniforms for the W Hotel female bar staff through her fashion label L.A.M.B.; and Sonia Rykiel designed a collection for H&M. They all followed the brief based on the parameters set out by the other companies, and they interpreted it to contribute their personality and philosophy to new products.

Limited-edition Coca-Cola Light bottle illustrated by the designer Karl Lagerfeld in 2010.

There are as many types of briefs as there are works that can be commissioned. Any creative brief can be restricted, requiring the designer to produce very specific and detailed work, or open, allowing more flexibility in the search for creative solutions. In general terms, the basic information that should be contained in a brief is, on the one hand, the information related to the company one is working for (product or service, market, and consumer), and, on the other, that corresponding to the work to be carried out and its aims.

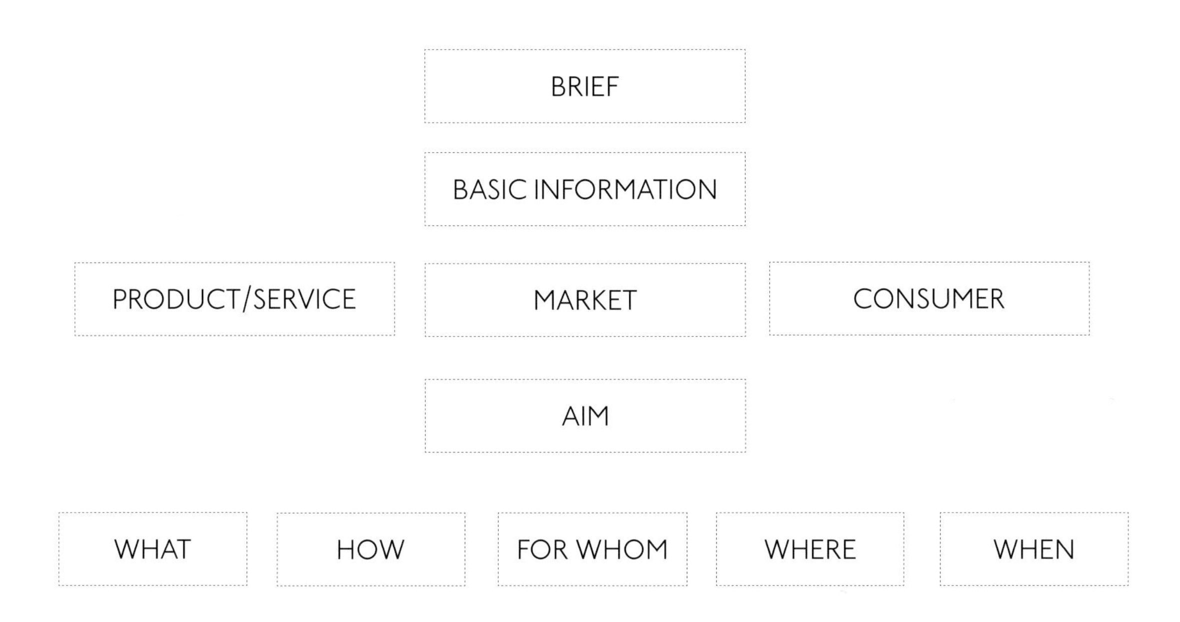

For example: a fashion designer signs an agreement with an airline to design the uniform for its cabin crew. This is an idea associated with the airline's tenth anniversary and with the aim of conveying an image of quality, design, and consolidation.

PRODUCT: airline.
MARKET: airlines.
CONSUMER: passengers.

WHAT (reasoning): renewing the image and making design and quality into emblems of the company.
HOW (language): by designing uniforms characterized by a marked style and functionality.
FOR WHOM (public): a designer uniform will provide enhanced value to service, the consumer of which will be passengers.
WHERE (means): on the airlines' planes, offering an excellent image of customer service.
WHEN (timing): as of the coming year.

Above, Anna Delgado and Macarena Buil at the presentation of their collection for Lladró. **On the right**, a model poses with one of the presented designs. **Below**, a gorgeous jumpsuit from the collection.

A BRIEFING FOR EL DELGADO BUIL

Designers Anna Figuera Delgado and Macarena Ramos Buil founded their label El Delgado Buil in Barcelona in 2004. Their clothes are versatile and can be worn by both men and women. They have featured in trade and runway shows such as Rendez-Vous Femme in Paris, Circuit in Lisbon, Cibeles Madrid, and 080 Barcelona Fashion with designs deserving of awards like those they have received from L'Oréal and *Marie Claire* magazine.

They are experts in developing special pieces in collaboration with other brands, for which they start with a briefing. PlayStation, Kipling, and Escorpion are some of the brands with which the name of El Delgado Buil has been associated.

In 2009 they created the spring/summer 2009 Porcelana collection, inspired by the prestigious Lladró porcelain company. Their collection featured floral prints in the pastel colors typical of Lladró pieces, in addition to the details and cuts that follow along the

Above, two uniforms designed for different departments in the hotel. **Below**, El Delgado Buil at the presentation of the uniforms designed for the EME Catedral Hotel.

lines of their signature collections. A highly acclaimed collection, it was presented in the Boutique Lladró store in Barcelona in 2008.

In the same year Anna Delgado and Macarena Buil were chosen to oversee the design of the staff uniforms for the EME Catedral Hotel. This magnificent luxury hotel is located in the heart of Seville, Spain. To date, this establishment has always shown its enthusiasm for fashion and has been the venue for significant productions by magazines like *Vogue, Glamour, L'Uomo, Marie Claire,* and *Elle,* among others, who chose it as the stage for showcasing important works by renowned professionals.

Following the guidelines set out in the company's brief and inspired by the urban and contemporary spirit with which the hotel was created, El Delgado Buil designed practical and cutting-edge outfits for men and women with the needs of each of the hotel's departments in mind.

2 Inspiration and research

"Nothing is more harmful to creativity than the passion of inspiration." Umberto Eco

Inspiration and research are the starting point in the creative process. They are highly relevant for the rest of the process, and therefore require time and meticulous study using the available sources. Every fashion article or collection is developed from a concept, whether it is set out in a brief or chosen at will by the designer.

Inspiration: One's upbringing or cultural setting, historical references, and personal experiences, plus ongoing exposure to the media, cause our minds to process information constantly and to be influenced by hundreds of stimuli. Inspiration is the stimulus received at a given moment that encourages creativity. However, as reflected in the words of Umberto Eco, this is not to say that the resulting idea is necessarily the most suitable. Thorough research and perfecting of an original idea is a necessary step if inspiration is to take us down the right road.

Research: Research becomes necessary in order to turn the stimuli that compel a fashion designer to work on an idea into the right ones, leading to the proper development of a collection or product. Consequently, a designer should follow two lines of research: research into materials and research into the concept.

The following chart will allow you to analyze what materials and concepts a designer should research when defining a collection. You will also see what sources stimulate a designer's mind towards new directions in design.

- Research into materials
  - Fabrics
    - Fabric composition
      - Natural fibers of animal origin
      - Natural fibers of plant origin
      - Synthetic fibers
  - Color
  - Prints and other finishes

- Research into the concept
  - Cultural influences
  - Historical influences
  - Trends

- The search for trends
  - The Internet
  - Magazines and books
  - Trend-forecasting agencies

Above, an image of the fashion designer Hanna ter Meulen's inspiration, with references to classic tailoring.
Below, one of the vampire images that inspired the latest collection presented by London-based designer Ara Jo.
On the left, the moodboard for Taro Horiuchi latest collection, representing minimalist elegance.

Right, blouse inspired by the Japanese technique of origami being created by Alexandra Verschueren.

RESEARCH INTO MATERIALS

FABRICS

A good choice of fabric is essential when designing a garment. It is important to take this into account because the quality and durability of the garment depends on the fabric. There are many kinds of natural fibers (of animal, plant, and even mineral origin) and synthetic fibers, which are produced from the chemical transformation of natural products using cellulose polymers, proteins, and other materials. The fabric should be compatible with the concept being conveyed, in its composition, and with the presence or absence of prints and other finishes. For example, if a fashion designer plans to make a shirt inspired by the Japanese origami technique, he or she needs to find a fabric with enough body to hold the desired structure; however, if it is too stiff, it will be uncomfortable to wear. Printed fabrics are always the riskiest, but they can turn a good collection into a sublime one. Leading labels and prestige designers have their own fabric design and printing departments, although there are also many fashion designers who specialize in prints who make up their own designs, adding added value to their clothes. One of the most important showcases for trends in fabric is Première Vision, an event held in Paris twice a year. There you can find the best international offering of textiles, which is organized around four trends every season. Moreover, this Parisian show has become so consolidated that fabric shows are currently being staged under the Première Vision brand in New York, Moscow, Tokyo, São Paulo, Shanghai, and Beijing.

select 1546

Fabric composition

Fibers are the filaments making up threads, and therefore, fabric. They can be divided into two large groups: natural fibers and synthetic fibers.[1] The former are those of animal or plant origin, which only need certain processing to enable them to be used in fabrics; the latter do not exist in nature but are manufactured in an industrial process. The following describes the most common of these:

Natural fibers of animal origin

Silk. This is a fine, soft, and elegant natural fiber with a delicate sheen. There are references to its use dating back to 3,000 BCE in China, and this fabric is highly valued in many cultures.

Wool. Fabric made from this fiber provides a sensation of warmth and makes good thermal insulation. It is elastic and wrinkles little. Wool should be washed in lukewarm water and dried flat, or dry cleaned.

Alpaca. Fabric made from this fiber is soft to the touch with a noticeable sheen. It comes from the fleece of the alpaca, an animal native to the Andean regions in South America.

Angora. This is a very soft and very fine fabric. The fiber comes from the long-haired rabbit that originated in the Angora region of Turkey. Its name often leads it to be mistaken for the fleece from the Angora goat. To avoid confusion, the cloth produced from the wool of this goat is known as **Mohair**.

Cashmere. The fabric made from this fiber is soft to touch, light, and silky. It comes from a goat originating in the Asian region of Kashmir. This is one of the world's most highly prized animal fibers; in fact a 100 percent cashmere garment is considered a luxury article.

Natural fibers of plant origin

Cotton. Cotton is one of the most widely used textile fibers, as it is one of the cheapest and most comfortable. It is easily dyed and printed. Present technology allows cotton fabrics to undergo chemical treatments to give them non-shrink and wrinkle-free finishes.

Linen. This fabric is commonly used for making summer weight clothing. Breathable and lightweight, linen garments are cool and comfortable, although fabrics can also be made with greater consistency than linen, such as linen sailcloth.

1. De Perinat, María: "Las fibras textiles," *Tecnología de la confección textil* [CD-ROM]. Spain: EDYM, 2007.

On the left, fabrics chosen by Manuel Bolaño for one of his designs. Among them is a prized mohair cloth. **Below**, silk and cotton used by Omer Asim for his latest collection.

On the left, white neoprene fabric used by Moisés Nieto in his fall/ winter 2010/11 collection. **On the right**, a mixture of sinthetics and natural fabrics. SS 2009 collection by Zazo & Brull. Photo by Gustavo López Mañas.

Synthetic fibers

Spandex (elastane). This fiber is very flexible and resistant. It is normally added to other fibers for flexibility and comfort. it is better known as Lycra, a brand name of the Invista company.

Nylon. Nylon caused a revolution in fashion industry the moment it appeared, an example of which was the production of stockings. It is generally used in fashion combines with natural fibers to cheapen production and increase the wear of garments. It can be matte or shiny.

Rayon. This was the first manufactured fiber produced from cellulose. This fiber was sold as artificial silk at the start of the twentieth century until it the name rayon was adopted in 1924. It is also known in Europe as viscose. It has similar characteristics to cotton, but with less quality.

Polyester. This fiber is elastic, warm to the touch, more opaque than nylon, comes in matte or shiny finishes, and is easy to dye, it is not very breathable and is therefore not recommendable for warm and humid climates.

Vinyl. This is a highly elastic synthetic and resistant polymer with a slightly plastic appearance.

Ritratti, a leading high-end lingerie producer, is the first Italian label to create a complete collection using Lycra 2.0 tape: The elegant Sensation 2.0 collection.

INNOVATION IN SYNTHETIC FIBERS: LYCRA® 2.0 TAPE

Synthetic fibers continue to evolve. Research and technological advances often give rise to new fibers on the market or, rather, they are combinations of fibers and new ways of applying them. In the case of Invista, one of the largest producers of polymers and fibers, mainly nylon, spandex, and applications for polyester, they have launched countless products on the market, which have become powerful tools for fashion labels.

We ask Invista about their latest advance in innovation with Lycra technology: Lycra 2.0 tape: "Lycra 2.0 tape is a polyurethane-urea elastic film with the qualities of perfect fit and recovery power. Lycra 2.0 tape replaces narrow and bulky elastics in hems and seams by means of heat-activated bonding at low activation temperatures. Seams using this adhesive tape keep their shape, even after regular washing. This technology is used to obtain smooth, comfortable, and lasting garments that fit the body perfectly."

COLOR

When choosing the dominant colors for a collection or a garment, it is important to take into account the psychology of color, the concept being developed, and trends. Depending on what is being expressed through the garment, color can be a fantastic medium. For a piece required to convey sensuality or passion, red is a color that never fails. White is the perfect color for highlighting purity, while black brings a somber elegance to whoever wears it. It is necessary to carry out a detailed study of the concept being developed in order to know what colors identify with it. If a designer is inspired by gothic punk, it is obvious that black should predominate in the color palette. A collection inspired by the Mediterranean will be influenced by cool shades like the blue of the sea, neutral shades like those of the whitewashed houses in seaside towns, and the warmth of its sunsets. Color is so important that it is turned into signature emblems of many fashion houses, even taking on the mane of the label. This is the case of the legendary Valentino red,[2] the red created and used for decades by the famous Italian designer Valentino, with a mixture of carmine, purple, and a bright cadmium red. Every season the fashion industry dictates that a new color will become the star color. Actually, these color trends are not new; they are shades that have already featured in other seasons, given an updated name when a color is to be launched as a trend. Examples of this are Klein blue,[3] which became fashionable in the 2008/09 season. Until then it had been known as ultramarine or electric blue, but it was rechristened with this name in honor of the blue patented by the French artist Yves Klein; and nude,[4] the ubiquitous color in the 2010/11 season. It is interesting to find that when the words "nude color" are typed into a search engine, there are countless hits indicating that this color is in, the latest – the essential color! These colors are always a safe bet for designers, but there is no reason why they have to feature in their collections if they do not identify with the collection's concept or philosophy at the time they arise.

2. Bela, Cristina: "Valentino, el rey de la moda," *Adessonoi* [online], November 13, 2009, <http://www.adessonoi.com/node/622> (accessed October 18, 2010.)

3. Zozaya, Pedro: "Rabioso azul Klein," *Vogue España* [online], November 27, 2009, <http://www.vogue.es/articulos/rabioso-azul-klein/2957> (accessed October 18, 2010.)

4. Caballero, Beatriz: "El *nude* es el nuevo negro," *Telva.com* [online], June 2, 2010, <http://www.telva.com/2010/06/02/gente/1275479412.html> (accessed October 18, 2010.)

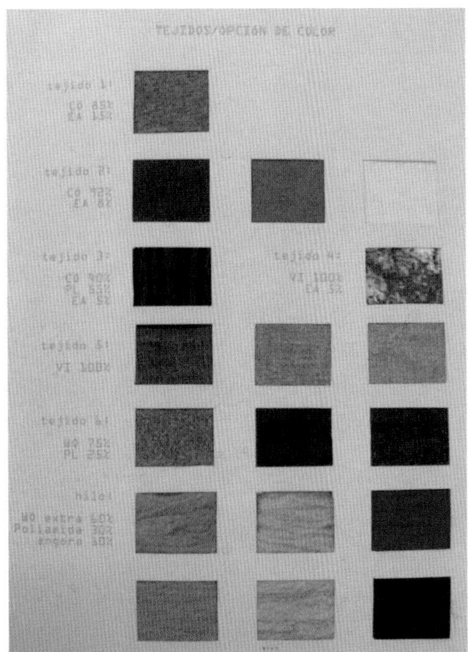

On the left, nude, featured in the fall/winter 2010/11 collection by Carlos Doblas. **Above**, study of color options by the designer Nerea Lurgain for her fall-winter 2010/11 collection. **Below**, ultramarine blue.

Fantastic 70s-inspired print by Avsh Alom Gur for the spring/summer 2010 collection surrounded by a print made by designer Thomas Engel Hart from magazine cutouts for the fall/winter 2010/11 season.

PRINTS AND OTHER FINISHES

As we pointed out at the start of this chapter on choosing fabrics, a well-chosen print, as with other finishes like embroidery or beading, can render a collection unforgettable. Its design should always take account of coherence with the concept of the collection or piece. Drawings made on fabrics can be hand painted or mechanically printed. Almost every designer has flirted with traditional craft techniques, working at one time or another with very exclusive, hand-painted pieces. However, textile printing – with its different techniques – is the most common means. We divide the types of printing into two categories, depending on the technique used to apply the colors and layout of the print.[5]

DEPENDING ON THE TECHNIQUE

Depending on the technique, textile printing is mainly done as direct printing or as resist dyeing, although there are other, less used ones. In order to make the right choice, you should keep in mind the kind of fabric you are using, the complexity of the drawing, and the number of colors, among others. Direct printing is where the design is applied directly over the fabric by means of stencils. There are several different direct printing methods: roller printing, heat transfer printing, screen printing, etc. and they are currently very developed industrially, although some of these techniques can be done in a more manual way. Reserve dyeing, however, involves long-standing manual techniques, such as batik, a technique originating in India, which is based on covering parts of the design with wax and applying different layers of dye. The wax is finally removed to leave an amazing result.

5. De Perinat, María: "Los acabados de las telas," *Tecnología de la confección textil* [CD-ROM]. Spain: EDYM, 2007

HORROR
MASK
THE HORROR
VAMP
MIDNIGHT
AUX
THE
OF
YOUR
Narcisse, aujourd'hui, est punk.
ATOMIC AGE
INSIDE
ENS
THE CREATURE GANG
MYSTERY
CABINET
THOMAS ENGEL HART
New York
THE EDGES

Print design and positioned print from Roomers collection
by Raphael Hauber, fall/winter 2010/11.

DEPENDING ON THE PRINT LAYOUT

Repeat prints are those that reproduce an image repeatedly to form a pattern. These are the prints you find under "printed fabrics" in fabric stores, although many fashion labels are increasingly incorporating their own print designers. On the other hand, positioned image prints are those where an image is placed in a studied manner on a specific part of the garment. An obvious example of this is the world-famous I Love New York T-shirt print created by Milton Glaser.

For textile finishes, countless techniques exist to make one fabric take on a great many distinct looks and textures. The most common are acid finishes, which are those producing aged or parchment-like effects on fabrics that are created through the use of acids. Coated finishes, such as starching, serve to add new properties to a fabric, stiffness in this case. Finally, there are aesthetic finishes that serve to alter the appearance and feel of cloth, as is the case of chintz, which is first waxed and then calendered under pressure to leave the fabric with a silky appearance and glossy surface finish.

RESEARCH INTO THE CONCEPT

CULTURAL INFLUENCES

Everything making up the culture of a place, music, film, literature, painting, and traditional costume, together with a cultural or artistic current from a certain time in history (like modernism or pop art), are likely to be used as a source of inspiration. In order to represent this cultural influence, it is necessary to research and obtain all the necessary information and then interpret it, according to the individual philosophy and style. Many labels and designers let themselves become absorbed by culture and resolve their creative projects based on this. Some find inspiration in music, like Converse and its latest designs, which call to mind Kurt Cobain and The Ramones. Others are inspired by a certain ethnic group, like Vivienne Westwood's spring/summer 2009 collection, inspired by gypsies. Perhaps one of the most memorable examples of the influence of culture applied to fashion is Yves Saint Laurent's Mondrian dress from the 1965 fall collection, inspired by the Dutch artist's Neoplasticism movement.

Sociology experts say that in periods of economic boom, there tends to be a leaning towards the technological, functional, or futuristic, while at times of economic recession, fashion delves into cultural roots, into ethnicity, and the purest forms of human expression as people unconsciously seek comfort in their origins.

Image from Zazo & Brull's samurai-inspired Bushido collection for the spring/summer 2010 season. Photo by Gustavo López Mañas.

Image from Isabel Mastache's Bulgarian Voices fall/winter 2010/11 collection, which draws inspiration from a combination of Indian, Central European, and Galician cultures.

HISTORICAL INFLUENCES

In any artistic discipline, history is essential to face the present and the future. Just as an individual needs to learn from past personal experiences in order to solve the problems they face, fashion designers need historical references to enhance their view of clothing and devise their designs with solutions that stimulate creativity. The history of clothes is closely linked to human history. Primitive societies used animal skins to cover and protect themselves. However, they did not follow "fashion" – they only satisfied a need. Great civilizations like that of Japan perpetuated their way of dress without significant changes for centuries. Fashion, as such, was invented in Europe, with three key moments in its history. In the fourteenth century there was an important differentiation between men's and women's clothes. In the nineteenth century haute couture was born in Paris. In the second half of the twentieth century the current fashion system was created. Delving into history through the history of clothes can be fascinating for any designer, and its interpretation can bring about incredible results.

A STORY WITH A PAST

Con el Corazón en Kyoto collection by Freddy Gaviria (freddygaviria.blogspot.com)

In the fall of 2008 designer Freddy Gaviria was given the opportunity to visit Japan for the first time including a visit to the Costume Museum in Kyoto, which has the world's most amazing and complete collection. The history of that place and the atmosphere pervading it still live on in his memory. Since that time, his spirit has continued to wander through the museum's galleries and the streets of the Gion district, famous for its okiyas, where aspiring geishas are lodged. An expert in the history of fashion, Freddy Gaviria began to associate the Oriental silhouette with the style created by Paul Poiret, the first great designer and pioneer and revolutionary of the current feminine silhouette, who released women from the corset back in 1910, allowing them to breathe. This collection revisits Poiret's work and his passion for luxury and the Orient. Gaviria's Italian training and technique contrast with the way he plays with color and his Latin exuberance in designs where Oriental style and European Baroque merge into one, and from which an architectural silhouette emerges constructed with clean and simple lines.

Freddy Gaviria's Con el Corazón en Kyoto collection, 2009.
Model: Xiao Qiu. Photo by Fernando Marrero.

No. 370

Image from the spring/summer 2011 trend notebook by the Paris-based agency Nelly Rodi and Copenhagen International Fashion Fair (CIFF).

TRENDS

Every designer has to be up to date with current trends and, in particular, with coming ones. The first thing is to be a good observer and know how to appreciate changes that occur in around you. Everything affects fashion, from art through to the economic climate in a place, including the appearance of new urban tribes. In fact, "trendsetters," such as specialized agencies, work with psychologists, historians, and designers, among others, to figure out how the fashion consuming society will respond to certain sociological, political, economic, and political changes. For a number of centuries it was the nobility and royalty who set fashion "trends." An example of this is when the French king Louis XIII began to use a wig to hide his baldness; soon all European noblemen shaved their heads and took to using hairpieces. Women's magazines in the nineteenth century were the first to announce trends, and screen idols and musicians in the twentieth century were the ones to set the fashion. Fashion today is in constant flux. It lasts a short time, which is why every designer should keep track of the aesthetic resources that will predominate in the following season. Hubert de Givenchy, founder of the French fashion house bearing his name, pointed to the globalization in current fashion, encouraged by media such as the Internet, which makes information on future trends available to any user with a click of the mouse. This enhances even more the fleeting nature of fashion. What is in fashion today will be out of fashion tomorrow. This means that experts constantly have to recycle their knowledge. Later on in this book we will analyze the resources designers have to research trends: magazines, books, the Internet, and trend-forecasting agencies.

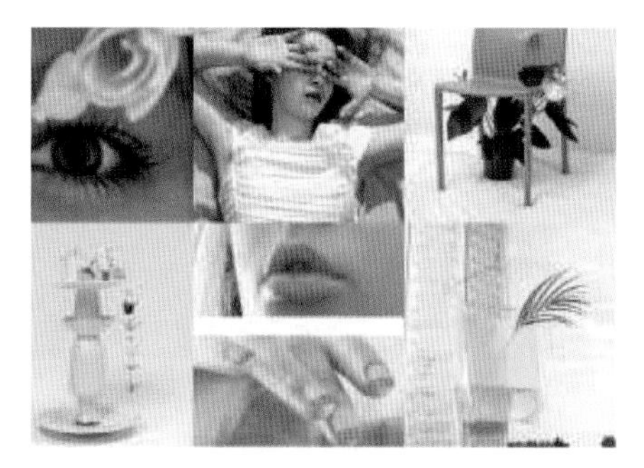

TINY PLEASURES
THE EMO HUMANS

SENSITIVE ROMANTIC POETIC TIMELESS SPIRITUAL
Modestly and patience, seeking to construct a tender refuge to escape from vagaries of the world, the brutality of events, the tumults and rumors of the outside world... At the crossroads of Asian refinement and Nordic humanist spirit, a fresh, respectful kind of design to the embellishment of daily lives...

Images by photographer and coolhunter Mike Madrid on his website Give Me the Shoot (www.givemetheshoot.com).

THE SEARCH FOR TRENDS

As we explained in previous chapters, inspiration can come at any time and anywhere, but you have to make sure the idea is a good one and to develop it by looking at background historical or cultural references, and trends. But where do you find them? The following shows you some of the most practical sources, such as: the Internet, books, magazines, and trend reports.

THE INTERNET

The Internet has become an important ally of fashion. At first it was unthinkable that fashion labels and designers would take the step of concentrating a great deal of their advertising, PR, and sales into this great medium of our time. However, today we can buy fashion from the world's best designers online, together with one-off pieces by young designers who sell their work exclusively on the Internet. More and more companies each day are being set up to sell fashion online. It is now possible to purchase designer labels such as Marc Jacobs at discount prices on fashion websites like Yoox in Italy. In addition, the concept of coolhunting has moved from the street to websites such as Chictopia and Lookbook, where it is possible to find hundreds of designs from hundreds of people who show photo images with their most contemporary looks. It is amazing how runway shows like those taking place in New York, Milan, London, and Paris can be streamed live or a few hours after they take place over the Internet and via online television channels such as FashionTV. Social networking sites and blogs have also enabled the ins and outs of the latest fashion and trends to spread instantly. Designers, PR firms, and many other companies connected with fashion utilize these media, which are the fastest and most economical way of becoming the name on everybody's lips. These and many others are reason enough to find hundreds of resources on the Internet with just a click.

March 2009 cover of *Vogue Paris*, a special edition dedicated to Coco Chanel. In the photo, model Iris Strubegger photographed by Mert Alas and Marcus Piggot.

MAGAZINES AND BOOKS

Libraries and newsstands are places where a designer can find a lot of information – both graphic and written – on fashion and trends. There are many books about fashion, which, unlike the Internet, compiles a great deal of clear and well-ordered information in a single volume. A search through libraries and bookstores can lead to discoveries of books on very specific fashion subjects, including fashion illustration, color, new technologies, and a long list of others that will stimulate the creativity of anyone undertaking a fashion project. Fashion magazines have been around since the seventeenth century, although it was only in the nineteenth century when they became more complete and better-illustrated publications that explained how to dress appropriately for every occasion. Over the years, fashion magazines have become the great disseminators of trends. Known as the fashion bible, *Vogue* began publication in 1892. Today there are editions of this magazine in more than a dozen countries and it is considered the most influential fashion magazine. There are now a great many magazines with very interesting content regarding fashion, such as the highly renowned *Elle*, *Marie Claire*, *Cosmopolitan*, and *L'Officiel*, among others, and other significant trend-revealing publications like the British *Dazed & Confused* and *Another Magazine*. Increasingly more publications are focusing on men's fashion. Newsstands around the world have been selling such magazines as *Men's Vogue* since 2008, in addtion to *GQ*, *Another Man*, and *L'Officiel Hommes*, and the list goes on.

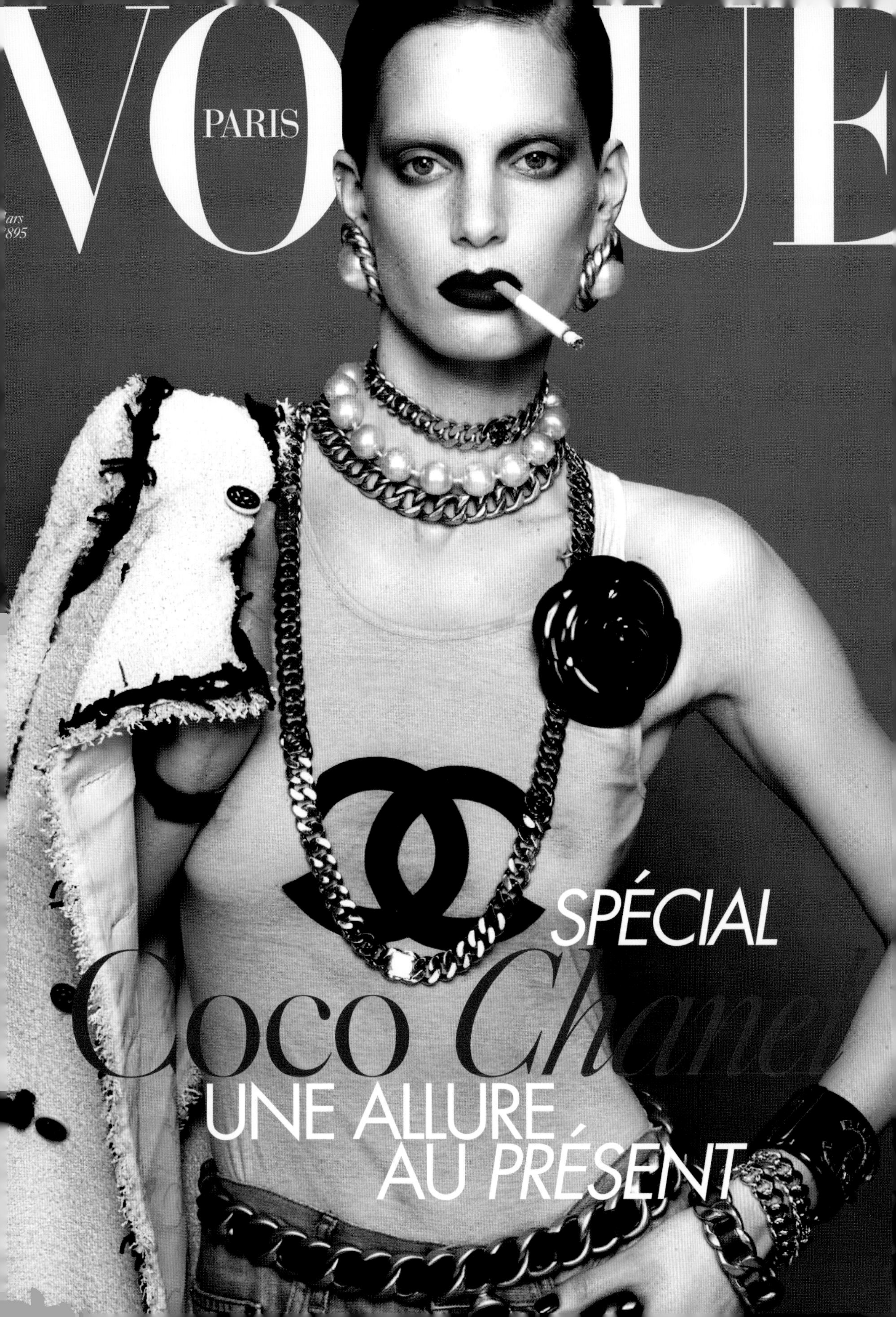
PARIS
SPÉCIAL
Coco Chanel
UNE ALLURE
AU PRÉSENT

INTERVIEW WITH RAMÓN FANO

Editor-in-chief of *Neo2* magazine

***Neo2* is undeniably a true coolhunting magazine that presents us with new talents in fashion, art, and culture every month. What ingredients do you think a fashion designer needs to succeed?**
I believe they need to have a very personal creative style and faultless workmanship, at the same time having a general insight into all the ins and outs of fashion, with a good capacity for work and the intuition to find social contacts and to present their collections and designs at suitable events.

***Neo2* recently celebrated its 15th year. Congratulations! During this time you've launched many young designers who have since made an important niche in fashion. Any particular anecdotes you can tell?**
These 15 years we've learned that we form part of a chain where our role is to be a support for showing outside work that we consider interesting, and also our own ideas that we put into practice together with collaborators. We are a means by which many creative people can reach other places. The only anecdote I have is that the people who are oblivious to where they come from probably won't get anywhere.

Men's fashion is particularly well represented in *Neo2*. Do you think that part of the secret to your success has been specializing in showing the latest for men?
We've actually been paying more attention to men's fashion because it's what has evolved more: it's where more new and interesting things are happening. This is probably because the fashion industry has discovered a new market to explore, that of men. Maybe it's because the world of women's fashion is more predictable and more exploited. It takes a lot of inspiration from past decades and collections and it isn't progressing as much as men's fashion is.

You have a blog and profiles with the main social networking sites. That's preaching by example by keeping up with the latest in communication trends. Has it been hard work adapting to new formulas in recent years?
Yes, it has. It's what has to be done. We have an online version of the magazine and blog, with its own content, which is different or complementary to what's in print, and it's updated daily. We also put out our own audiovisual guidebooks showing different cities through the eyes of their creatives. And, naturally, we receive feedback from all of this through our presence on social networking sites – Facebook, Twitter, and Spotify. We've been adapting to everything. We started at the time of the digital technology boom, but with analog backgrounds. We love to experience and enjoy our time.

May 2009 cover of *Neo2*. Photo by Paco Pelgrín.

NEO2
ATIVE GENEORATION
o 09 3€(Spain)
Austria:
Canada: 10,25
Engla
Espa
Franc
Germany:
Italy:
Mexic
Morocco:
Sweden:
Switzerland
Tahiti:
0008
9 771138 562005

Image from the spring/summer 2011 trend notebook by the Paris-based trend-forecasting agency Nelly Rodi and Copenhagen International Fashion Fair (CIFF).

TREND-FORECASTING AGENCIES

In the second half of the twentieth century, when the fashion system we know now was established, the fashion industry became an unstoppable machine, with a rate of production that was difficult to keep up with. This fast pace means that the textile industry has had to become increasingly professionalized and specialized as the only means it had to cope. Thus appeared the trend-forecasting agencies specializing in fashion. Many have spent decades accompanying large companies in the sector in their creative processes. These agencies draw on experts in different fields: sociologists, psychologists, historians, designers, coolhunters, etc., who use historical and sociological benchmarks to define and predict the trends for the coming seasons through annual reports.

A specific report for a client can cost as much as 20,000 euros ($27,000). Nevertheless, many companies invest in them, knowing that it is a safe strategy for the success of their collections, and the best guarantee to minimize uncertainty and reduce margins for error.

Companies ranging from large distributors such as H&M and Inditex to luxury houses like Givenchy trust in the advice given by trend-forecasting agencies when creating a new collection. Not only do clothing companies trust in them, but, more importantly, so do textile manufacturers. Bear in mind that if Baroque-style prints feature heavily in the coming seasons, or metallic effects, or jade green, fabric producers need to have these parameters on hand two years earlier.

Some of the most influential agencies in the world are Promostyl, Nelly Rodi, Peclers Paris, Carlin International, and WSGN.[6]

6. Tungate, Mark: "That's the power of the cloth," *The Times Online* [online], July 21, 2005, <http://women.timesonline.co.uk/tol/life_and_style/women/fashion/article546009.ece> [accessed October 18, 2010].

PROFILE OF A TREND EXPERT:
Nelly Rodi (www.nellyrodi.com)

Since 1985 the Paris-based agency founded by Madame Nelly Rodi has been made up of professionals from different fields to achieve creative interaction. They have a series of authentic globetrotters who travel the world detecting and interpreting signs of change, new iconographies, and documentation on textiles and other fashion areas. They also have correspondents in more than nineteen countries. Nelly Rodi is held in great esteem in both the French and international fashion industries, and counts among its achievements the development of a unique method for clients, known as MarketingStyle®, which combines marketing, creative intuition, and decoding of new behavioral patterns among consumers.

3 Creation

"Success comes from what one does not learn."
Coco Chanel

After researching and compiling all the information related to the concept of the collection or the garment that is being developed, the next step is to design – to turn the information into a piece, to give it shape, to interpret it. The quote opening this section reflects the notion that you succeed because of what you are, not because of what you learn. Obviously, innate talent is essential in fashion design, but only a good interpretation of everything you have researched and learned is a good indication that the design will be a success. A designer can develop this process individually or as part of a team, and in a way that is more or less elaborate depending on the scale of the project or the type of company they belong to. In the case of haute couture – a term protected in France by the Chambre Syndicale de la Haute Couture and which is only granted to companies that comply with their rules – the piece is designed to order from a client, generally using craft techniques that require a great deal of time, a prior choice of excellent materials, and painstaking attention to detail. Prêt-à-porter fashion, also known as ready-to-wear, is not designed for an individual client, but great care is taken with the materials and work and the label offers certain exclusivity. Finally, mass-produced fashion for the general market uses much cheaper materials and means, with a large proportion being machine made and for standard sizes. Nevertheless, these garments are creatively designed and can create a good effect at a reasonable price. Part of this success is due to their design being copied in many cases from the main prêt-à-porter labels. The following section looks at a number of points in this creation process such as design (sketches), pattern making, making up the garments, and fitting.

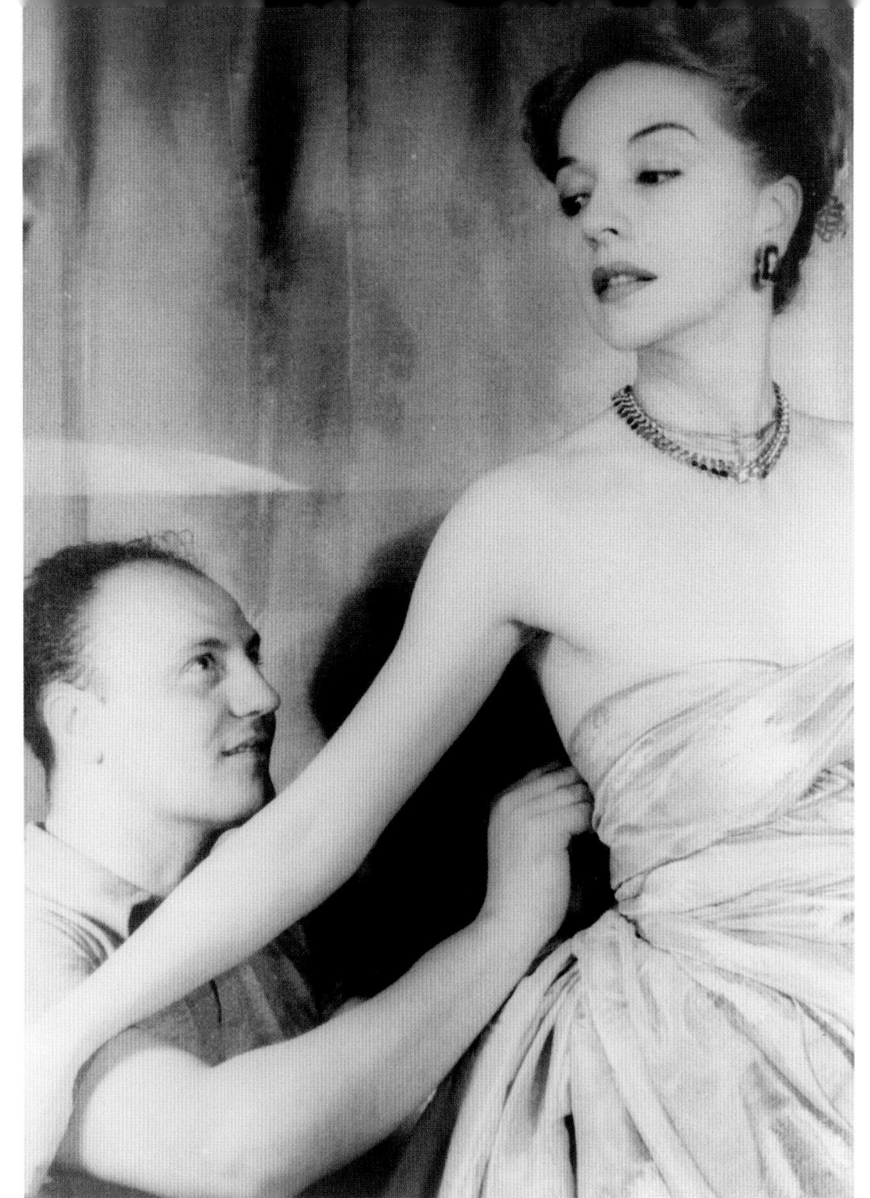

Pierre Balmain adjusting a dress on the model Ruth Ford in 1947. Library of Congress, Prints and Photographs Division, Carl Van Vechten collection.

HAUTE COUTURE IN FRANCE

In France the term *haute couture* is protected by law and defined by the Chambre de Commerce et d'Industrie de Paris. Only fashion houses that appear on the annual decree issued by a commission of the Ministry of Industry may use the term *haute couture* in their description or for publicity purposes. Pierre Balmain, Chanel, Christian Lacroix, Yves Saint Laurent, and Jean Paul Gaultier have all appeared on this list over the years. The following rules, specified when making up this list, were established in 1945 and revised in 1992:

- The design of made-to-order and made-to-measure garments for private clients.
- Designers may sell only one design of each creation per continent.
- The design house must have a Paris atelier employing at least twenty full-time technical people.
- The presentation each season of a collection containing at least thirty-five designs before the press in Paris.

Image from the Sposa collection by the Italian designer Valentino for the Spanish bridal house Pronovias.

NEW CONCEPTS IN FASHION CREATION: PRÊT-À-COUTURE
Between prêt-à-porter and haute couture

"Fashion is essentially a dream; but the times we live in are driving designers to show less abstract dreams and ones that are more real and specific." John Galliano[7]

Fashion is created in an environment of cultural and social influences, in a specific moment in time.[8] Today, the lifestyle of many consumers, particularly women who buy from important fashion labels, have made it necessary for designers to have to streamline their method of working. Haute couture, as we saw previously, continues to be as demanding as ever in its requirements to form part of its list. As a result, from the dozens of haute couture houses in the 1950s, those remaining can practically be counted with your fingers. Most of these women have no time for several fitting sessions and waiting weeks to receive their order. Consequently, in recent times there has been mention, acknowledged by fashion experts, of the new term "prêt-à-couture," which combines the French expressions "prêt-à-porter" and "haute couture." This is an intermediate solution, where designers present semi-finished pieces for finishing with the client by means of minor adjustments. This enables them to adapt to demand, while still offering something unique or at least with a large degree of exclusivity. This is a much more sophisticated version of ready-to-wear, but created in the spirit of haute couture and produced in relatively limited numbers. An example of this change comes from the Italian house of Valentino in association with the Spanish company Pronovias, which created a marvellous bridal collection in 2010. Just as Valentino's prêt-à-porter line featured reminiscences of haute couture, these wedding gown designs represent the label's craftsmanship and refinement.

7. Montes-Fernández, Jesús María: "Un nuevo sistema, el pret-a-couture," *elmundo. es* [online], October 16, 2005, <http://www.elmundo.es/suplementos/magazine/2005/316/1129315910.html> (accessed October 18, 2010).

8. Schroeder, Dominique: "Pret-a-couture, la opción de moda para los impacientes", *Perfil.com* [online], January 22, 2008, <http://www.perfil.com/contenidos/2008/01/22/noticia_0017.html> (accessed October 18, 2010).

FASHION SKETCHES AND ILLUSTRATIONS

Fashion houses in the nineteenth century hired artists to make sketches or to paint the designs of their clothes. These were then shown to customers. They were much more economical than showing samples previously made up in the shop. If the customers liked the design, the piece was ordered to be made up for them. The tradition of fashion drawings started as a practical way of economizing, and this is not far from the lookbooks used in the present day.

Fashion sketches and illustrations are the visual tools to assist in the understanding of a garment for pattern making and making-up the piece. These drawings can be done by hand using different techniques such as pencil, watercolor, and gouache, among others, or with design software. But do all designers have to know how to draw perfectly? Those sketches that are more stylized and respond to canons of beauty that border on the abstract are always more pleasant to look at. However, the important thing in practice is not how pretty the drawing looks but how easily it can be interpreted for better technical translation.

There have been cases of fashion designers who admit to not being good at drawing; nevertheless, with a simple outline they can express the features of the garment perfectly. The use of computer-aided design (CAD) software that make fashion design easier is gaining more and more adepts. However, there are those who use both techniques and prefer to make an initial sketch that can be uploaded onto a computer so that their designs can be seen in different colors and textures more quickly and effectively. There is a wide variety of software for creating fashion illustrations, whether stylized or technical. However, most experts agree that the most complete and perfected program for these illustrations is CorelDRAW.

Sketch by Vittorio & Lucchino for their spring/summer 2010 collection.

Above, design by Chris Liu. On the left, sketch of a male by Sjaak Hullekes. **Below**, on the left, Diego Binetti drawing in his New York studio. **Below**, on the right, digital illustrations by Rachel Freire.

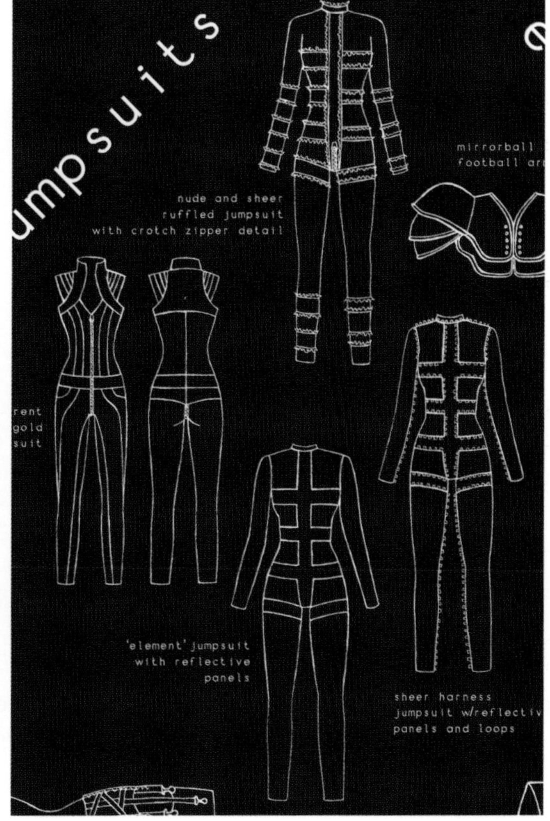

VIEW OF AN EXPERT IN COMPUTER-AIDED FASHION DESIGN
Anna María López López (www.anna-om-line.com)

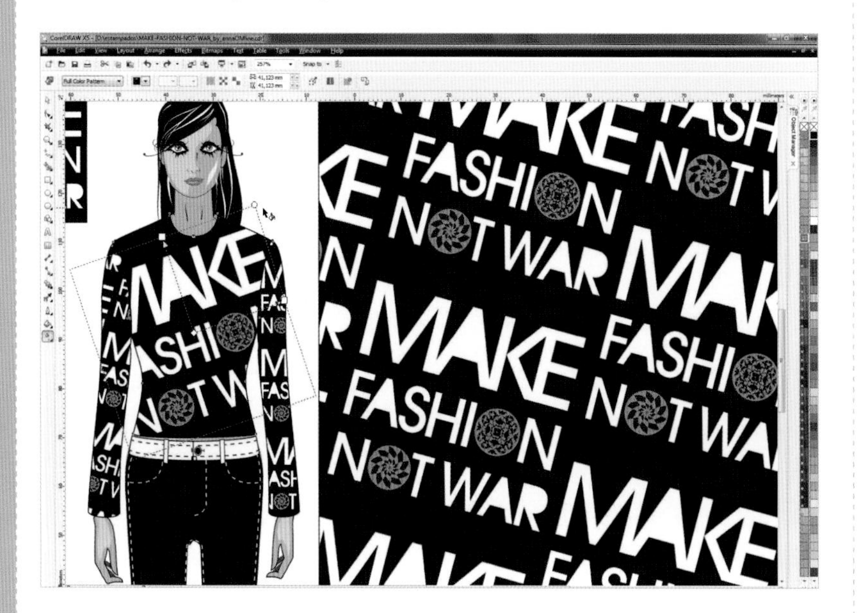

Anna María López López is a well-known designer who is a specialist in computer-aided fashion design using specific CAD/CAM solutions for the world of fashion and the author of several specialist books (see bibliography). She admits to being a fan of fashion design with CorelDRAW.

Anna María, why do you recommend this program as a fashion tool?
Personally, I think CorelDRAW is the leading program in computer-aided fashion design for several very specific reasons. Besides being one of the most intuitive vector-based design programs on the market, it features several exclusive functions that are indispensable for a fashion designer:

Interactive fill tool. The interactive fill tool makes it possible to preview what a print design will look like on a garment directly on the screen. Interactive controls showing changes in real time allow you to modify the position and rotation angle of the print design. This makes the task of creating a presentation of the design far easier.

Automatic vectorization with incorporated color reduction. When creating designs for positioned image or repeat prints, it's always a good thing to reduce the number of colors in the repeated pattern, or rapport, in order to lower production costs. Well, CorelDRAW comes with PowerTRACE, a bitmap to vector convertor producing vector-based images that are very faithful to the original. But what makes PowerTRACE the best option for a fashion designer is the possibility

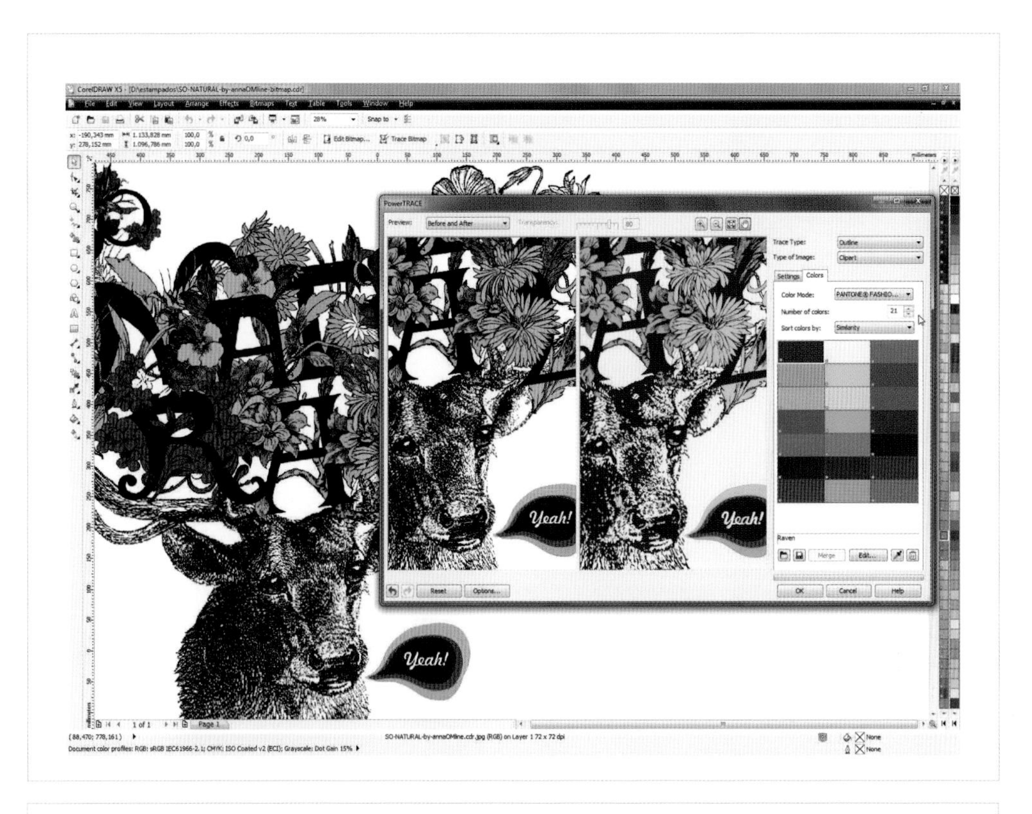

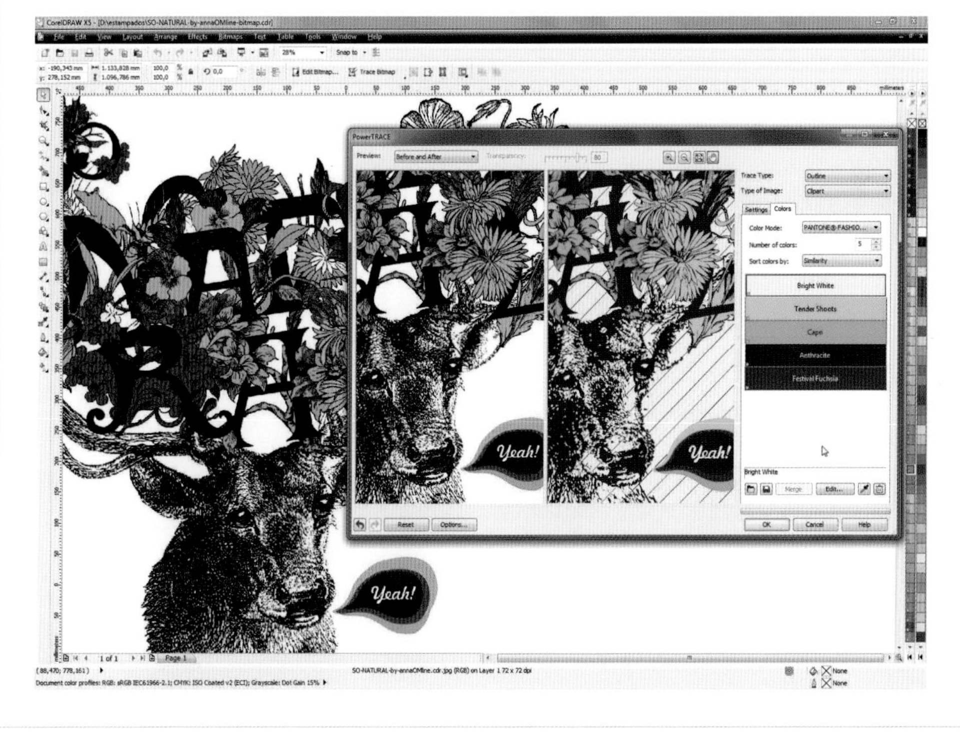

These screenshots offered by Anna María López show the use of the different tools explained in this section: **On the left**, the interactive fill tool, and, **above**, the automatic vectorization with incorporated color reduction.

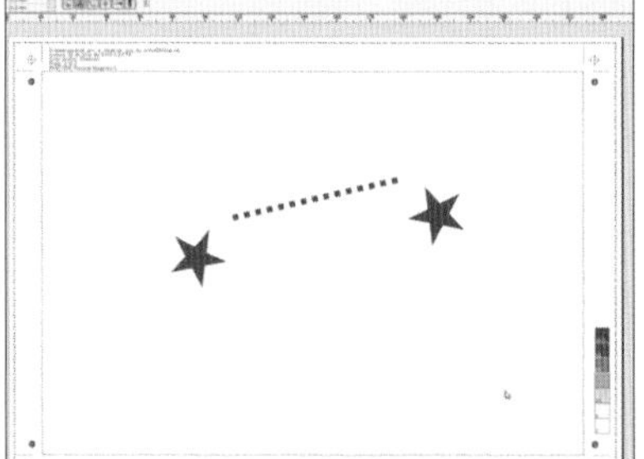

Images showing color separation.
Designs made with CorelDRAW.

you have of reducing the number of colors on the bitmap image during the vector conversion process. You can even designate a specialized color palette, such as Pantone Fashion+Home. When the vectorization process is complete with PowerTRACE, in addition to obtaining a vector-based image, you also have an optimum design for printing with the least number of colors.

Direct preview of color separations. One of the most common printing techniques in the fashion industry continues to be screen printing, which makes it very important to check whether the colors in the design being created can be correctly separated onto plates. With CorelDRAW there is no need to have a design printed to check whether the color separations are correct. You can see the generated color plates by using the print preview window, which will also give you all of the necessary instructions for correct printing.

Possibility of running VBA macros. CorelDRAW enables you to run macros in order to automate common processes. In a fashion designer's daily routine there are certain tasks that are repeated over and over again, for which certain companies have created certain macros or accessories for CorelDRAW using VBA technologies specifically for professional fashion design. One example is My Online (www.my-online.es), which offers specialist utilities such as My Confección, an accessory for CorelDRAW that allows you to mark out backstiches, which can be turned into coverstitches, zigzag, zipper, or any other element with a simple click. A simple click on the mouse will also

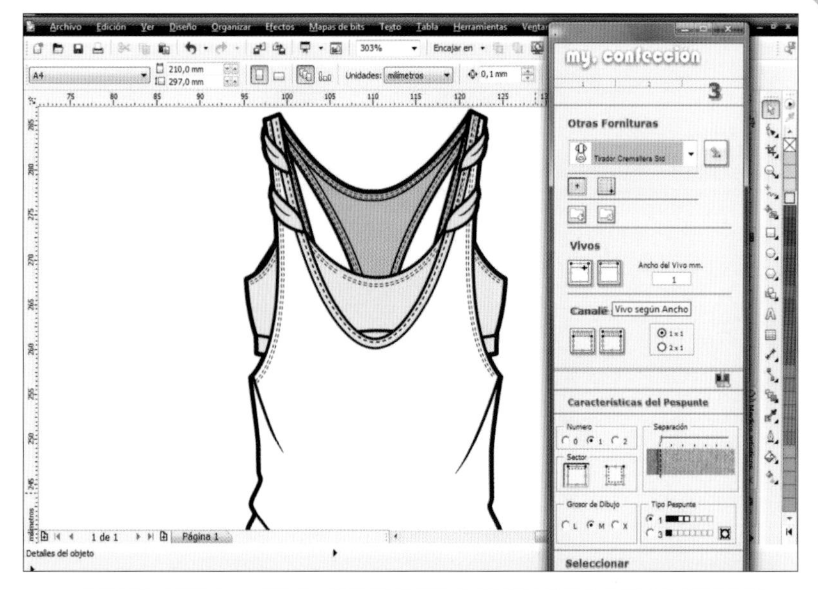

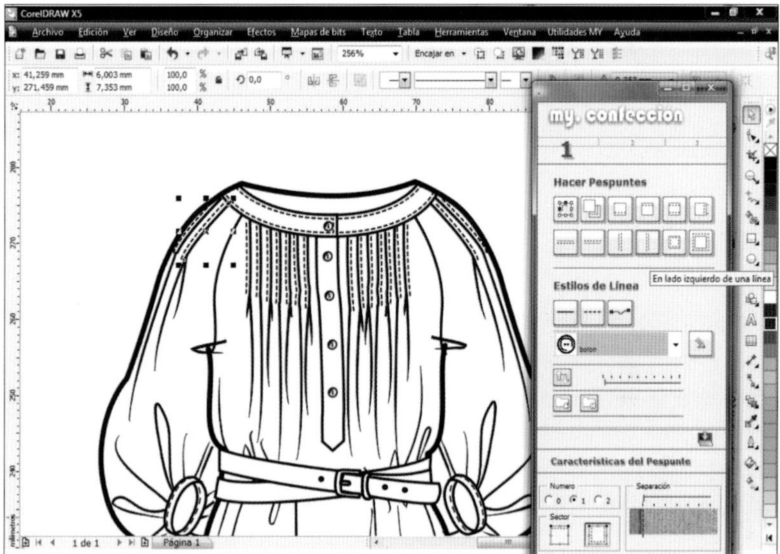

Designs made with My.

enable you to position buttons, apply pockets, trimmings, and to create piping and other effects. The aim of the My Online accessories is to save as much as possible the time needed to design with CorelDRAW, particularly when creating a flat drawing of garments for technical specifications. It is important that a program be able to follow your pace and, especially, make a task as easy as possible. CorelDRAW has been around for more than twenty years demonstrating that it is the fashion designer's best friend. In short, the best formula for choosing one program over another is to see which one best adapts to your real creative needs.

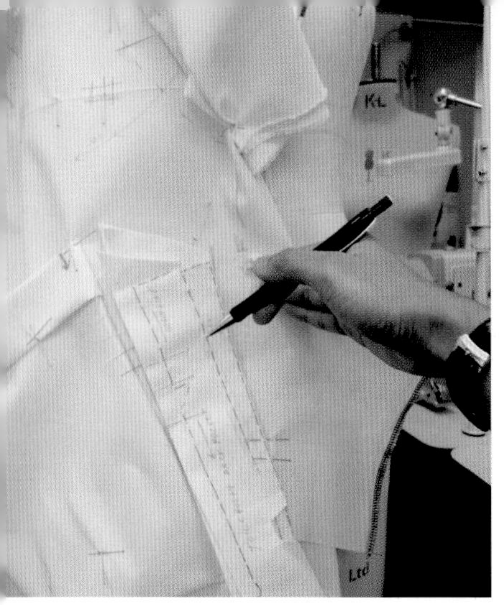

On the left, designer Lesley Mobo checks the pieces of a garment with the patterns. **In the center**, Kilian Kerner drapes cloth over a dummy. **On the right**, a member of the Bora Asku staff prepares patterns over fabric for cutting.

PATTERNMAKING

Patternmaking is to fashion what architecture is to construction. It is how the plans of what is to be a garment are developed. The designer, or the patternmaker, as the case may be, needs both the technical and strategic means of correctly preparing the patterns. Depending on the type of garment being made, whether it is an haute couture gown or ready-to-wear dress, for instance, different techniques will be needed to move from the sketch stage to the making up of the garment. Although there are several methods, for non-industrial patternmaking and tailoring, the most common way is to work on a basic pattern or block and modify it according to the required model and measurements. Likewise, one can work with a flat paper pattern, or with pattern draping, constructing a "model" of what will be the final garment over a dummy. In industrial patternmaking, the patterns are prepared with a cutting line, i.e. with the seam allowances included and with all of the necessary details to enable mass-production processes to take place (marks such as buttonholes, for instance). Patterns also have to respond to industrial size charts adapted to the population of the target market. Therefore, besides the art of interpreting a design, patternmakers need to master the technique of grading or scaling. Like with fashion illustration, there is a variety of different patternmaking software that helps to make this process much faster and more precise, enabling them to improve their productivity and keep up with the vertiginous pace of fashion.

MAKING UP GARMENTS

The process of making up garments, understood as the process from the moment the fabric is cut until the last details are finished, varies depending on whether the garments are made using a traditional or industrial systems. Even so, there are certain points that should always be taken into account.

Cutting. Before cutting any piece, the fabric should be prepared bearing in mind a number of points, such as what is the right side and the back of the fabric and its direction. The direction the fabric is cut in is determined by the garment design. In the case of velvet, you would need to take into account the direction of the nap or the preferred perspective, given that different effects can result from different positions. Likewise, it is important to analyze the pattern to know whether the fabric is to be cut as a single or double piece, or symmetrically, etc. It also necessary to follow the direction marked by the pattern, whether straight-grain (parallel to the selvedge), cross-grain (perpendicular to the selvedge), and on the bias (diagonal). Finally, the positioning of the different pieces is essential for making the best use of the fabric. Software used in industrial processes determines their placement for the greatest efficiency.

Making up garments. Depending on the type of process, traditional or industrial, the methodology and finishes can be very different. In some fashion firms, cutting and sewing are done by a specific team or, in most cases, particularly in ready-to-wear and mass-produced industries, by external factories. In recent years many companies of a certain size have sent production to countries where fabric prices and labor costs are cheaper. This requires constant supervision of production to monitor that the processes and finishes suffer as little as possible.

TOOLS FOR AN EXPERT IN INDUSTRIAL PATTERN MAKING AND GRADING

Iñaki Blanco (www.inakiblanco.es)

This freelance patternmaker has more than twenty years' experience in fashion. He carries out patternmaking and grading independently for all kinds of companies dedicated to clothing manufacturing. He also works on the management of samples, production, quality control, and production process coordination We asked him what software he uses for patternmaking and grading.

PGS Model. This software is specific for patternmaking and grading, incorporating latest-generation tools for creating new patterns and modifying old ones. It also enables a client's patterns to be digitized for computer processing later modifications and grading.

Kaledo. This is drawing software with specific applications for designs, fabric prints, technical specifications, color, etc. It's also a good complement to 3D Fit, and it is used to prepare the scanned fabrics, for drawing the trimmings on garments, such as bows, embellishments, and logos, for subsequent viewing on the dummy.

Modaris 3D Fit. This software is for 3D viewing of virtual two-dimensional prototypes. This tool allows decisions to be made before the prototype is cut out, and it has different means for checking: garment measurements compared with the dummy to check free movement, thread deviations in the fabric, garments in forced positions, the fall of different fabric compositions in garments, tests for garments in different sizes after grading, etc.

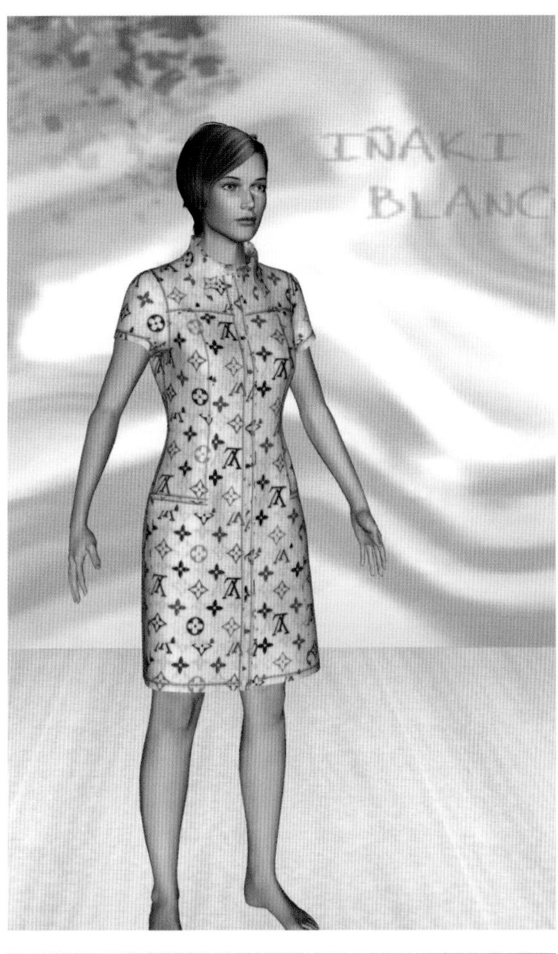

The design of a virtual prototype made by Iñaki Blanco. On the previous page, screenshot of Iñaki Blanco working with colors and prints on Kaledo software.

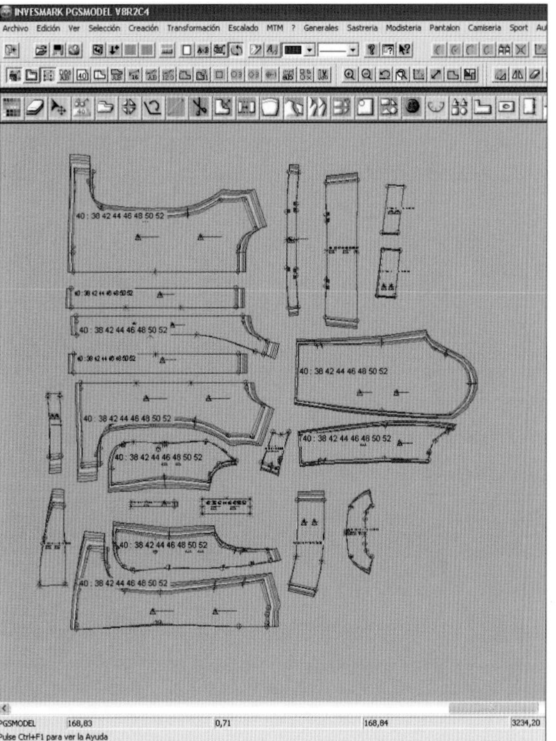

Screenshot of Iñaki Blanco working on a garment with PGS Model software

FITTING

In the more traditional settings, fittings are a part of the process from start to finish. Haute couture requires a client to have two or three fittings between ordering and delivery of the finished piece, where the designer adjusts the dress to her body shape and tries different techniques to complete the design. In the field of prêt-à-porter, designers usually fit a garment several times (although it is for no client in particular), normally on a dummy, and finally on a model. This allows them to make small adjustments such as correcting pleats or narrowing the waist, and to check that the fasteners are well positioned. Fitting clothes on a model gives more complete information, as a person's movement resolves questions such as comfort, which is an essential quality in clothing. Agencies exist now, particularly in the major fashion capitals, that cater to this need by providing professional fit models of different sizes and with good experience. Fashion firms and designers normally use inexperienced friends, family members, or the expensive services of standard modeling agencies with a limited range of sizes for this process. Fittings agencies fill this niche by providing a perfect service that responds to all the requirements designers might have.

On the left, designers from The Individualist(s) during a fitting with a model. Below, a member of Taro Horiuchi's team fits a dress on a dummy.

PROFILE OF A FITTING EXPERT
Fittings Division
(www.fittingsdivision.co.uk)

Fittings Division is one of the leading fittings agencies in the UK, supplying professional and experienced fitting models to the fashion industry since 2003. It was the first agency of this kind, and was created by the brother and sister team of Gemma and Alex White. Located at the heart of London's rag trade, it has a huge range of professional models of all shapes and sizes and an extensive client portfolio, having worked with firms like Puma, Fred Perry, and Jonathan Saunders, among others. It has female models from UK sizes 4-28 (US 2-18) and male models from XS-XL in different age groups. The business was set up to fill a large void in the market by providing a greatly needed service to the fashion industry.

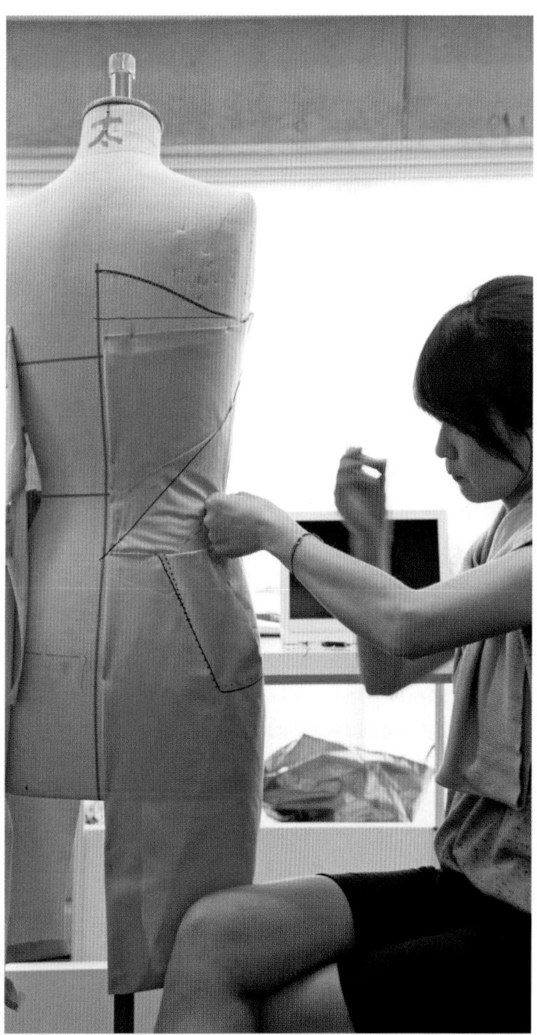

4 Result and presentation

Every creative process ends with a result. In the case of fashion, the process finishes with a presentation, which can include being part of a fashion show, a catalog, or a lookbook. Here the selling process begins and the collection enters the market.

RUNWAY SHOW

The runway show is the showcase where a collection is presented to the world. It is the way of showing the result of months of work by a designer and his or her team. In the last fifty years the term "fashion week" has spread around the world, and there are few countries that do not have a fashion week. This is a way of turning a city into a fashion capital for a week, and focusing much greater media attention on the work of designers than with independent presentations. Fashion weeks are held twice a year. The designs for the spring and summer of the following year are shown in January and February, while the fall and winter collections are shown in September and October. This enables the fashion industry to become more organized, and for each label to schedule periods for design, production, and sale revolving around these events, always one year in advance. The cities with the most prestigious fashion weeks and with the most media impact are Paris, London, New York, Milan, and Tokyo. However, many cities around the world present very interesting fashion shows, such as Berlin, Hong Kong, Rio de Janeiro, Madrid, Sydney, and Copenhagen, and a host of others. Milan and Paris have been pioneering fashion weeks exclusively featuring menswear.

On the left, The Individualist(s) fall/winter 2010/11 show during Tokyo Fashion Week. On the right, image from the runway with a design by Victorio & Lucchino. Below, a Mongrels in Common show.

Above, Lemoniez runway show, February, 2010, Madrid Cibeles Fashion Week. Photo by Mike madrid. **On the right**, Zazo & Brull show, Bushido collection, 080 Barcelona Fashion.

Runway shows are a powerful means of promoting collections. However, they are very expensive to stage and involve a tremendous amount of effort—all for only a few minutes in the public eye. Media impact and economic returns are not always assured. For this reason, it is necessary to choose the show format wisely, depending on the label's doctrine and the target audience. For example, there are designers who prefer to take part in alternative shows to the official fashion week program because the audience attending these identify with their designs and habitually purchase clothes in this category. On the contrary, there are other designers who present collections at more than one fashion week, a case being that of designer David Delfín, who shows in Cibeles Madrid Fashion Week and during New York Fashion Week. The show will be a success as long as the press shows interest in the designs and sales of the collection increase. A collection with a poor runway show can bring harsh reviews and a setback in a designer's career. Organizing a runway show involves many professionals (designers, agencies, models, stylists, stage designers, audiovisual technicians, photographers, etc.) and when it comes to choosing, it is recommendable that you choose ones whose work and experience is more in tune with the philosophy of the label or the collection being presented. Likewise, good PR is important. You need to count on the services of a good press agency that knows how to convey what is being presented and what makes the event newsworthy. Finally, the event organizing team must be very aware of the availability of relevant figures for the label to attend the event, such as fashion editors and buyers, and they should not coincide as far as possible with others who would make their presence impossible.

Above, image from Avsh Alom Gur spring/summer 2010 collection. **On the right**, photo from the Homini Emerito (HE by Mango) launch catalog, 2008.

LOOKBOOK

A lookbook or collection catalog is an important tool for a designer or label to use when presenting a collection. It is important to put together a professional lookbook, as this will help, for example, sales staff in a boutique to provide a suitable complement to the pieces from a collection through the ideas proposed in it, or to advise customers on the different options they have. Good styling, well-directed photography, a model who responds to the body form the target market identifies with or admires, and spectacular art direction can enhance the qualities of a garment and turn it into the start piece of a collection. Many labels entrust their image to celebrities or international models for the season's lookbook. Others hire renowned photographers or artists to turn their catalog into a work of art. Both options, despite the sizeable investment required, are compensated by the publicity they receive from the media. An example of this is the lookbook featuring the model Anouck Lepère for Stella McCartney's 2010 cruise collection, or the one featuring model Jon Kortajarena to launch Mango's menswear collection in 2008. PR and advertising agencies working for fashion labels are turning more to the Internet as a means of showing their work through original ways of connecting with the public. Quicksilver, for instance, has taken good advantage of young netizens' interest in fashion to promote the brand's female line. To this end it has chosen style ambassadors in different countries around the world. These are special girls with great potential and style, who have become "moving catalogs" for the company.

HE

WHAT NO FASHIONISTA SHOULD MISS

MAGAZINES

A Magazine
www.amagazinecuratedby.com

Another Magazine
www.anothermag.com

Bon Magazine
www.bonmagazine.com

Cosmopolitan
www.cosmopolitan.com

Dazed & Confused
www.dazeddigital.com

Elle
www.elle.com

Fly
www.fly16x9.com

GQ
www.gq.com

Harper's Bazaar
www.harpersbazaar.com

H Magazine
www.hmagazine.com

L'Officiel
www.officiel.com.ua

Lula Magazine
www.lulamag.com

Marie Claire
www.marieclaire.com

Neo2
www.neo2.es

Numéro Magazine
www.numero-magazine.com

Nylon Magazine
www.nylonmag.com

Plastique Magazine
www.plastiquemagazine.com

Status Magazine
www.statusmagonline.com

Tank Magazine
www.tankmagazine.com

Tendencias Fashionmag
www.tendenciasfashionmag.com

V Magazine
www.vmagazine.com

Vanidad
www.vanidad.es

Vogue
www.vogue.com

Wad Magazine
www.wadmag.com

BLOGS AND WEBS

A shaded view of Fashion
www.ashadedviewonfashion.com

Chictopia
www.chictopia.com

Facehunter
www.facehunter.blogspot.com

Fashion&Style on *New York Magazine*
www.nymag.com/fashion/

Fashionisima
www.fashionisima.es

Fashion TV
www.ftv.com

Garance Doré
www.garancedore.fr

I can teach you how to do it
www.icanteachyouhowtodoit.com

Inside am-lul's closet
am-lul.blogspot.com

Kate loves me
www.katelovesme.net

Lookbook
www.lookbook.nu

Mensencia
www.mensencia.com

Not Just a Label
www.notjustalabel.com

The Fashionisto
www.thefashionisto.com

***The New York Times* Style Magazine**
www.nytimes.com/stylemagazine

The Sartorialist
thesartorialist.blogspot.com

Trendslab bcn
trendslabbcn.blogspot.com

Trendtation
www.trendtation.com

StockholmStreetStyle
carolinesmode.com/stockholmstreetstyle

Style
www.style.com

Style Cliker
www.styleclicker.net

Unlimited Clothes
unlimited-clothes.over-blog.com

50 CREATIVE SOLUTIONS

ALEXANDRA VERSCHUEREN

www.alexandraverschueren.com

Born and raised in Antwerp, Alexandra Vershueren was always interested in fashion. She studied at the Royal Academy of Fine Arts in Antwerp, an institution she chose for its good reputation: it was the school that produced the Antwerp Six in the eighties and, in the years since, designers such as Bernhard Willhelm, Peter Pilotto, AF Vandevorst, Veronique Branquinho, and Bruno Pieters. After graduating among the top in her year, she went to New York as an intern at Proenza Schouler, where she stayed for one month before starting work as a junior ready-to-wear designer at Derek Lam. In the meantime, she sent an application to participate in the International Fashion and Photography Festival in Hyères. Once chosen, she decided to return to Belgium to prepare for the event. In the festival, which took place in April 2010, she was awarded the Jury Grand Prize for her collection, Medium, which was judged by such persons of note in the fashion industry as Dries Van Noten, Sarah Mower, María Cornejo, Olivier Lalanne, Charlotte Stockdale, and Pascalle Mussard, among others.

MY IT

I don't think I really have only one *It girl*. Firstly, I never really start designing with a specific woman in my mind. Concept and the translation of materials and techniques are my first priority. Only after that the woman I see in the collection emerges. I like a strong, mysterious woman, who has integrity, who is different without trying to be different, who doesn't need to say much to make her point. A woman who is passionate and attentive for detail, who appreciates a garment for what it is and embraces the piece her whole lifetime.

INSPIRATION

In general there are a lot of things I find to be inspiring, and in all different fields. It doesn't necessarily need to be fashion. It can be also art, design, crafts, science, and literature. Love, friendships, artists, books... They all do the trick for me. For the Medium collection I got inspired after seeing the work by German artist Thomas Demand. He recreates objects out of everyday life into paper, such as kitchens, empty offices, and bathrooms, and then he takes photographs of them. As a viewer you see the picture and realize something is off, but only after close inspection you realize it's fake. It's not a vacuum cleaner you're looking at, but a recreation of a vacuum cleaner. He really plays with your interpretation of reality. And I like the fact that paper is used in this case as a strong medium to lay bare the artificiality. Also, as a designer you're confronted with paper all the time (to note down ideas, to sketch on it, and to cut your patterns). Then I started thinking how I could translate and push the idea of paper into the garments. I tried treating the fabrics as if they were paper. I applied folding techniques found in Japanese origami to the garments . That way unusual shapes emerged, without ever having had the intention to create sculptural pieces. Also paper allowed me to do all kinds of prints, like blots of ink on blotting paper, the crude first strokes in children's drawings, and the blue lines of notebooks. In short, my collection is about paper as a medium and I only used fabrics, like felted wool (with polyester), and cottons that I starched and strengthened with Tyvek. The colors were decided on the basis of the three general ballpoint pen colors – blue, red and green – but also blots of ink on pink blotting paper, blue ink, and then more natural colors like gray, camel, and black for the coating to balance out and complement the bright colors.

CREATION

It was quite challenging translating these foldings in paper on fabric and onto a female human body. I didn't want the body to disappear, so I really tried making the pieces quite tailored. The creative process and the techniques I use play an important role in the development of my collection. The work that needs to be done to translate the concept is as important as the end result itself. I try to use fashion as my medium, and I try to study the numerous ways one can look at and think of garments. I try to keep both concept and form/shapes in my mind while working on a collection and see how those two things interact with each other. Designing garments absolutely amazes me in many ways. I feel inspired by the medium itself. I feel the tendency to take it apart, like a little kid who wants to see "what's inside." I feel challenged by the boundaries of garments and how far I can push them without losing touch with the reality of it and the wearability of the clothing itself, and the girl/woman wearing the garment. I try to work meticulously and research-based, using an experimental approach, an approach that also provides the poetry of trying and failing. This is an essential part of my work. I want to leave traces of the making in my garments, referring to the process and to myself on the other side of the garment. That's why I also try to do as much manually as possible. As a designer, you have to try to reach things not initially attainable, to be creative and find solutions, working on a vision that doesn't exist yet, without having a clear idea of the possible

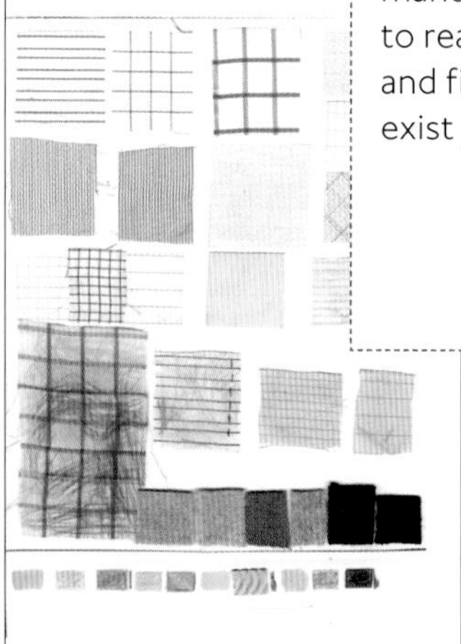

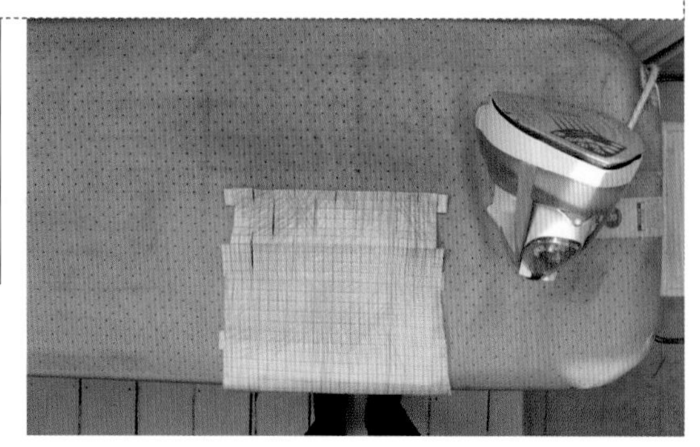

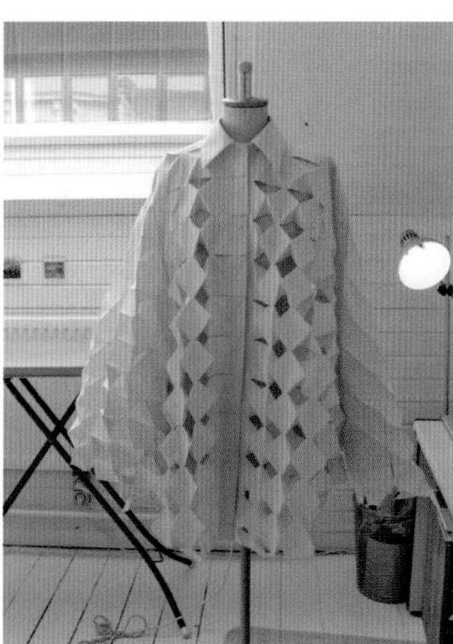

LOOK

The final look is the translation of this collection. Alexandra wanted the garments to be the focal point. She didn't want them to look to weird or funny, but wearable, something anyone could wear everyday. That's why she wanted the girls to look quite serious and neutral, complementing the garments this way.

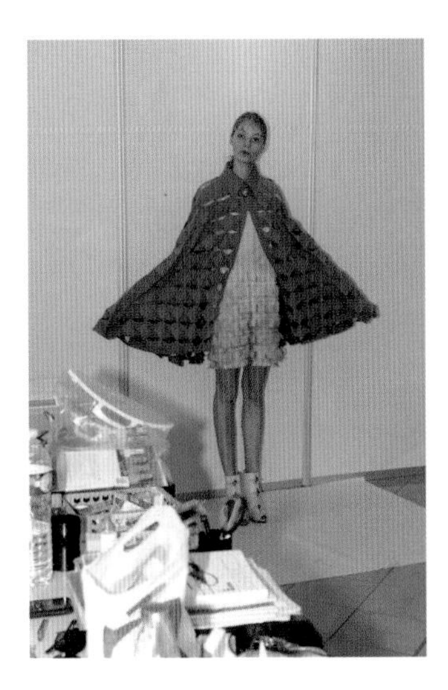

ALEXI FREEMAN

www.alexifreeman.com

Alexi Freeman was born in December 1978 in Hobart, Australia. He earned a degree in fine arts at the University of Tasmania, graduating in 2004 with a major in printmaking and sculpture. His artwork has always taken references largely from the concepts and aesthetics of fashion. Freeman produced limited-edition prints and garments until 2005, when the Tasmanian government, through its Arts Tasmania institution, provided him with funding that enabled him to open his own brand, Alexi Freeman, in 2006. Currently based in Melbourne, the firm's womenswear collections are characterized by their incorporation of printed and hand-decorated fabrics, and the use of draping juxtaposed with tailoring. Freeman has produced eight ready-to-wear season collections to date, which have been distributed to a growing list of retailers and private clients in Australia, New Zealand, the US, and Europe. His collections are a graphic homage to the world we live in and their raison d'être is to fuse together fashion and art, to enhance the misunderstood avant-garde, and to popularize the concept of urban couture, in addition to paying tribute to the modern woman.

MY IT

She's a star of the no-star generation, a post-punk revolutionary enamored by the beauty of a bygone era whilst lusting after the must-haves of an unknown future, so she keeps everyone guessing by lacing her basics with a hint of luxury, and dresses down her couture with urban utilitarianism. Integral to the experimental jet set, she's a cosmopolitan aesthete who roams the concrete jungle turning trash into treasure, and treasure into tomorrow's trends. She works, she plays and she doesn't have time to get changed in between, and if it doesn't make her feel sexy she doesn't even bother. She's an old fashioned girl who has just seen color for the first time and still has stars in her eyes.

INSPIRATION

In the 1940s Christian Dior unveiled the H-line skirt, which became commonly known as the "pencil skirt" in the 1950s due to its slim fitting shape, signaling a return of the fetishism of femininity through physical constraint. The classic suit was then brought back with a vengeance in the 1980s as a figure-hugging component of the shoulder thrusting power suit, heralding the rise of women to positions of power in business. With the onset of the 2010s I identified the need for yet another review of the modern woman's suit, and I proposed for my *It girl*, battling the glass ceiling, a shotgun overhaul of tailoring juxtaposed with sportswear elements to give a new look and feel. This is achieved by teaming a classic pencil skirt and blazer combination (doused in geometric print) with graphic leggings, a mesh backed jersey singlet and a supple leather clutch. In addition, a monochromatic palette of shades of greige is highlighted by black silk-screening, creating a print on print on print effect. The wool/cashmere used for the blazer and pencil skirt is sourced from Italy and then printed in my own geometric "mini-flapper" motif. The print is stripe matched through the seams creating some optical construction effects. Both pieces are fully lined with natural toned acetate, which is also printed in the same motif. This is teamed with an Australian greige merino wool jersey and cotton/polyester diamond mesh singlet, and accessorized with a white leather clutch and oiled cotton belt with adjustable studded fastenings.

CREATION

I wanted to create a modern take on the classic suit, so I looked for a range of fabrics that could work together to re-invigorate what has been a staple of women's fashion for over sixty years. I've always loved woven motifs such as herringbone and houndstooth, but I wanted to create my own, so I designed the "mini-flapper" as a response to these classic textile motifs. I then substituted the classic woven blouse for a merino jersey singlet, and the hosiery for Lycra leggings and voilà – my signature AF suiting was born. I feel I have offered an alternative for women who want or need to wear suiting, but don't want to subscribe to the tried and tested formula worn for generations.

LOOK

The look is achieved in the form of a black and shades of greige phantasmagoria of print on print mayhem both inside and out. Not a layer is left unadorned in this anomalous mix of fabrics, silhouettes and influences. Not for the faint hearted, the result is a thoroughly modern take on classic tailoring: a sophisticated, elegant suit with a contemporary sportswear twist.

BRATTLE
BOOK SHOP
KENNETH GLOSS
PROPRIETOR
WE BUY AND SELL
FINE LIBRARIES

AMAYA ARZUAGA

www.amayaarzuaga.com

Amaya Arzuaga is currently one of the Spanish fashion designers with the greatest international following. In little more than fifteen years since she launched the label bearing her name, she has presented her designs in London, Milan, Paris, New York, Barcelona, and Madrid. Her collections are also sold in over twenty-five countries, and she has more than 200 stockists in Spain. She received the Spanish Gold Medal for Merit in Fine Arts in May 2005. She is also the recipient of Best Designer awards given by fashion and lifestyle magazines *Telva*, *Elle*, *Woman*, *Glamour*, and *Cosmopolitan*, in addition to the *El Mundo* Visual Arts Prize, the *Expansión* Young Entrepreneur Prize, the *Arte de Vivir* Prize, and the Cibeles First Prize, among others. She has taken part in a number of fashion exhibitions and designed the costumes for Pedro Almodóvar's movie *Live Flesh*, in addition to the dress worn by Cruella De Vil for the fifteenth anniversary of Disneyland Paris. Amaya Arzuaga is a versatile designer who always surprises. Her collections feature pure, highly structured forms that challenge the limits of physics.

MY IT

My *It girl* would be Karen O, the vocalist of the New York indie rock and punk garage band Yeah Yeah Yeahs. I like her great charisma, which is reflected in her music, her attitude and her theatricality. Her style of dressing is very personal and she is constantly experimenting – changing and evolving it.

INSPIRATION

Metamorphosis as a sublimation process has its paradigm in the transformation of a silkworm into a cocoon, and then to a silkmoth. This duality is intrinsic to everything, including beauty. Any sequence of time modifies the universe and involves a movement, like the subtle beating of dragonfly wings. My inspiration was the movement made by butterfly wings. In this case, we needed a weightless fabric, one that was light and with movement but somewhat stiff at the same time. This led us to choose a mix of two fabrics: resin-treated viscose and pleated tulle. I chose black for the color simply because I think in black.

CREATION

I needed to design a dress that wrapped around a women's body as naturally and comfortable as it could without making her feel enclosed by the piece. Using a semi-stretch fabric like viscose allowed the dress to fit and mould her silhouette. Also, the idea of a dress without zippers or any other type of fasteners adds to this sensation of freedom. We'll work the pleated tulle around the mannequin to reflect a shape insinuating the lightness of butterfly wings.

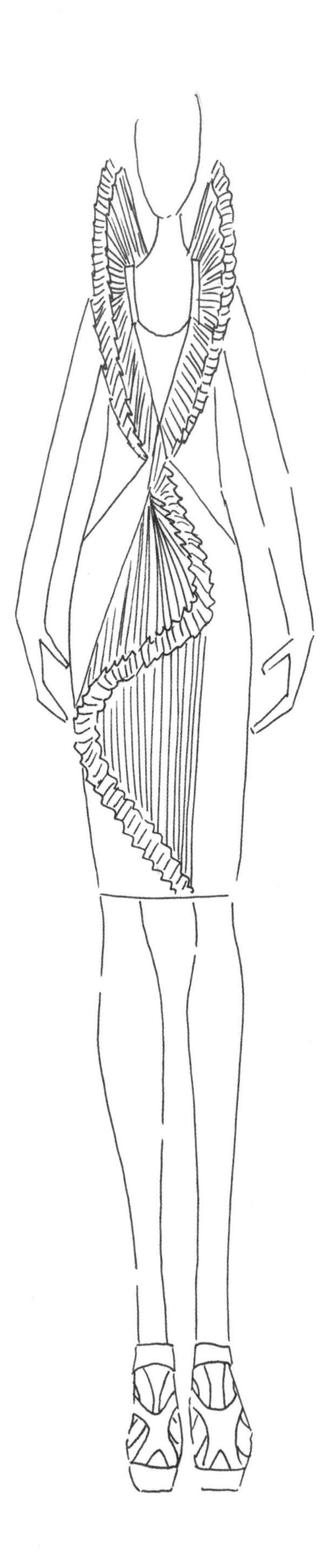

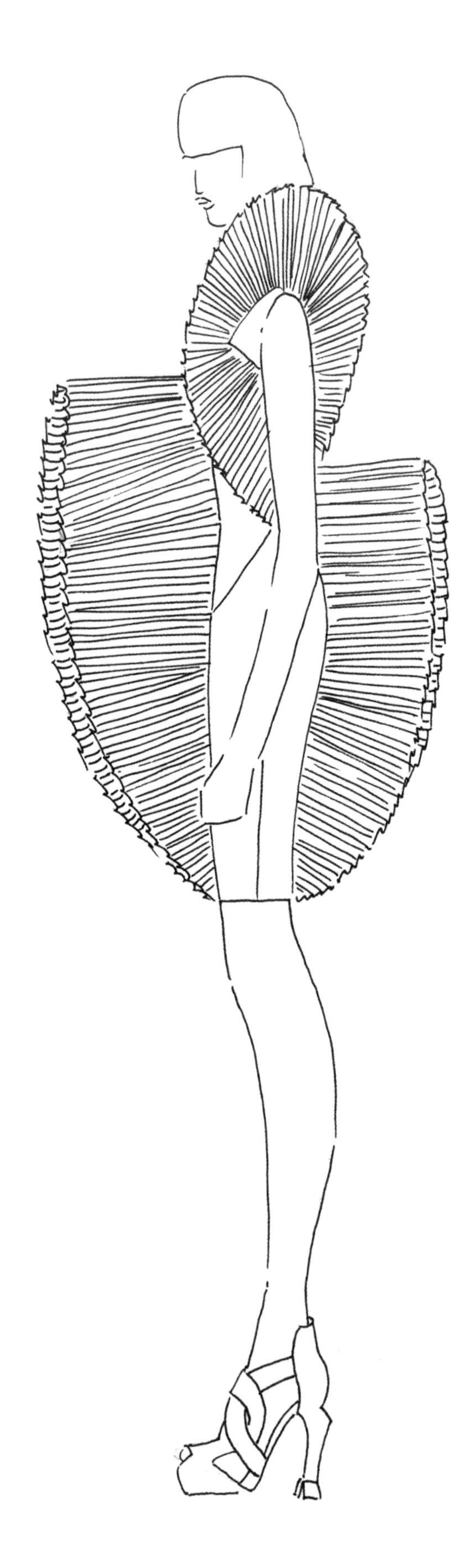

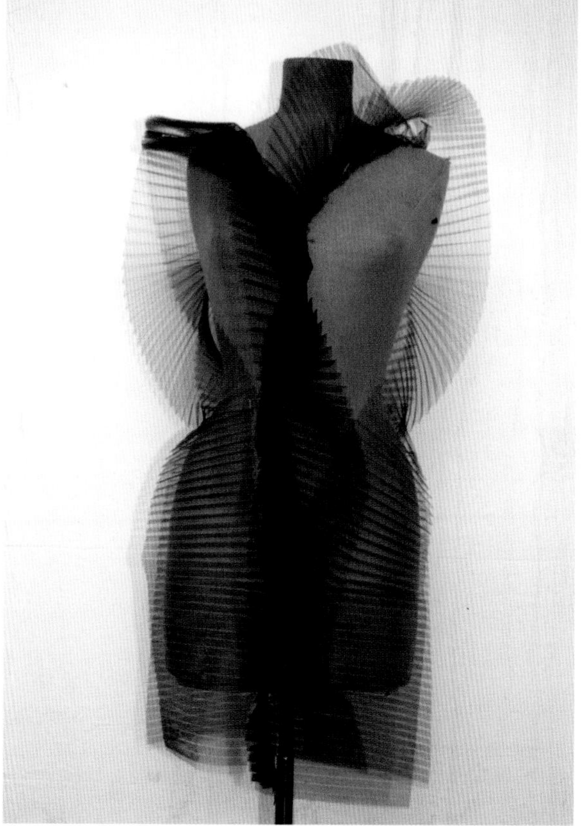

LOOK

The result is a dress that is easy to wear and which suggests femininity, lightness, and elegance. Faithful to the concept created by the designer, its appearance is as fragile and subtle as the movement made by butterfly wings. The footwear designed by Amaya Arzuaga always embodies quality and originality. An example of this is the shoes we propose to accessorize the look, which belong to the same collection. The first two models are patent leather platform sandals with interlaced straps in black combined with sky blue, nude, or pearl gray, with sculpted heels. The third is a three-colored sandal with ankle strap with yellow and silver combining with black to give a spring touch.

ANDREA CAMMAROSANO

www.andreacammarosano.com

Andrea Cammarosano was born in Trieste, Italy, in 1985. After studying the first year of fashion design in Florence, he decided to transfer to the Royal Academy of Fine Arts in Antwerp, Belgium, mainly owing to its reputation for alternative ideas, which, according to Andrea, attracts ambitious students with a more cutting-edge view of fashion. After graduating, in 2008, he began work as an assistant to Walter Van Beirendonck in Antwerp, helping him with the creation of new collections. The project featured in this book belongs to Bury Me Standing, his first collection after graduating, through which Andrea toys with the idea of dressing for "protection" and "identity," a work that has been exhibited around the world at such relevant venues as MoMA in New York and the MuseumsQuartier in Vienna. He has also collaborated with artists such as Narcisse Tordoir and Fischer Spooner. He is currently working on a new collection titled "I'm a monster."

MY IT

He is young and silly, sexy, well built, with fantasy and a sense of originality. Menswear is sometimes very boring. I definitely am not into the skinny boy minimalist aesthetics, just because I find it a bit dry and repetitive at this moment. I've been anorexic for a short period and after that I relate skinniness to a very deep sadness and frustration. You have got to eat carbs to be happy – it's a scientific fact.

INSPIRATION

I'm not always sure where my inspiration comes from. I guess ideas can stick to the walls of your brain for a very long time, until at the end you have a clear image of what you want – and after that, if you analyze the whole thing a bit, you find out that there was a reason for everything. But analyzing can be dangerous – it creates many words and it bleaches the ideas. I see a lot of people around me, not only in fashion but also in arts, who work with "themes" and call them "concept." But a theme is not a concept. The seaside, Kubrick, the 1970s, nostalgia, these are all themes. You can develop a really good collection around them, and you can also mix them in an interesting ways. A concept is something different. This project is about battles. You can fight hunger, or you can fight anorexia, there are many battles in the world. In all of them there are uniforms like an identity. Fashion is all about uniforms, and about how to break them. But even to break them, you must use the right language and the right code, or you won't be understood. I have considered memorials knowledge too. In the past, some of the dead had beautiful rooms adorned with paintings and full of the objects that could be useful to them in the afterlife. If you have to leave – because of a war, or because something occurs that you couldn't foresee – you must be ready, choose your dearest things, the ones strictly necessary to live… your home in a pocket. Finally it's just about hope. Otherwise you wouldn't even have started that battle, would you? Maybe at the beginning you really thought it was a hopeless adventure. Well, you might still be able to succeed, as long as you choose the right allies and fight with true hope. Be happy with what you've got, but always be ready to go further.

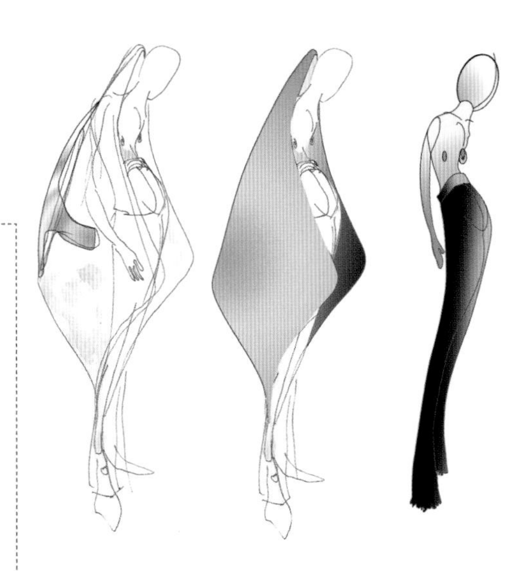

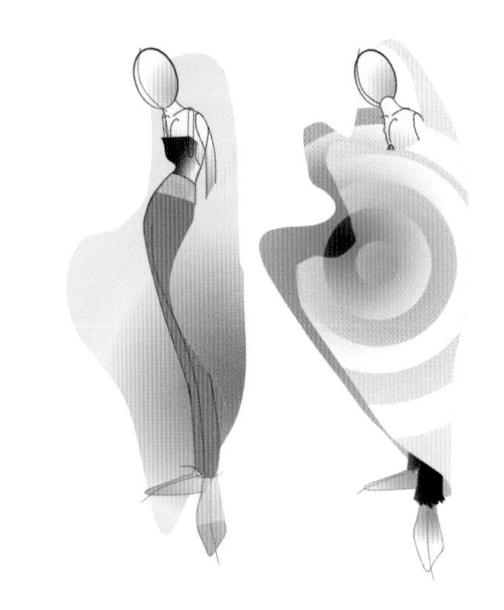

CREATION

My design process is very abstract. As I say, once things come out I can kind of see where they trace back to, but they can all gather up from different places and times. I've always been very attracted by food, but this of course concerns more the "feeling" I have towards fabrics, shapes and textures than the final look of clothes. I guess in food I recognize the pressure of the body. The body is not a hollow skin, but is a very plump object. Sometimes, when you squeeze it in the right place, you get all the effect you need. A belt that is slightly tighter than it should be can be a very sexy thing, of course. In fact, the body is my major source of inspiration. I try to chop it up, to deform it and to cover it. I guess this is why my work is very "sculptural" – a remark that many people have made. I think you can say a lot through volumes. When it comes to fabrics, I really, really, really love colors. They give me such joy. I like the contrast between opposites – say, furry and chubby materials versus a very light chiffon, or technologic materials versus natural, rough textures. In the collection portrayed here, I really enjoyed using organza because it can be so transparent but so stiff; and I reinterpreted military clothing through a transparent, feminine sensitivity mixed with sequins and gold. This of course was a theme. The concept of the collection, though, was to frame these silhouettes in some abstract, empty machines that would force the body in a different position. These are the polyester cocoons that you see in the pictures. They were some sort of walking frames meet coffin meet backpack, something to re-frame the body to portray it from a different point of view and understand it better.

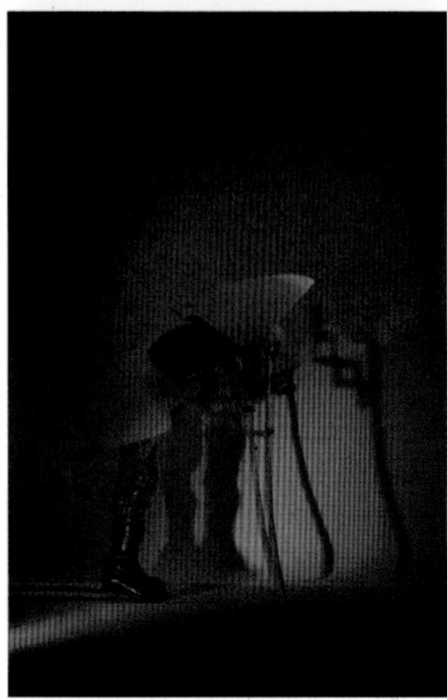

LOOK

In this look Andrea's model is a tiny but well-built guy. Andrea likes the way the shirt makes him a bit clumsier, with all this oversized smock work on the waist. The boots were deliberately chosen to clash with the gold and the organza. The model suffered a bit inside that plastic shell, but then again, as Andrea said, "if you don't suffer, you don't feel your body!"

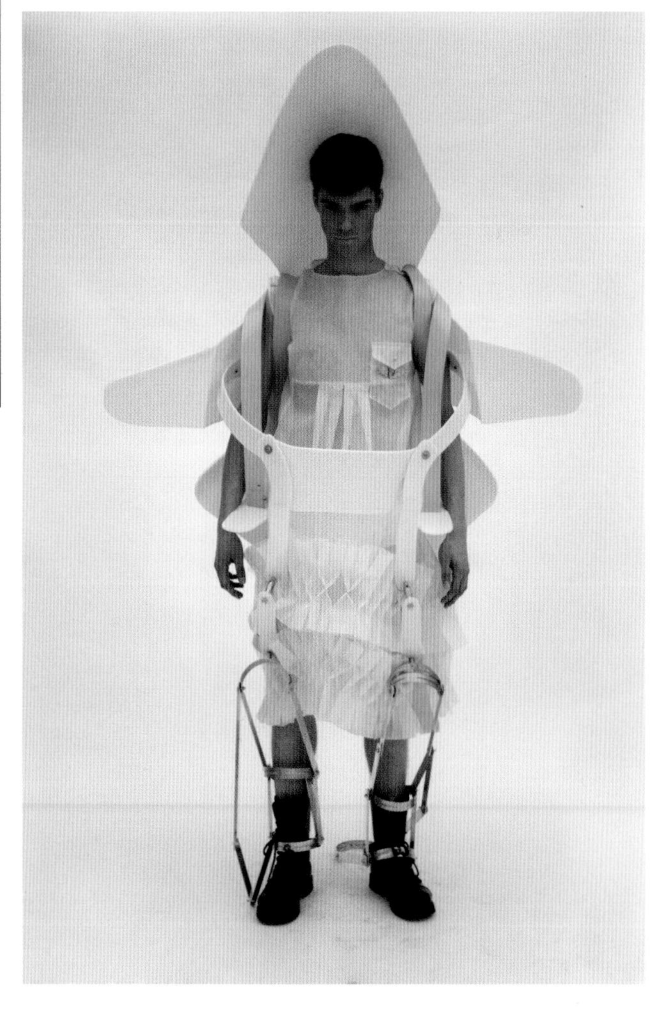

ARA JO

www.notjustalabel.com/arajo

A graduate in fashion design from the prestigious London art and design school Central Saint Martins, the South Korean designer Ara Jo based herself in the British capital after finishing her studies in order to set up her own label. Despite being new to the fashion world, some of her dreams have already come true, such as dressing the new queen of pop Lady Gaga and other celebrities, the likes of Jamelia, Leona Lewis, and Buttafly, which means that her name is on everyone's lips in London. Since showing her degree collection, the press has received her with great enthusiasm and has publicized her creations, which are currently featured in fashion columns in magazines such as *Neo2*, *InStyle*, and *Nylon*, among others. Ara Jo is obsessed by mysterious creatures, fairy tales, and using beautiful references, such as muses, in her designs. Ara Jo's designs show her crazy side, which she balances with intricate detailing and very delightful effects, together with an amazing choice and combination of fabrics, which adds to her personal touch of sensuality.

MY IT

My *It girl* is a vampire, a magnificent woman who has lived since the nineteenth century. Naturally, I believe vampires have been living in our society since the classical age. She's a woman who is very self-assured, and she loves to play seduction games. She likes to dress romantically and with sophistication, and always with elegance.

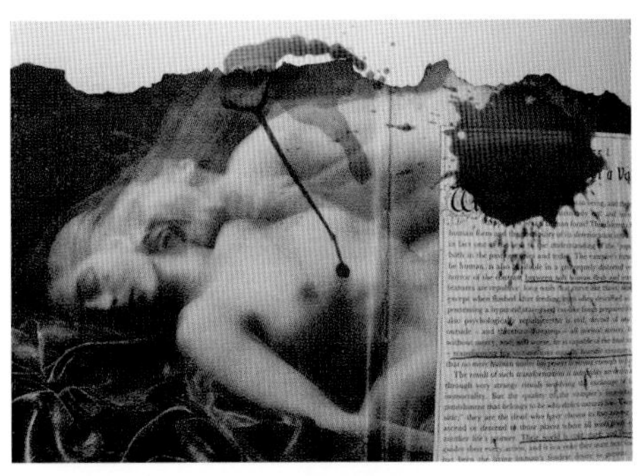

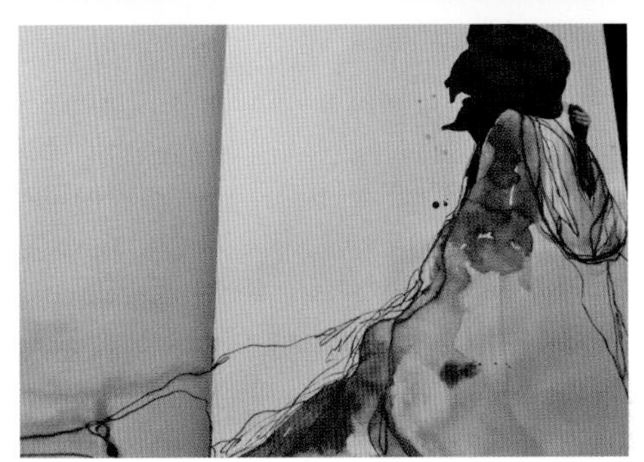

INSPIRATION

In dressing this charismatic *It girl*, I found inspiration in vampires and the reinterpretation of their classic references: fangs, batwings, bite marks, and blood. The vampire straddles the limits between the human and the divine, between what is permitted and what is forbidden. I take some references from Gothic and Romantic literature, such as fantasy, extreme emotions, the struggle between good and bad, and sensuality. The fabrics I use are those that convey a sense of mystery, gloom, or sheerness, such as bleached silk and cotton velvets, Lurex, and tulle, with accessories like brooches, buckles, and hooks. I tend to use deep colors such as burgundy combined with black, gold, and silver.

CREATION

With so many artistic references, the design work is very creative, but it also requires an in-depth study so as not to overdo the pieces. I play with volumes and shapes to come up with a highly theatrical look. First I make several sketches that evolve until the design takes the desired shape. In this case, the sleeves will have a considerable volume and they will be structured to imitate a lion head. So first I work with a toile. Then, once the pattern is made and the required modifications are made on a dummy, I start to sew the garments. The fitting shows that the result corresponds to the design as far as form and comfort are concerned. Finally, I try to bring the best out of each piece with the finishing details.

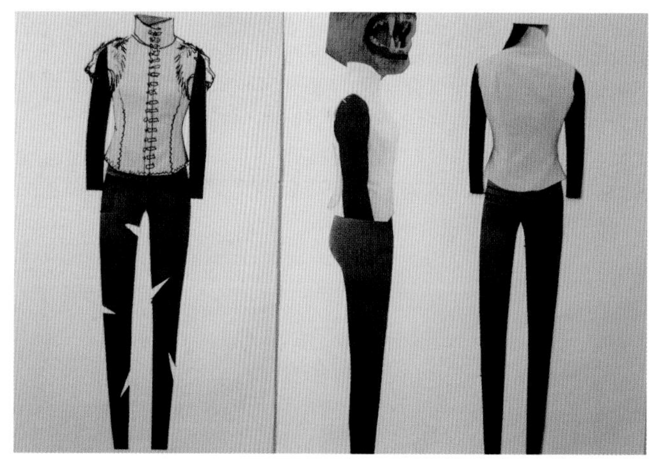

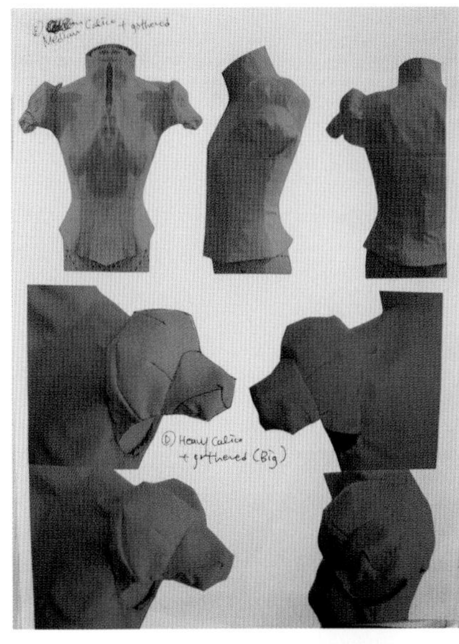
Medium Calico + gathered
Heavy Calico
+ gathered (Big)

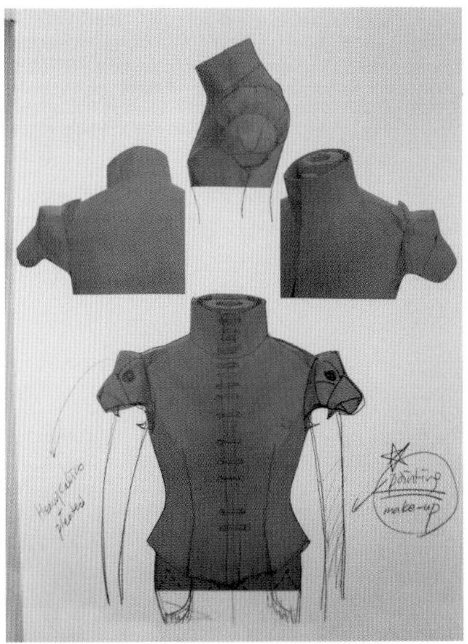
painting
make-up

Pages 100+111 Photography: Andreas Waldschuetz. Styling: Adia Trischler. Make-up: Stefanie Lamm. Hair styling: Patrick Glatthaar. Digital retouch: Christian Friedrich

LOOK

The result is an outfit made up of a bleached velvet skirt, topped off with a wide gold belt used as a sash. The back slit allows the wearer to walk comfortably. The back velvet top is cut to just below the bust. The high neck gives it an austere touch and lengthens the silhouette. The volume is structured in the shoulders, which imitate two lion heads. Finally, the accessories – shoes, bracelets, rings, and a spectacular gold pendant – accompanied by meticulous styling, turn the model into an authentic chic vampire, an awe-inspiring *It girl*!

ASGER JUEL LARSEN

asgerjuellarsen.blogspot.com

Since graduating with distinction in 2009 with a menswear degree from London College of Fashion, Danish designer Asger Juel Larsen has enjoyed huge media attention, in addition to being listed among the finalists of the prestigious Mittelmoda fashion award. Inspired by historical events such as the coronation of the last Russan czar, Nicholas II, and movie figures like *Terminator*, his degree collection reinterprets the themes of medieval warfare. The pieces are marked by hard contrasts that explore expressions of masculine strength. Stiff structures are softened by a silhouette that is transformed into two opposing ideas: the voluminous and the slim. This dichotomy is also reflected through futuristic materials such as leather, PVC, rubber cords, and different metals. Asger Juel Larsen is currently working on his 2011 spring/summer collection while completing an MA in menswear at the London College of Fashion.

MY IT

He's in his mid-twenties and has some quite unusual hobbies. He still thinks highly of the old sci-fi collection of toys he collected in the 1980s. His favorite movies are *Creature from the Black Lagoon, The Element of Crime* and *Terminator II*. He also likes very much to dress up and feel good about himself and go out and rave with his friends.

INSPIRATION

The hero is confronted with the raw industrial architecture of a future past, reminiscent of Richard Rogers' apocalyptic TSB Lloyds building in East London. Cables, tubes, shafts and elevators pervading the building like bones and veins – an aesthetics that is applied to his very own corpus, covering him in metallic safety panels and wire-like structures. Here, the visual worlds merge and unite with the visuality of the film *Titus* by Julie Taymor, marked by its dark and grotesque costume design. As eclectic the far and severe future appears, as crucial is protection in the dispiteous fight for survival. Elements of riding and fencing uniforms are therefore translated as the protagonist's armor. The construction of fencing helmets, 1970s and 1980s bicycle equipment as well as horse hoof protection are mirrored in the elaborate details and craftsmanship.

CREATION

For me, the whole design process is connected from initial ideas to the final pieces. It's about jumping back and for while working on the different parts of the process and still keeping the focus on what the initial ideas were. Before designing, I do thorough research into a specific theme. In this case, futuristic architecture and sci-fi movies. I read, draw, visit relevant exhibitions, take photos and notes and speak to people who have a different knowledge and point of view about the chosen theme. This always helps me to understand what I'm working with. At this point, I start developing my rough sketches into actual designs. While doing this, I find relevant fabrics and materials, so designing and collecting fabrics go hand in hand. Then I start making my toiles and figure out what works and what doesn't. When working with metal or any alternative material, it's very important to test, test, and test. For my *It boy* I wanted to create a strong masculine look for a grown-up boy with an adventurous mind. It should be a structured look where the silhouette is fitted from the bottom and grows larger from the waist, so it ends up in a V-shape. The trousers are made in soft neoprene with a chunky visible metal zip and two press studs. Quilted vertical stitching is applied, so the trousers connect with the waistcoat. As for the waistcoat, it is made in the same fabric as the trousers and it has quilted shoulder panels that combine the twenty-eight tubes with the hemline. Rubber cords with metal studs are put on through small eyelets on each tube to structure the waistcoat in any way you like. Two metal buckles in the neck and hem opening are stitched on before the 8m (26 ft)-long chrome metal tubes are applied. I cut the metal tubes in different sizes by using a grinder, so the movement of the tubes becomes irregular when moving your body.

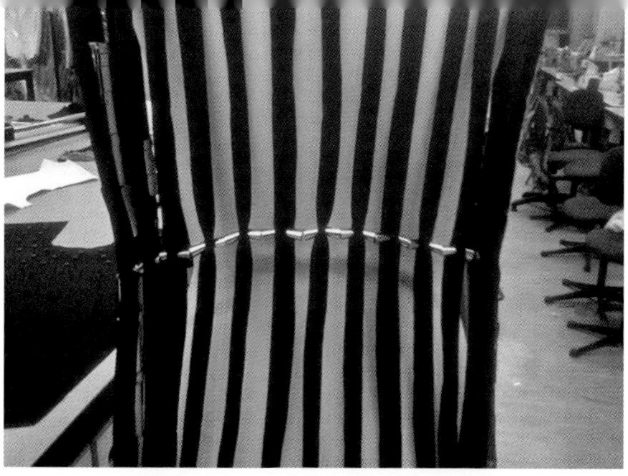

LOOK

Asger defines this outfit as "an adventurous look for a daring life." The outfit really responds to each of the aspects that inspired the designer. Here is the image of a hero faced with industrial architecture, an armored rider from the future. This delicate work is constructed from neoprene, metal, and wire, with a subtle Gothic touch that conveys a certain nostalgic feel in this image. The look is a convergence of the past, the present and the future, and a combination of different sources of inspiration perfectly embodied in it. It is a look for a tough and masculine guy, for those willing to live out new experiences.

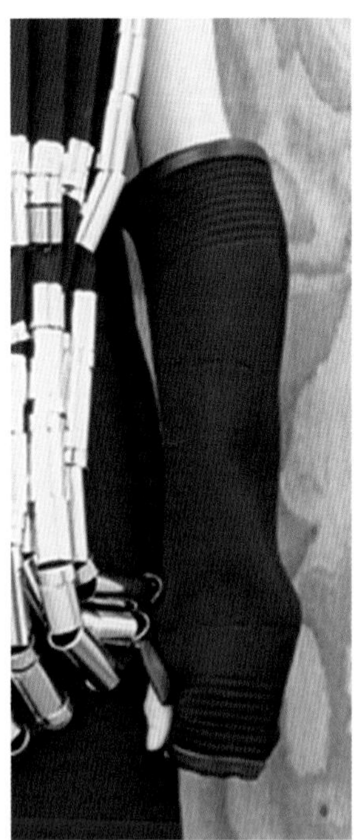

AVSH ALOM GUR

www.avshalomgur.com

Avsh Alom Gur is a London-based fashion designer. He graduated in fashion design with distinction from Central Saint Martins and joined the team at Donna Karan after his graduation as a designer of evening gowns, his main line. He has also rendered his services as a freelance fashion consultant to such leading fashion houses as Roberto Cavalli, Chloé, and Nicole Farhi. His most recent collaboration was as creative director at Ossie Clark, where he oversaw the relaunching of one of the most emblematic British labels. Avsh Alom Gur launched his own label in 2005 and has presented his collections off-schedule during London Fashion Week in the last ten seasons. His designs, a very urban combination of Eastern and Western elements, have won for him the New Generation Designer award given by the British Fashion Council and Topshop for three consecutive seasons.

MY IT

My *It girl* would be someone who challenges traditional ideals of femininity and beauty. She is a playful and independent modern woman who dresses to express her personality. I create garments for women who treat their wardrobe as though they were a curator of a gallery.

INSPIRATION

I take inspiration from anything and everything from my daily vision! I can usually find something unique and beautiful in what others might think of as mess or dirt. I have found inspiration from the landscapes of urban London, from disposed packaging, empty drinks cans and other general litter found on the streets. These work beautifully when combined with the arts and crafts of tribal ethnic cultures. In this occasion, challenged by the illusion of Op Art (Optical Art), I give movement to black and white prints, offsetting them with bold injections of color. Colors should be odd, beautiful, rich and dirty at the same time. I usually go for a group of colors from the same family in order to create shades for a playful result. I also like to throw in an accidental color to offset the harmony. I love fabrics that are made from natural fibers such as cotton, linen and silk. In the past I have bought fabrics in greige stage and then manipulated them with silkscreen printing, dyeing and distressing, according to my needs. I usually like to combine different textures and weights of fabric within the same garment.

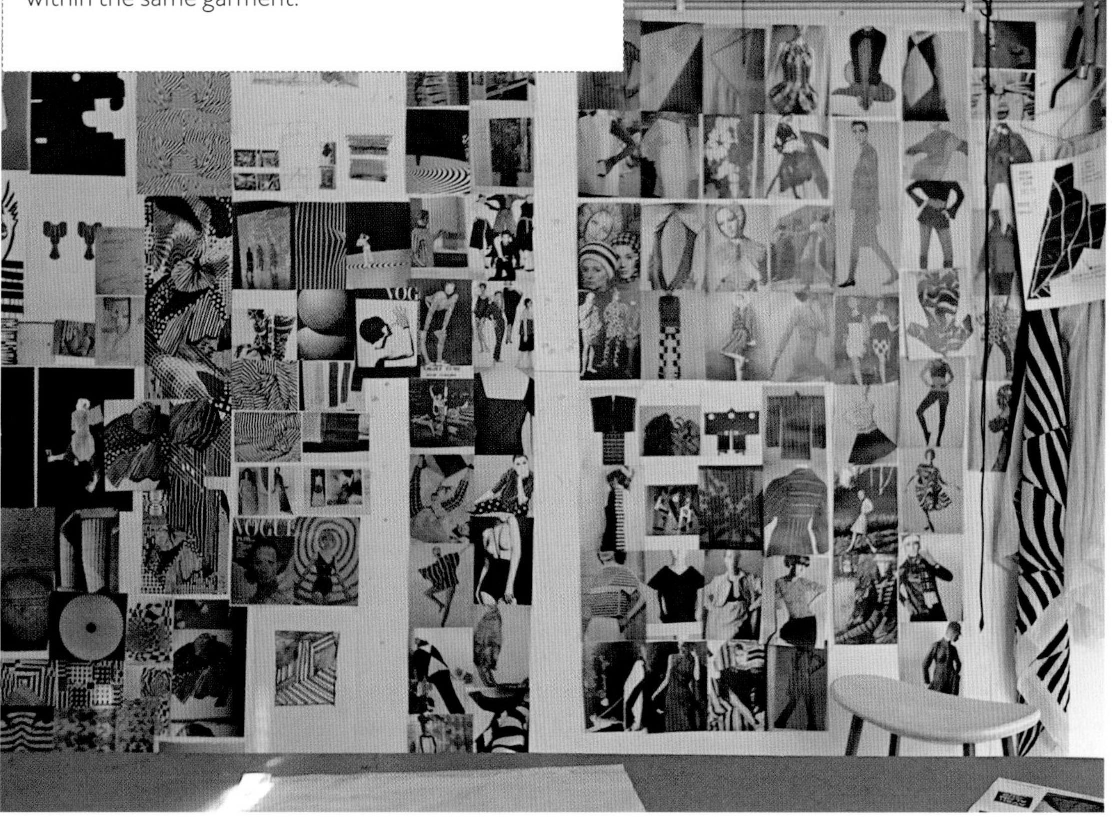

CREATION

For me it is always about a story, a fantasy, a scenery or a backdrop. Once these are in place, they act as guidelines, which help me to curate and "cast" the rest of my fantasy colors and materials. Choose a story, close your eyes and imagine what garments a beautiful girl would wear. Then start creating. I usually create the collection in an organic form and with a true collaboration and design dialogue with my closest team and freelance-contributing designers. Each garment and accessory is individually constructed in the Avsh Alom Gur production studios in East London and/or sourced first hand and closely monitored by the Avsh Alom Gur design and production team to ensure the highest quality and uniqueness of product. From the initial process of dyeing, printing and treating fabrics to the stitching of garments and to the fine finishing of each product, most Avsh Alom Gur mainline garments and accessories are currently produced either in-house or nearby in studios in London by experienced and talented professionals. My workplace is an organized chaos. Masses of fabrics, materials and equipments hanging from the ceiling alongside objects found in the streets. It is an open space that hosts both creative and technical personnel.

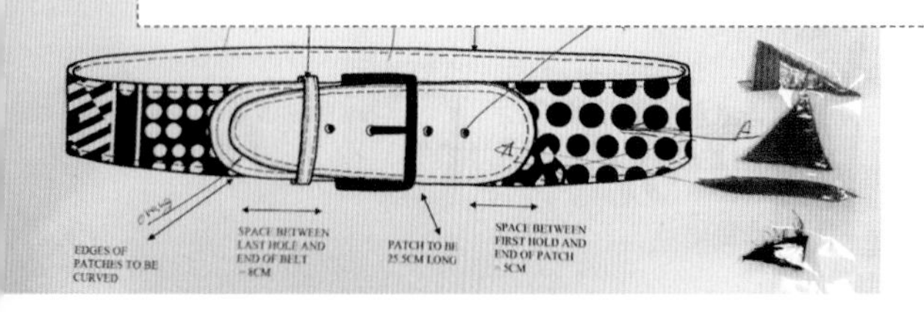

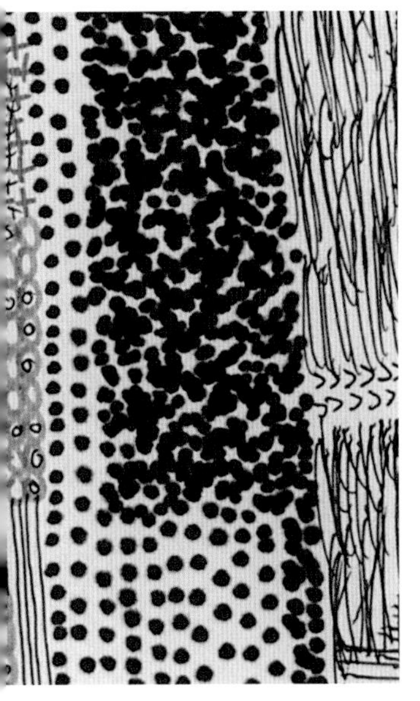

LOOK

This is a clean, modern silhouette, built on simple lines and geometric shapes. A simple, fluid cut, it breathes life into dresses and separates. Sensuality and comfort come in the form of effortlessly feminine dressing. Silk jumpsuits and dresses, in simple graphic shapes, for an individual and timeless style. See-thru prints flirt with light and shade, casting a silhouette against the skin. The complements, such as bracelets or belts, combine with each of the proposed dresses.

BOESSERT/SCHORN

www.boessert-schorn.de

Designers Sonia Boessert and Brigitte Schorn studied fashion design together at the Burg Giebichenstein University of Art and Design in Halle, Germany. It was there that these two talents realized they had to combine their taste in aesthetics and their view of fashion to create a single label, Boessert/Schorn. Their debut took place at the 18th International Fashion and Photography Festival in Hyères, France, in 2003. This event was without a doubt a turning point in the label's development and later consolidation. Since 2006 Boessert/Schorn have presented their designs twice a year in cities like Tokyo and Paris. For their most recent collection, for the 2010/2011 fall/winter season, the designers decide to cross the pond and introduce themselves to the American market by showing in New York, where they received great acclaim. Boessert/Schorn pieces are on sale in select stores around the world. Their style is a result of their love of combining textures and fabrics, among which knits of all kinds feature strongly. They work with special craft techniques, those of knitting and dyeing, which are largely inspired by antiques, crafts, and folk costumes.

MY IT

Our *It girl* is a mind of her own and she is sometimes a bit bullheaded. She prefers a rough aesthetics in a discreetly feminine way. She likes comfortable clothes that surround her like a house in which you just feel good. Her style is rough, inaccurate and nonchalant.

INSPIRATION

The inspiration of Boessert/Schorn is everyday life, craft, old things and traditional costumes. We prefer irregular structures. That is why we abstracted a landscape beyond recognition, until you could only see some blurry spots. We combined this rough structure with a very fine one, which reminds us of blurred and handmade brushstrokes. We like to use very rough-textured drapery, especially when they have a natural structure like wool, cotton or silk, in a harmonic combination of warm colors, like yellow, ochre, and other earth colors.

P.126+127_Photography: Stefanie Schweiger. Make-up and hair styling: Bettina Colmsee. Shoe design: Volker Atrops

CREATION

The strokes look real but aren't. They were made with digital printing. This is one of the contradictions we like to work with. We work a lot with knitting. Also the jacquard of the winter jacket is knitted. It is a mixture of a rough wool yarn and cotton. Through the different materials the knitted becomes more structured. In this occasion we have designed a very wide winter jacket. It is warm but very comfortable at the same time, and it allows movement. We have created very skinny trousers, but a little flexible, looking always for comfort. In addition, the trousers are framed by pieces of knitting which gave them a touch of sport and originality. The maxi shawl is also printed with another kind of brushstrokes. It adds some red and green tones to the set.

LOOK

The result is a very natural work, both for the fabrics and the handcrafted work. It is a very current and sophisticated design, a bet of the designers of Boessert/Schorn that fills the feminine wardrobe of happy colors for the fall/winter season. The big lapels of the coat raise to turn in maxi neck and play with the shawl and the scarf. An additional detail of this fantastic look are the original shoes, created by Volker Atrops, an artist who is an habitual collaborator of the signature, who has created jewelry pieces too, for their latest collections.

Pages 128+129 Photography: Stefanie Schweiger. Make-up and hair styling: Bettina Colmsee. Shoe design: Volker Atrops

Photography: Philipp Forstner

BOGOMIR DORINGER

www.bogomirdoringer.com

Bogomir Doringer was born in Belgrade, Serbia, in 1983. He studied sociology for three years at the University of Belgrade, focusing his interest on research into social and political issues and in the contradictions in the media regarding fashion. The post-war period caused a change in social values, and clothes took on an important role in society. This observation gave rise to Doringer's fascination with clothing. He realized it could be a perfect tool for making strong criticism in the eyes of the so-called high society. At the age of twenty-one he moved to Amsterdam, where he earned a degree in fine arts at the Gerrit Rietveld Academie (audiovisual department). His work *Deranged #2* was one of the designs representing Serbia at the Venice Biennale in 2009. His clear cinematographic influence and his critical analysis of the media were reasons behind his being invited to take part in an experimental master's degree at the Netherlands Film and Television Academy in Amsterdam. Doringer has forged his own unique creative identity that helps him to satisfy his "Robin Hood syndrome," using it to denounce injustice or to question certain moral aspects. He is intersted in interactive public participation, finding fashion the perfect accomplice for conveying his values and opinions as a multidisciplinary artist.

MY IT

I will have to play with the meaning of *It*. Once vocabulary is defined, it becomes limited, so I would use the term *It* as the *It* from the horror novel by Stephen King. Precisely that is my *It*. I work with the uncanny subjects that do not cuddle up to the audience, and the same audience mostly ignores them. Everybody is invited, everybody has this *It* that I am hunting with my work. The only problem is that most people pretend that this *It* is not part of them. That is why I work with fashion, because mass media is hooked on it. After very long mass media manipulations and the power of fashion magazines, the audience is in a specific mood. If you are an artist, you will have to deal with *It* in a way you can and you feel you should.

INSPIRATION

After working on the *Deranged #2* I created a new video installation that again uses fashion as a language, which will have an outfit made from 100 percent hair as its result. When I started devising it, I realized that all the sketches coming out of my brainstorming sessions looked like burkas. Far from wanting this, I decided then to take away any sign of gender from the person wearing it and to make the clothes only from hair, like wild scribbling covering a blank page. On the other hand, I was also inspired by a story from my childhood written by Ivo Andric called *Aska and the Wolf*. It's about a lamb called Aska who danced and danced until almost fainting, and succeeded in not being eaten by the wolf. This was the reason why I invited the ballet dancer Anreas Kuck to choreograph the project.

CREATION

Once the idea was outlined, we started to develop it. A video recording would show a character – without gender – played by a ballerina, who dances like Aska, exhausted and deranged. And with every movement her hair would grow and dress the person until the asphyxiating dress is created as the final look. Practically until today I've been regretting not having contacted the designer Iris van Herpen at the time because then, when I was doing *Deranged*, Iris was finishing her collection made from hair. That collection was exactly what I was looking for. Once designed, the sculptural dress of long metallic black hair was specially made in China with 2m (6ft)-long hairs. Because China was affected by the earthquake at about this time, the outfit arrived late... Hours of costume, makeup, and choreography tests, among others, resulted in a very satisfactory piece of work.

LOOK

Deranged runs for eight minutes in which there is a succession of very mechanical movements choreographed by Andreas Kuck for the ballerina Anouk Froidevaux. The recording shows the dress apparently creating itself until the final result is achieved: a spectacular hair dress wrapped around an ultra-white body. It is a fusion of artistic disciplines where fashion plays a surprising leading role and ends up trapping and deranging viewers.

BORA AKSU

www.boraaksu.com

The London-based Turkish designer Bora Aksu graduated with distinction from an MA fashion course at Central Saint Martins in 2002. Aksu's degree show was a turning point for him, since the press rated his designs very positively, and some of his pieces were even purchased by Dolce & Gabbana. And to top it off, this presentation was rewarded with a sponsorship that led him to create his own label. His debut was with the 2003 fall/winter collection, which was shown off-schedule during London Fashion Week in February 2003. CNN defined Aksu as the new emerging name in fashion and *The Guardian* rated his runway debut as "one of the five best shows in London." After presenting this collection, Bora Aksu was awarded the prize for Best New Generation Designer by the British Fashion Council and the popular fashion clothing chain Topshop. Since his first appearance, Aksu has received this acknowledgement four times.

MY IT

My *It* is a girl who customizes her prom dress on the way to the ball. She was called a tomboy during her childhood. She is romantic, but with a darker edge. She is a total individual with a unique taste.

INSPIRATION

My inspiration catches the flavor of late-adolescence and mixes it with the edginess of street-smart Goth. I wanted to redefine the term "beauty." And I wanted to create strangely beautiful textures and shapes. For me, beauty is more than just a word to define someone or something. When you search beyond the mainstream meaning of a word or quality, you begin to look at everything in a new way. Beauty isn't as rare or superficial as you may have once thought. By discovering the beauty in even the smallest, meaningless thing, beauty then transforms into a more definite quality. My aim was to create a dress with an abstract way of seeing the detailing rather than the obvious overall look. The inspiration features a 1960s constructional approach, with sculptural detailing.

CREATION

I experimented with different techniques creating demi-couture dresses with a twist. Environmentally friendly fish skin pieces provide a leather-like look. The skins are sourced from local fish restaurants and specially treated by Brazilian fish farmers to create an attractive and tactile new fabric. As more and more individualism is becoming the new trend, people are searching for the uniqueness. In other words, everyone has a different approach to fashion, which makes the whole dressing concept much more interesting. I am a designer who really does not follow trends. I believe that trends and fashion dictations used to play a huge role in the past, but now people are much more aware of whom they are, which also opens a great space for individual designers.

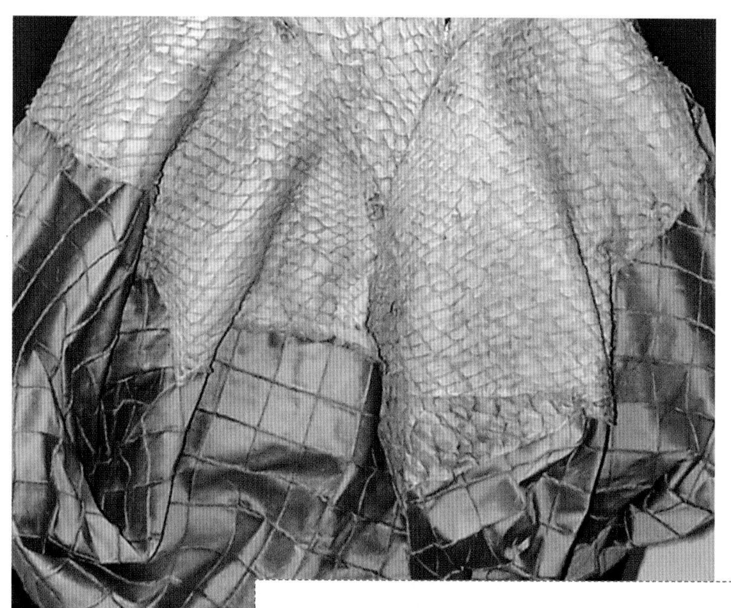

LOOK

The result is a sleeveless dress with a round neck and puffball skirt in a spectacular combination of fabrics and textures. This exciting cut emphasizes the waist and enhances the hips with fun shapes. The nude color blends elegantly with the metallic tones, including gold and copper. A casual, Gothic touch is provided by deconstructed black leggings and covered platform shoes, which underscore this *It* girl's "roguish" past.

BRYCE D'ANICÉ AIME

www.bryce-danice-aime.com

From an early age, this French designer knew his passion was the arts, and drawing, painting, and anything related to creativity soon took a privileged place among his interests. Once out of his teens, he moved to London to study at Central Saint Martins, where he discovered a new passion – fashion and this school's extravagant atmosphere, which motivated his ideas and stimulated his talent. During his years of study, Aime always venerated and found inspiration in Thierry Mugler, admiring not only his vision, but also the Mugler woman and her world. Since graduating, Aime's love for modern architecture as a source of inspiration and his technically challenging design have been his principal resources. He admires labels like YSL and Balenciaga, and considers French and British *Vogue* to be his personal fashion bibles. Aime belongs to the group of designers that take every last detail of their look into account, resulting in his special acceptance and recognition by lovers of fashion. All this, plus invaluable advice from friends and family, have led the label to a new level of development, culminating in the opening of the Bryce Aime boutique in London in November 2009.

MY IT

There isn't a perfect woman. Therefore, the idea of *It* remains partially fictional, and that's a great thing! It's a very good starting point... She is modern and confident, groomed and aware. She isn't afraid of being unconventional and to stand alone. On-trend or off-trend is only secondary. Her personality makes everything on-trend and charming. Above all, she is admired. She is the main inspiration.

INSPIRATION

Egyptology was the name of my fall/winter 2010 collection. Ancient Egypt is back to life for turning mummification into the new black, featuring graphic prints representing bandages and wraps in wine red and ash gray. Arch shape hemlines run through the collection in reference to doorways and coffins. The collection includes soft tailoring, long blouses, structured dresses and collars, leggings and jersey tops. I have used light and heavy wool, silk jersey, and Lycra. Matt and gloss black and wine, dark purple and black and white prints are the colors I've selected. Trims are studs and zippers in black and copper.

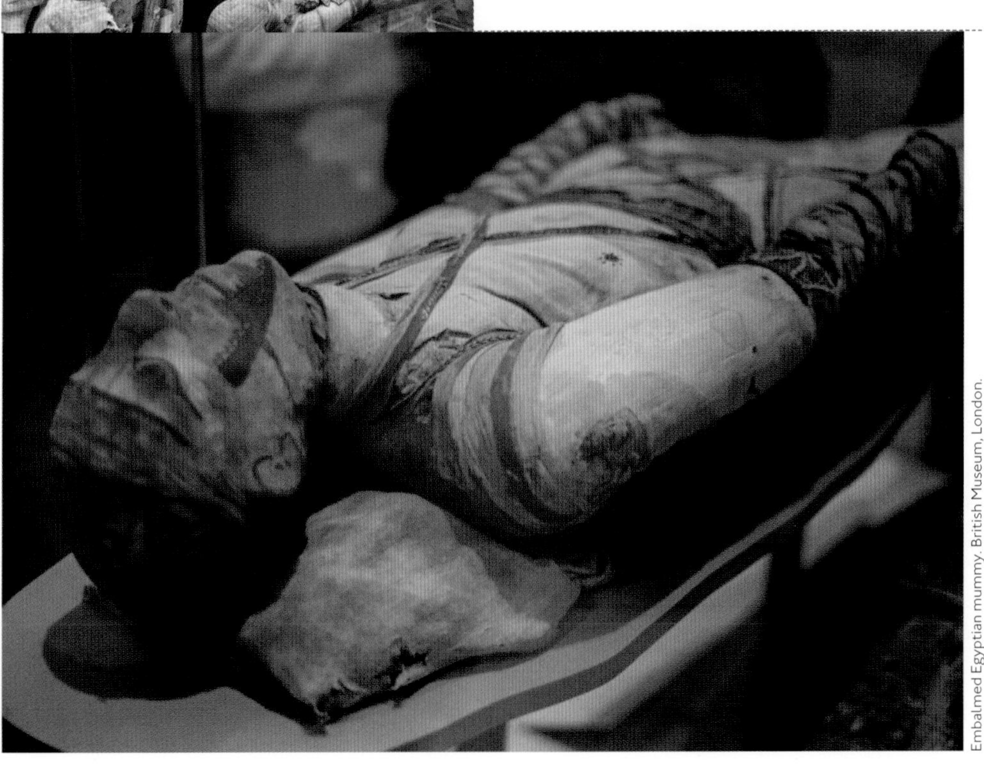

Embalmed Egyptian mummy. British Museum, London.

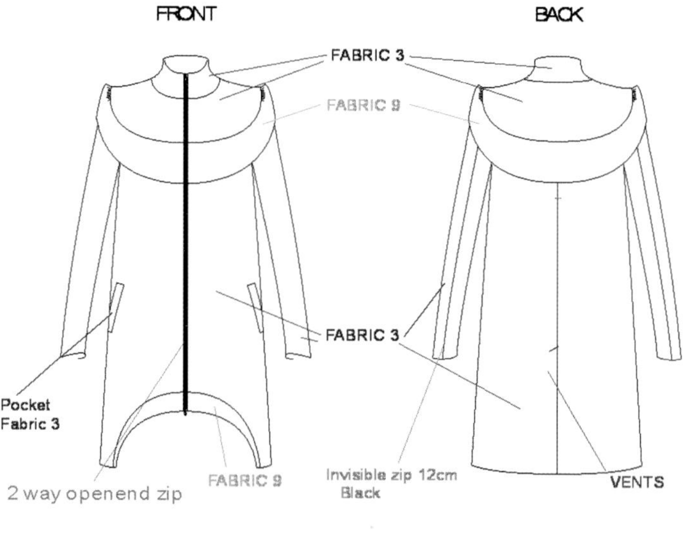

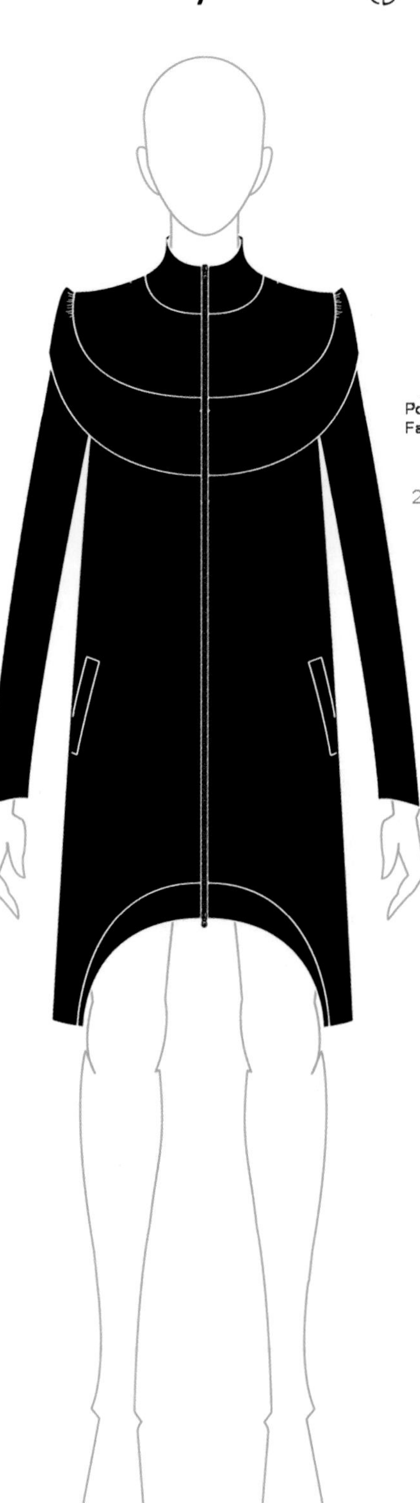

CREATION

As always, I took the essence and its philosophy. I then tried to translate it in "tomorrow's style." I have my favorite subject in every inspiration: architecture. My approach is quite graphic and shaped throughout cut lines and silhouette. I think of clothes construction to be interesting, simple and sharp. The collection has to reflect a modern and edgy look but individually simple and commercial. Egyptology was an inspiration for this season, but overall the style is an ongoing work in progress for each and every season. Behind the inspiration there is a continuity and always the same question: What would she be wearing? I know her personality but I have to guess a wardrobe every season... And the starting point was: What would the Egyptian back then be wearing today? (Something that she would wear in all occasions.) The references are here, but never in your face, except maybe for the showpieces. After all, it doesn't matter how it's done, it's about complementing her personality. When I reach this conclusion, it usually means that I am done with it.

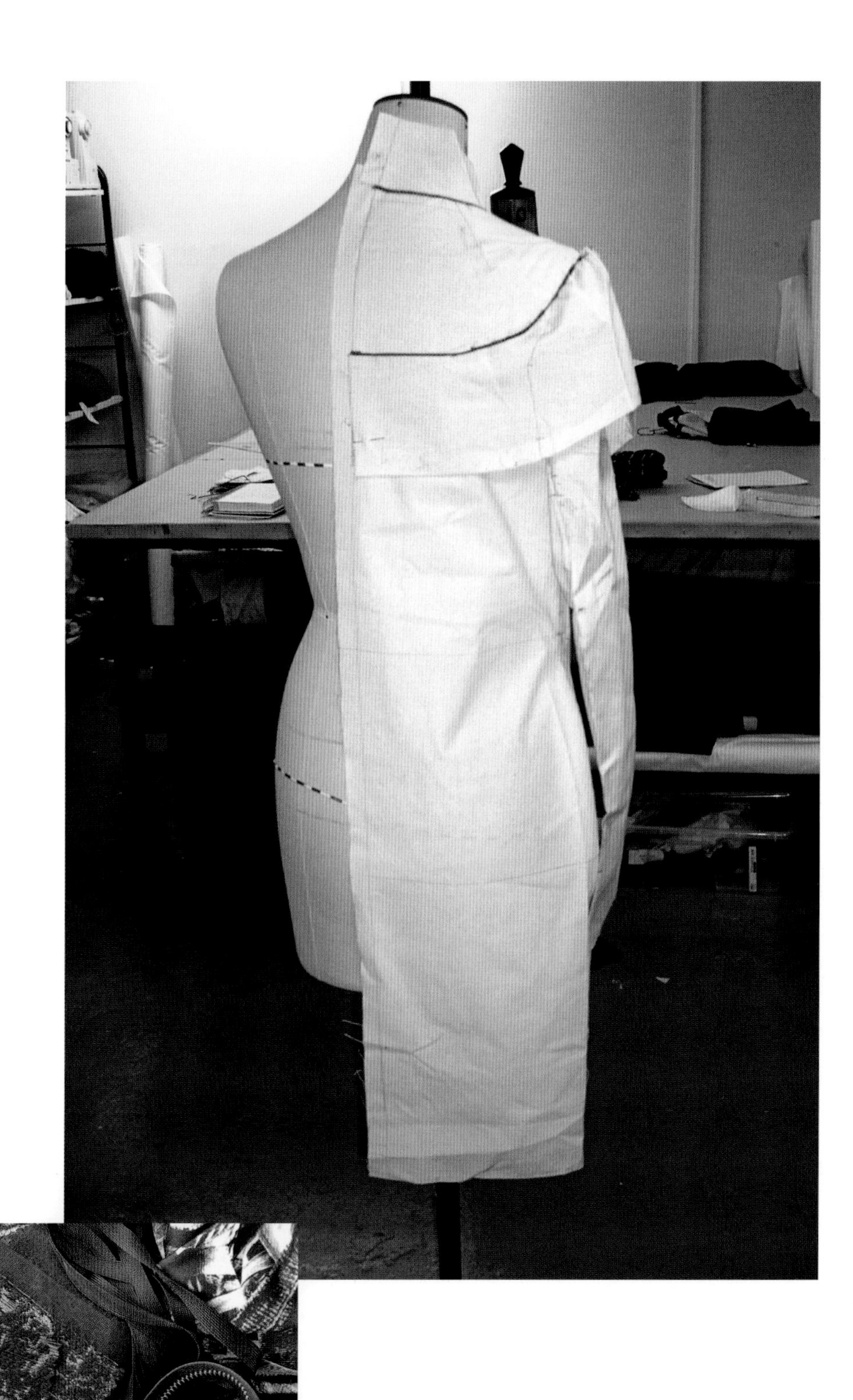

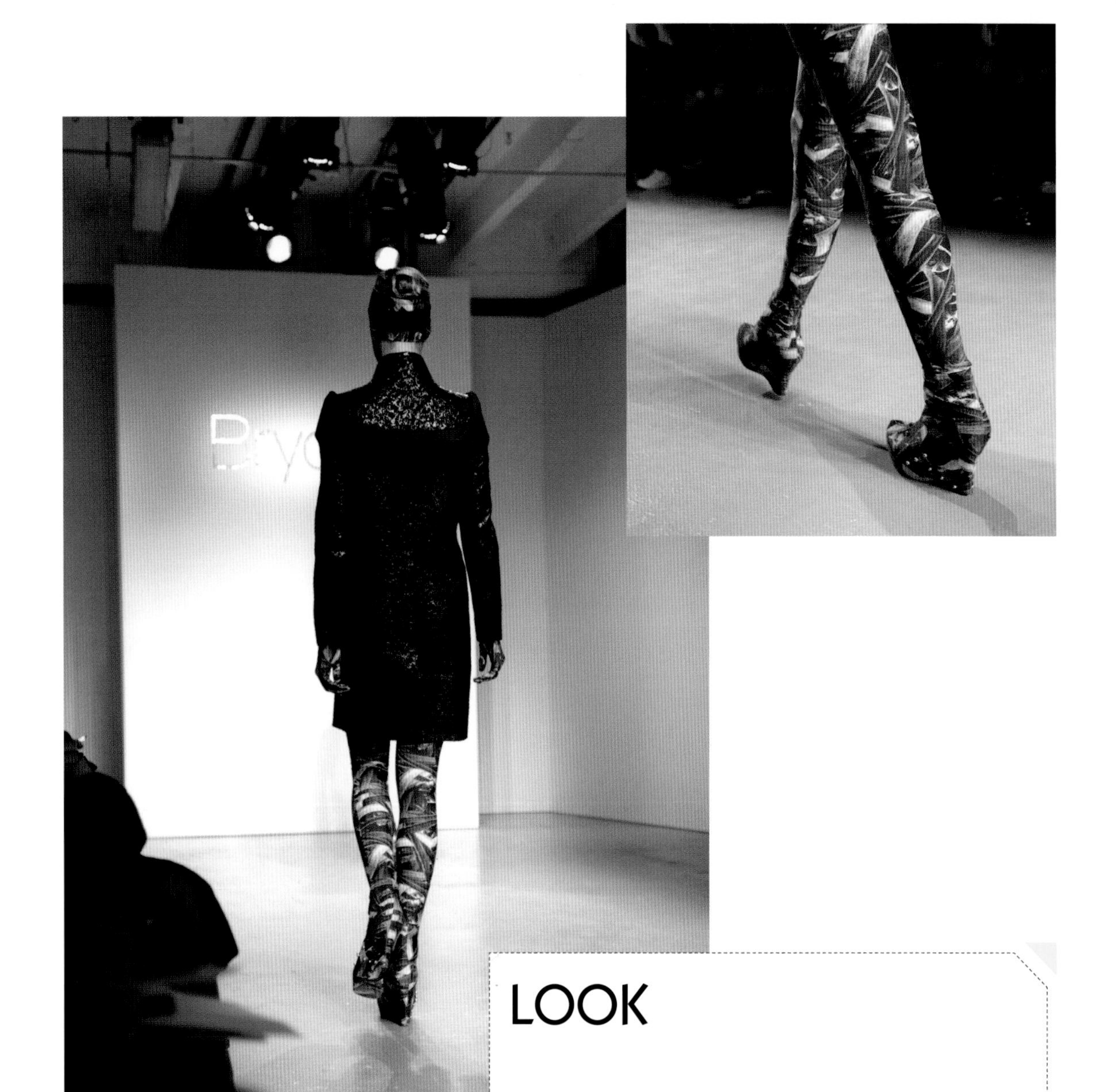

LOOK

This fantastic outfit is truly original. Violet is the color of mysticism, of unity, and of magic. These attributes, combined with the print, inspired by mummy wrappings, evoke the magnificence of Ancient Egyptian culture. The black coat conveys austerity with dual impact, through shiny and matte effects, and through different, perfectly combined textures. The circular shape of the neck is also a reference to the necklaces used in this ancient culture. This magnificent outfit sees Bryce Aime marking a difference and showing his passion for detail and the exquisite. It is a carefully designed and perfectly finished outfit for a modern, elegant, and sophisticated woman.

CARLOS DOBLAS

www.carlosdoblas.com

Designer Carlos Doblas was born in Seville, Spain, in December 1987. Drawn to art and fashion at an early age, he graduated from high school with a baccalaureate in art. When it came to choosing his college studies, he decided to take fine arts in his hometown, where he completed the first stage of his degree. Once Doblas had built up an aesthetic and artistic base, he felt that his place was in fashion, moving to Madrid to study fashion design at the Institución Artística de Enseñanza design school, where he is currently in his final year. Since arriving in the Spanish capital three years ago, he has combined his studies with work as a design assistant for David Delfín, with whom he has had the opportunity to participate in the designs for the collections shown during New York Fashion Week and the Cibeles Madrid Fashion Week. Carlos Doblas had his solitary debut in the El Ego de Cibeles program during the 50th Madrid Fashion Week in September 2009. He repeated in February 2010 with his second collection and is currently expecting to present a third collection with his label.

MY IT

When I design, I normally start with aspects that are more intangible than physical as far as a person is concerned. I think of the woman I want to dress based on her demeanor, her thoughts, what she does, her tastes, and especially, her preoccupations. Naturally, I want to address a public who appreciates everything from the good cut to the finishing of the garments and the details. It's something I take very much into account. I like people with initiative, who decide, and who make efforts. Hard-working, fun people are my role models.

INSPIRATION

I often use minimalism as the starting point for my work. It's evident in this case. Austerity, neutral colors, and clean and straight lines coexist and merge to create a suit that appears to be completely simple, but it is loaded with features that were already done by the first minimalists back in the 1990s. Inspiration can come from anywhere, from a feeling or a thought or from a piece of furniture or architecture. Most of the time I discover what my inspiration was when I finish what I'm doing. I design on impulse. The fabric I used was wool because it has hundreds of possibilities for finishes. In this case the wool was treated very carefully and the result is an impeccable fabric, so much so that it looks like a fabric used in tailoring. Its elasticity enables me to create both loose and fitted clothes. The poplin lining gives the jacket more structure while being pleasant on the skin. The fabric is the determining factor for achieving the desired effect in each piece. Lastly, I chose nude for the color because it's neutral, soft, and subtle. For me, it has something to do with nudity, with flesh. The sensation you get when it merges with the skin is as flattering as it is elegant. There's a trompe l'œil effect going on so you don't know where the body begins and the garment ends. It contrasts perfectly with black, but without shocking. The resulting look is somewhere between melancholic and futuristic.

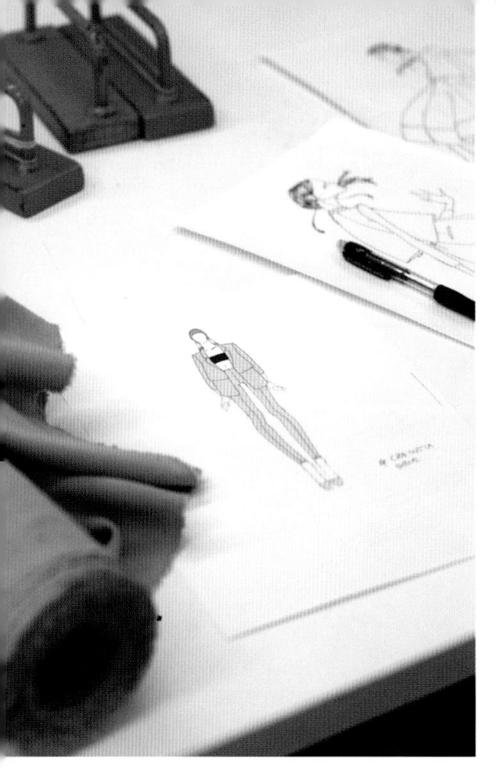

CREATION

I think it's fundamental that the sketch lets me communicate with my team, that it lets me represent the fabrics and pieces as they are so we can actually create something as similar as possible to the sketch. My drawings are mostly closer to illustrations than to sketches in order to provide maximum representation of the details and shapes. At times it's necessary to work with technical specs to obtain something much more accurate in regards to measurements, cuts, pleats, or other details that might be unnoticeable in freehand drawing. The jacket is made on two overlapping levels; the first finishes at the waist, and the second appears from inside and falls as far as the hip. The pants have a rib sewn down the middle of each leg a couple of millimeters wide to give a lengthening effect and to make the piece a little more special. The contrast between the movement and the volume of the jacket and the simplicity of the pants works by focusing attention on the top part of the jacket. As the silhouette doesn't hug the body, it suits any woman's shape. The crotch doesn't need to be raised. The three-quarter sleeves give it a more contemporary look.

STOCKMAN

LOOK

Carlos Doblas presents a fresh, dynamic, and versatile look. Color is no impediment or restriction to adapt to any moment of the day. The black top makes it a little more casual without becoming vulgar. It suits any age or situation in combination with other pieces such as a basic white shirt or flat shoes. This look is as comfortable as it is attractive and contemporary. The neutral shade suits and flatters any skin color.

CHRIS LIU

www.chrisliulondon.com

During the 1990s, Chris Liu studied at the Auckland University of Technology, in New Zealand, and worked as a designer for the Sabatini knitwear label for four years. He then moved to London to work for Burberry Prorsum, followed by a design consultancy with Christopher Bailey. In 2003 Liu graduated with distinction from the London College of Fashion with a masters degree in fashion design and technology. With funding from the London Development Agency, he established his clothing label Huan by Chris Liu that same year, which he presented at a fashion show in London City Hall in August. The collection was well received and was sold immediately after to such prestigious establishments as Harvey Nichols and Joseph in London and Maria Luisa in Paris. Some of the celebrities who have chosen to wear his clothes are Maggie Cheung, Angelica Cheung, Shu Qi, Michelle Yeoh, Kylie Minogue, Sade, Jamelia, and Sophia Myles. In 2005, he left Huan and created his own label, Chris Liu. He was shortlisted for the 2009 Big Ben Award for the first Ten Outstanding Chinese Young Persons in the UK, and was a finalist for the British Business Awards in the Alumnus category. Liu is also a visiting tutor at the London College of Fashion.

MY IT

Britta Burger. As a fashion stylist, she doesn't need clothes to express who she is, but instead as an added luxury. Amazing dresses are her favorite garments because she can put them on quickly and they don't need accessories. Britta thinks she could wear a couture gown like a dirty white T-shirt she just picked up from the floor. This always looks hot. I do share Britta's view – style is about how you wear something rather than what you wear.

INSPIRATION

When *Star Trek* meets Narnia – an erupted city, volcano ash, fractured landscape and buildings falling down. You are forced to grow up when fairy tales are no longer in your dreams. It is my passion to always have a Chris Liu collection for these grown-up women. They are women who enjoy the life, and the small things are, definitively, what make them grow every day. They know what they want. For them, knowing how to wear a garment is far more important than the garment itself. Confidence is very sexy! As for fabrics, I used fractured cut out detailed polyester plastic film material. Loud orange and rave red represent the heat and the force of the volcanoes.

CREATION

By means of subtle sketches, the ideas we had in mind were initially set down, taking into account the sources of our inspiration and, in this case, Britta's preferences and her passion for dresses. The sketch represents a cocktail dress to be made in plastic in hot colors from yellow to red, just like the lava from an erupting volcano. It is a very painstaking work, involving having to cut piece after piece in different shapes. Once interwoven and superimposed onto a transparent film, they'll take on a bright and sophisticated effect.

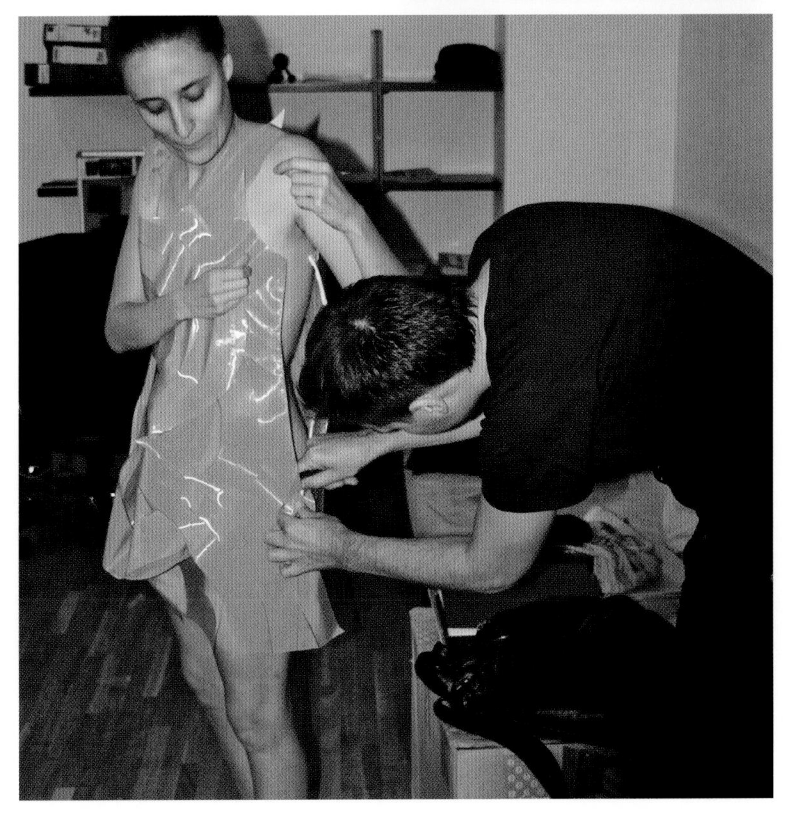

LOOK

Britta looks fantastic, fun, and especially very natural, which is just what she is. The orange dress is the result of an elaborate process. The dress is very comfortable, wearable, and original, with a touch of sophistication. It is also a very versatile dress, suitable for any occasion. It can be styled in very distinct ways to achieve different effects. Additionally, although it is a very special dress with personality, it is also a chameleon-like piece that adapts to the woman wearing it without taking attention away from her; rather, it brings attention to her. It is a way of discovering the volcano inside her. On the left, the same outfit in white velvet reinforced with white elastic.

CHRISTIAN WIJNANTS

www.christianwijnants.be

Born in Brussels in 1977, Christian Wijnants moved to Antwerp in 1996 to study fashion design at the Royal Academy of Fine Arts. After graduating in 2000, he won the Grand Prix at the International Fashion and Photography Festival in Hyères and began selling his collection in stores like Colette in Paris, Pineal Eye in London, Via Bus Stop in Tokyo, and Henri Bendel in New York. After working as a creative assistant for Dries Van Noten in Antwerp and Angelo Tarlazzi in Paris, he launched his own label in 2003, with which he has received such prestigious acknowledgements as the 2005 Swiss Textiles Award and the ANDAM Prize – presented by the Yves Saint Laurent Foundation – in 2006. Wijnants presents his collections twice a year during Paris Fashion Week. His clothing is manufactured in Belgium and is sold in exclusive stores around the world: Le Bon Marché and Maria Luisa in Paris, Mameg in Los Angeles, IT in Hong Kong, United Arrows in Tokyo, Belinda in Sydney, and Podium in Moscow. Christian Wijnants has also been teaching at the Royal Academy in Antwerp since 2005.

MY IT

It always makes me really happy when women that I respect and admire for their style and personality choose to buy my clothes and like to wear them. But I don't have a muse or an ideal customer in mind when I design my collections. My task as a designer is to propose a look to a woman who will adopt it and interpret it in her own personal way. I respect women that are true to themselves without following blindly what fashion dictates to them.

Photography: Camille Vivier

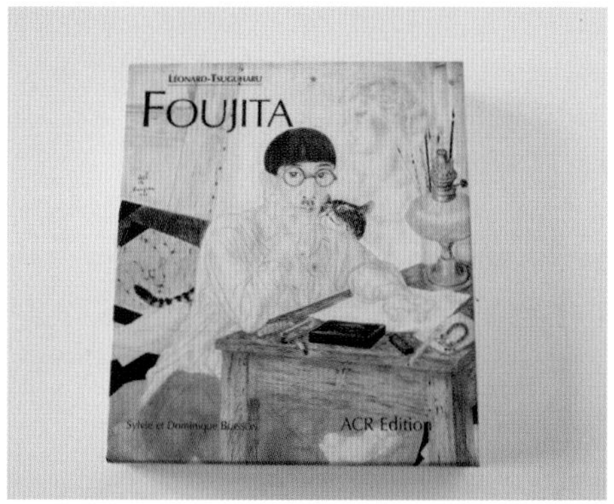

INSPIRATION

The inspiration came from a book I found about the French-Japanese artist Foujita. I loved the ambiguity between Orient and Occident in his work. Also the textures and materials in my collection were inspired by his compositions and his love for cats. I wanted to create a sort of texture that referred to fur and feather at the same time, some kind of animal fabric. I used organza silk, stain printed chiffon silk, fine ajouré knit in linen and silk, layered stripy organza, hand frayed layered georgette and chiffon silks, applications of different fabrics on double georgette, jacquard knits with cat fur design, and intarsia knits mixing fine cotton and heavy linen. Colors are fresh and subtle such as cognac, beige, mole gray, and anthracite, with a yellow accent.

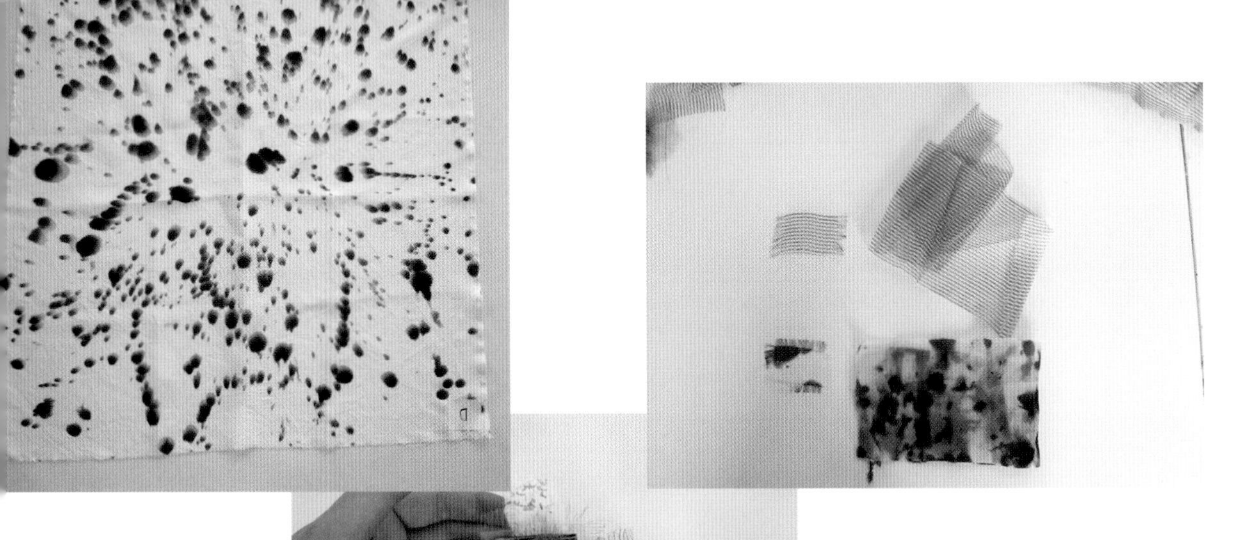

CREATION

I worked a technique using frayed silk stripes to imitate different textures, such as the feathers of the owls or the soft coat of cats, with a camouflage effect. Each application was made by hand in a very elaborate process. First the small silk pieces were cut and frayed. Then they were folded and pleated, and I made the correct combination of them to obtain the wished effect. As it is shown in the pictures, I marked in the dress pattern the position of the applications, which were then fixed on the dress. When the garment was nearly finished, I fitted it in Sabrina to verify and to correct the last details.

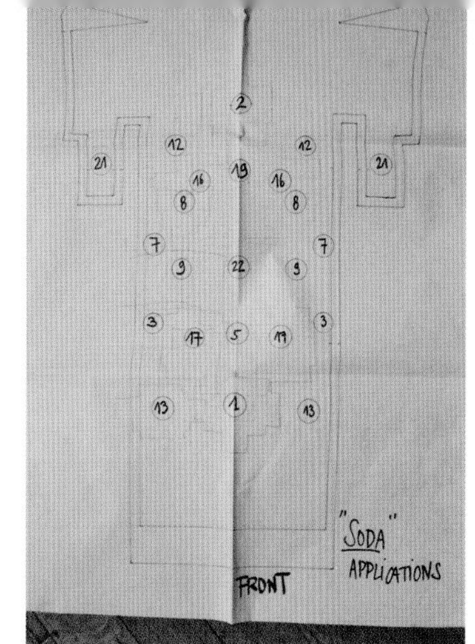
"SODA"
APPLICATIONS
FRONT

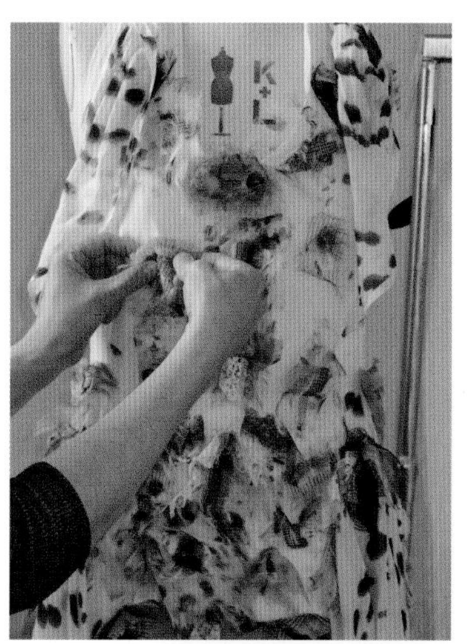

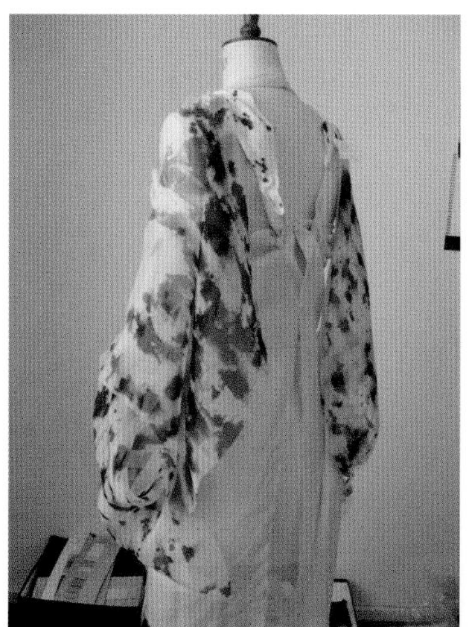

Page 165 Photography: Camille Vivier. Model: Anouk Lepere

LOOK

The dress has an unexpected and indescribable shape. It represents the spirit of the entire collection with its shape, colors and mix of textures. It has something mysterious and poetic. In addition, here we show some pieces of the spring/summer 2010 collection and a detail of the excellent layered scarf made from frayed silk stripes resembling owl feathers. With this design, a warm atmosphere and a perfect photo shoot by Camille Vivier, the result could not be better.

DICE KAYEK

www.dicekayek.com

Ece and Ayse Ege were born in Bursa, Turkey. Ece Ege studied fashion design in Paris and decided to make her home there. For her first collection, in 1992, she designed thirteen white poplin shirts. In the wake of the great success she had with her first designs, she launched her ready-to-wear line Dice Kayek with help from her sister Ayse, who has been in charge of managing the label since then. Her first showing took place at the Institut du Monde Arabe in Paris, and was inspired by tales from *The Arabian Nights*. The collection was well received by both the fashion world and consumers. Today Ece lives between Paris and Istanbul, so as to be able to divide her time between her Black Label and her Pink Label. Romantic and modern, and appreciated by celebrities such as Cameron Díaz, Uma Thurman, and Diane Krueger, the Black Label is designed in her intimate and refined Paris atelier/showroom. Haute couture detailing and good workmanship are the keys to this line, the collections of which are presented each season during Paris Fashion Week. Her second line, Pink Label, which is manufactured in Turkey, offers more urban designs with a fresh and feminine appeal. Ece Ege is currently considered one of the leading ambassadors of Turkish fashion.

MY IT

"For all girls who feel like a star," says Ece Ege smiling. She is a modern and feminine woman who appreciates a minimalist silhouette, refined cutting and sophisticated fabric work.

INSPIRATION

I'm strongly influenced by architecture, especially by Byzantine architecture. This dress is an interpretation – through the different folds and graphic lines – of the domes of the world-famous Turkish monument Hagia Sophia. I used silk-crepe because I find it to be as elegant as silk but with more body, which was essential for giving it structure without it losing its shape easily. I used nude because it's a subtle, neutral color.

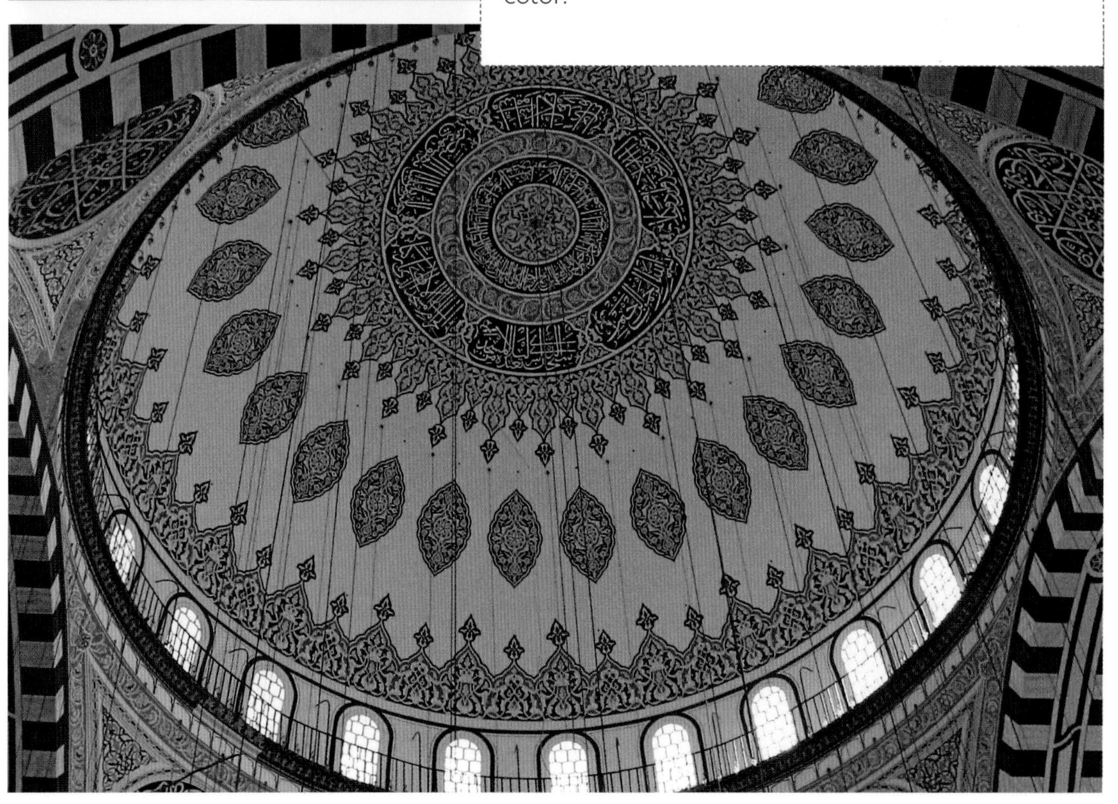

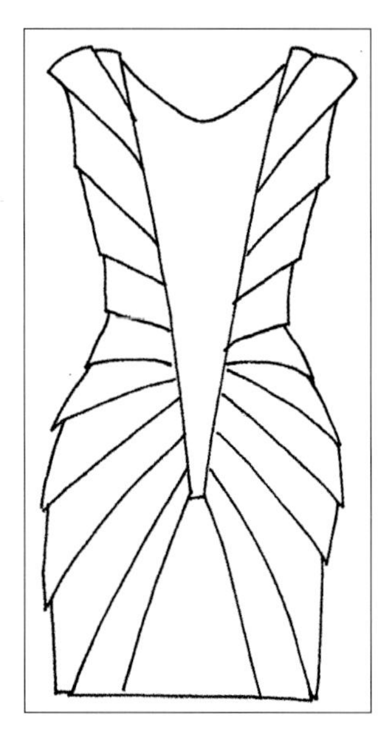

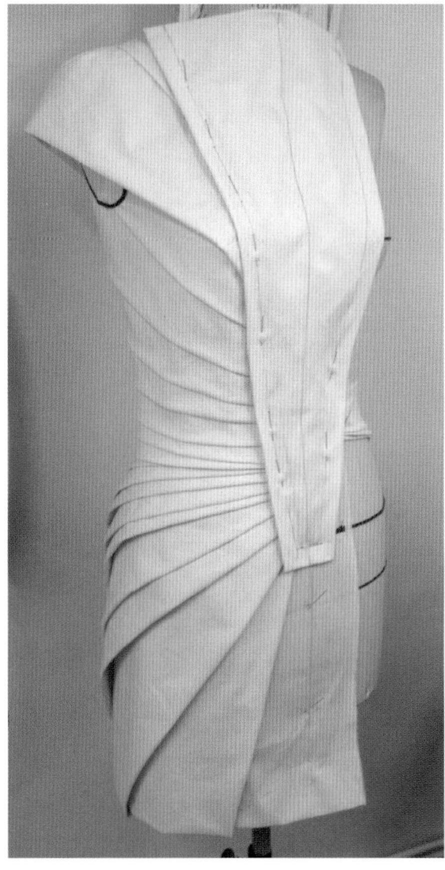

CREATION

To make up this design, I drew a complex structure of volumes and pleats that reflected the layout and grandiosity of the Hagia Sophia dome. The pleats are designed to end at the waist. That way it lengthens the silhouette and distributes the visual volume between the hips and the shoulders. This kind of dress is made in a traditional way in the atelier, with close attention to seams and finishing. The piece is handled very gently. When you work with volumes and shapes, it's difficult to define the piece as a flat-pattern, which is why we carefully drape it over the dummy, checking to see that all the pieces fit perfectly and respond to the original idea and effect we intend to convey.

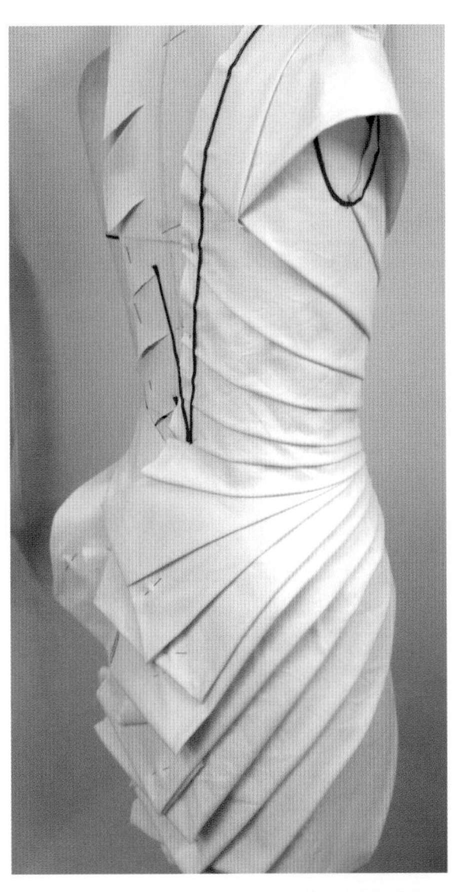

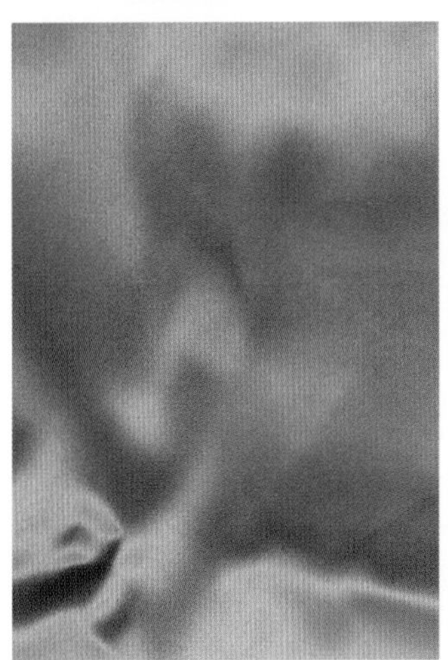

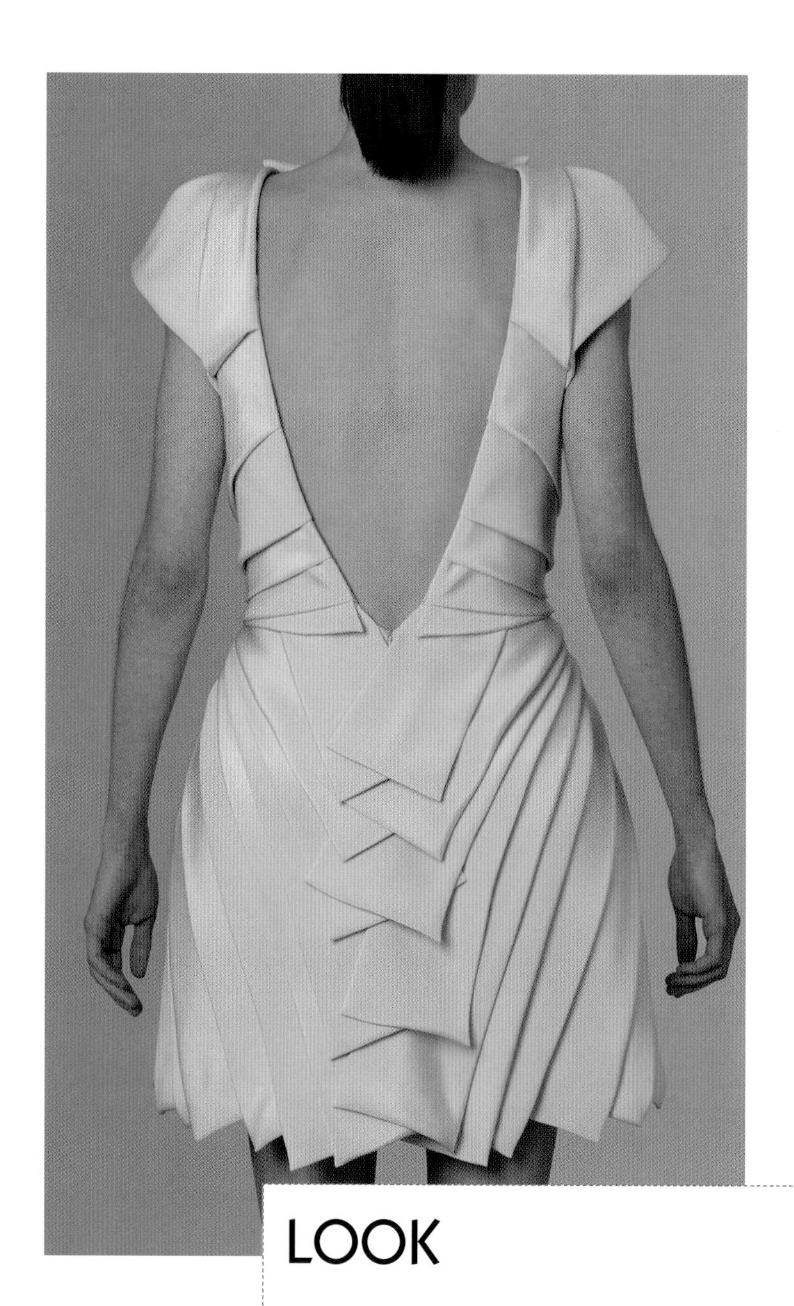

LOOK

This is a very sophisticated piece where architectural rationality coexists with a romantic atmosphere. Nude is a very current color and brings softness and elegance to the piece. Combined with other colors, its delicate nature and the subtle sheen of the silk-crepe can be enhanced even more. In contrast, combined with shoes in the same color, it can convey greater neutrality and a refined style. Ece Ege demonstrates her passion for complex shapes and her personal interpretation of architecture. She dresses very feminine women with a taste for original pieces.

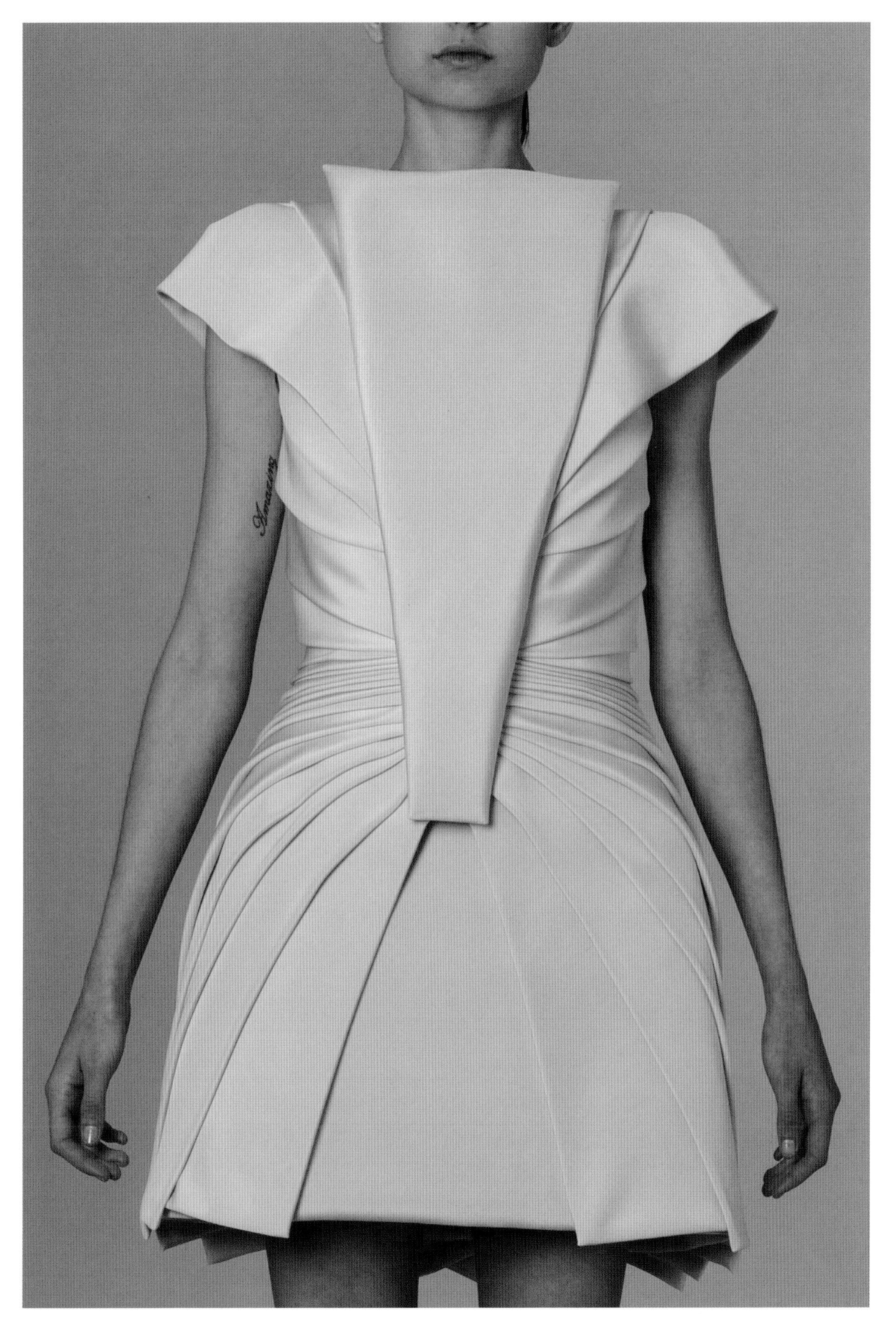
Amazing

DIEGO BINETTI

www.ilovebinetti.com

Born in Buenos Aires, Argentina, Binetti's first contact with fashion came at the age of seven, when he helped his mother with the decorations and embroideries for complex gowns for her clients. In this way he began to love and understand his mother's passion for fashion. At the age of fifteen he studied fashion at the Donato Delgado Institute in Argentina. After his family emigrated to the Florida coast, he graduated from Miami International University of Art & Design in 1991. He later moved to Milan, where he worked as an assistant to Antonio Bordonaro for such fashion houses as Bulgari and Paola Franni, and he continued to study at the Istituto Marangoni. At the age of twenty-four he moved to New York City, and one year later he was working as a designer for Jill Stuart, a position he held for five years. In 2001 Diego Binetti founded his own label, Binetti, and in 2008 he presented his diffusion label, I Love Binetti. The former label specializes in haute couture designed for jetsetting women of the world, while the latter is an alternative line for today's modern and fun-loving women.

MY IT

My *It* is a combination of the two seductive sexes of the human race. A man or a woman who captures that look or, better said, possesses that distinguished self-confidence. The *It* has empowerment in fashion and in society: a liberal self-expression, a metamorphosis, and a mélange.

INSPIRATION

A combination of a romantic Gothic punk, having tea with the Empress or a powdering party, she plays dress-up with Marie Antoinette and her buddies. The Empress, with her splendor and unique expression is the Gothic Punk, decorated elaborately with gems and embroideries. She projects independence and dares to live beyond the edge. Marie Antoinette transports me to the surreal, where clothing and society were so out of control: corsets that were used both by men and women to accentuate their waist, elaborated hairdos that were the talk of the town, and powdered faces where all were in disguise. I choose fabrics like satin and silk sashes, silk macramé pieces to be worn as over layers, metal work with incrusted mirror details, buttons and special ornaments. As for colors, I will use a unique range of blacks.

CREATION

The tailor suits are fitted from the cup of the sleeves to the hem, and an internal corset gives that very tight and masculine/feminine look to my *It*. The capes will be cut out in a circle, gaining that flow and swing: the details will enhance that opulence. The full gowns must be draped, creating that rich and delicate hand-coutured look. A well-fitted garment is a complete finish performance in this industry. I've dedicated my entire life to seeking the details that result in elegant pieces. It's very important to see the flow of the garment and the end result on the figure of a woman.

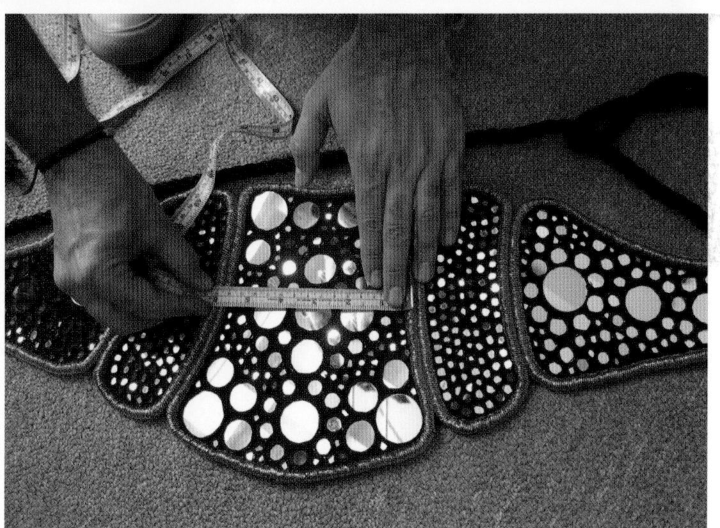

LOOK

This outfit is made up of several perfectly combined pieces. The top is a series of several superimposed layers. Sheer fabric exposes one of the arms, giving it a touch of mystery and sensuality. The metallic details, the bow at the neck, and the amazing mirror belt are an ode to sophistication, to a more bourgeois side, in coexistence with Gothic inspiration. The loose pants are combined with ankle boots to add comfort and strength to the look.

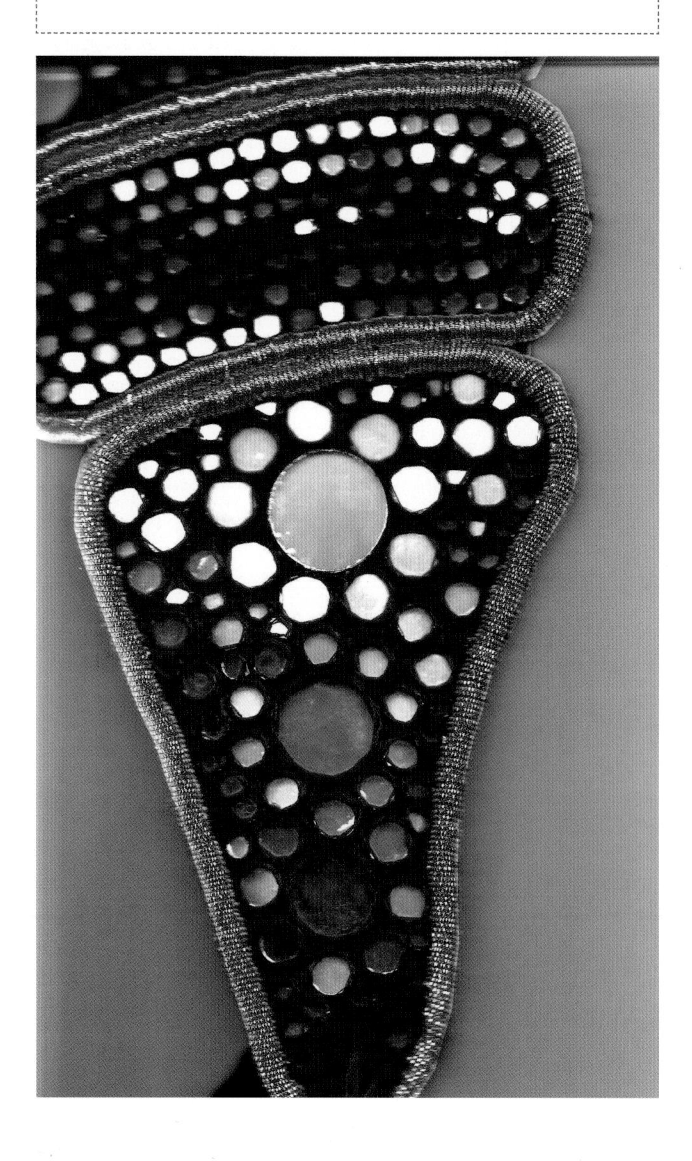

DOLORES PÉREZ

www.mygrandmotherssofa.com

Dolores Pérez was born in Argentina in 1981. As a young girl she was interested in art and fashion, which led her to begin her clothing design studies at the University of Buenos Aires. She moved to Barcelona in 2002 to broaden her training, taking courses in painting and fabric printing, and collaborating with different companies in the world of design. For the next seven years, her personal and professional learning experiences gave her the tools to take on her own collections, leading to the creation of the label My Grandmother's Sofa in 2009. She creates designs for unrepeatable one-off pieces that make use of recycled fabrics and elements that take us back to another age, but which give rise to modern and original pieces. Her collections show and suggest the story of her family and of people near to her, and immerse us in a warm atmosphere and dreamlike states. Dolores Pérez likes to reflect on the evolution of things and their change with time, taking the past into account, but wanting the story to continue.

MY IT

I don't have a particular *It girl*, although I like to imagine a woman who looks for authenticity, who believes in herself and knows what she wants when it comes to dressing. She's a woman with a romantic and sophisticated side, with a touch of sweetness, but with a firm nature who likes to make her own decisions. Naturally, she likes to feel feminine and sees her clothes as a way of conveying how she feels at all times.

P.178+179_Photography: Uauh, www.uauh.es

INSPIRATION

I find inspiration in everything around me, like my personal experiences when I look at a picture or discover new cultures. This collection takes its inspiration from a number of objects and fabrics that were used in my family's hotel in Argentina over thirty years ago. Most of the cotton fabrics are recycled curtains, printed bedspreads, and hotel sheets, combined with upholstery fabrics and viscose with different textures. The color palette I use mainly consists of earth tones, with crimsons, gold, green, and blues. Contrasts and shiny finishes also feature in some pieces.

P.180+181_Photography: Uauh, www.uauh.es

CREATION

Some old bedspreads my father kept in his hotel had been drawing my attention for some time so I decided to use them in my designs. These bedspreads had been witness to many different experiences of all the travelers who had passed through that place. I brought these fabrics to Barcelona, together with memories and the images my father passed down to me, which became my inspiration and the starting point when it came to designing my collection. I use illustrations to design very feminine, fitted pieces, with nipped waists and emphasized shoulders, but without shoulder pads. The garments start with patterns from traditional tailoring, with cutouts and overlapping between plain fabrics and prints, which have a theatrical, elegant, and baroque feel. Each piece is unique, with a history of its own and a story to be told. I worked the upper part of the piece in such a way as to present a harmonious symmetry, enhanced by the precise contrasting of the fabrics.

FASHION NOW

LOOK

Dolores explains that the resulting look transports us to a dream world of fairy tales full of princesses and princes. The combination of the green with its soft sheen and the prints in the same shade together with white and the lapels and buttons recalls clothes from another time, with military and Victorian reminiscences. The look is completed with ultramarine blue leggings and flesh-colored ankle boots to give it a more urban and sophisticated touch.

P.182+183_Photography: Santiago Guerrero

ELENA MARTÍN - MARTIN LAMOTHE

www.martinlamothe.es

Martin Lamothe is a ready-to-wear label for women and men's fashion founded by Elena Martín, who was born in Barcelona in 1978. Fashion and architecture have been two of her passions since childhood. She graduated from the famous Escola d'Arts i Tècniques de la Moda (School of Fashion Arts and Techniques) in Barcelona, later studying art history in the same city and at the Southampton Art School where she finished top of her class. At the age of twenty, Elena began a degree in fashion design at Central Saint Martins College in London, where she developed her special taste for structured looks and prints. Soon her first student collection left an impression on such important publications as *Self Service* and *International Textiles*. After graduating, she went on to work with Alexander McQueen, Vivienne Westwood, and Robert Carey Williams, experiences she combined with freelance styling for artists of the caliber of Kylie Minogue and Howie B, and with costume design for experimental theater and cinematographic productions in London. In 2006 Elena Martín launched her womenswear label Martin Lamothe, which became unisex in 2007. Martin Lamothe's design has a very British flavor in fusion with new forms and concepts. Features of the clothing produced by the label include prints, appliqué, and architectural forms.

MY IT

My *It girl* likes to dream, imagine, surprise, and be surprised. She's cutting-edge, transgressive, well-educated, and romantic. Her progressive nature lies in her taste for art and culture, and pop and folk music, among others. Aesthetic sensitivity is one of her greatest qualities. In this case, my *It* could be the actress Isabelle Huppert.

INSPIRATION

Thomas Lenthal, art director; Victoire de Castellane, creative director at Dior Jewelry; Charlotte Kemp Muhl, muse; Sean Lennon, musician; and Chloë Sevigny, actress, are some of the many names that make up my particular constellation of stars who fit perfectly with my idea of *It*. As Francesco Vezzoli says in *Self Service* spring/summer 2010 issue: "Celebrities are the immortal gods and goddesses of contemporary mythologies. Therefore, just like saints and kings for the painters of past centuries, they seem to me the most natural and genuine subjects for art." However, they are not gods but humans, and as such they share experiences as common and familiar as travel. These people travel constantly and attend events, but they also need to dress for everyday life. So they need multi-purpose clothes with an edgy feel. The spring/summer 2010 Cruise collection fits those requirements. Inspired by the rage for glam cruises in the 1970s, it represents a pop view of the present-day cruise, travelers, discoverers, and it is bold and romantic at the same time. As always, the Martin Lamothe figure defends the idea of multicolored pop without overlooking elegance in impossible mixtures featuring tops, boat-necks, and primary colors, together with the austere tones of navy and beige.

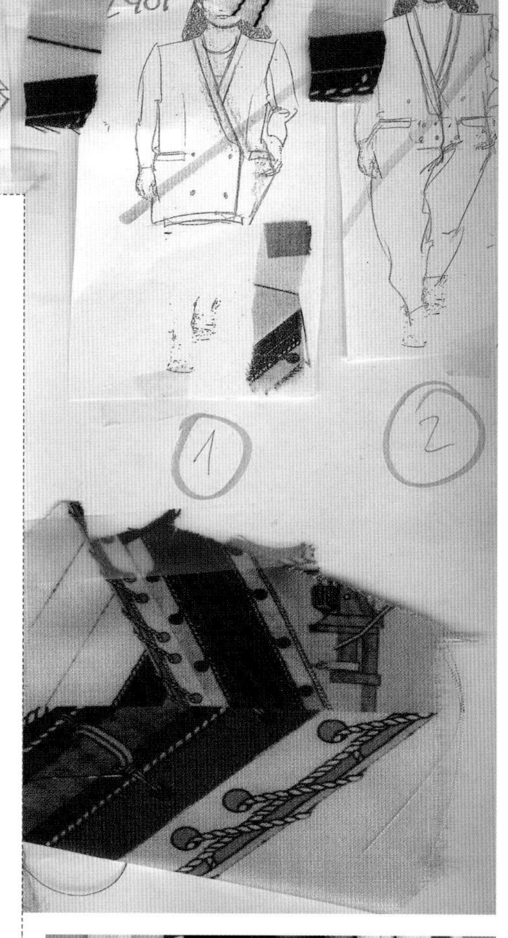

CREATION

Designs essentially need something old and something new, which is what *It* represents. There has to be room for ropes, cotton, and delicate handwork, plus sport and contemporary details, and so on. These designs have a degree of folk influence, expressed through classic shapes that have been updated. The palette features aggressive but pure primary colors, the ones that define people who come from nowhere, but whose charm or work lead them to set the standards. These colors belong to them. The fabrics range from the most commonplace and pop-inspired to the most delicate and brash. We feature everything from polka-dotted viscose, cotton poplins, printed cool wool, and flesh-tone organza to a very subtle cream Italian silk-crepe. For the look we present here, which is a two-piece outfit, we created a print with a retro feel made from an abstraction of other fabrics.

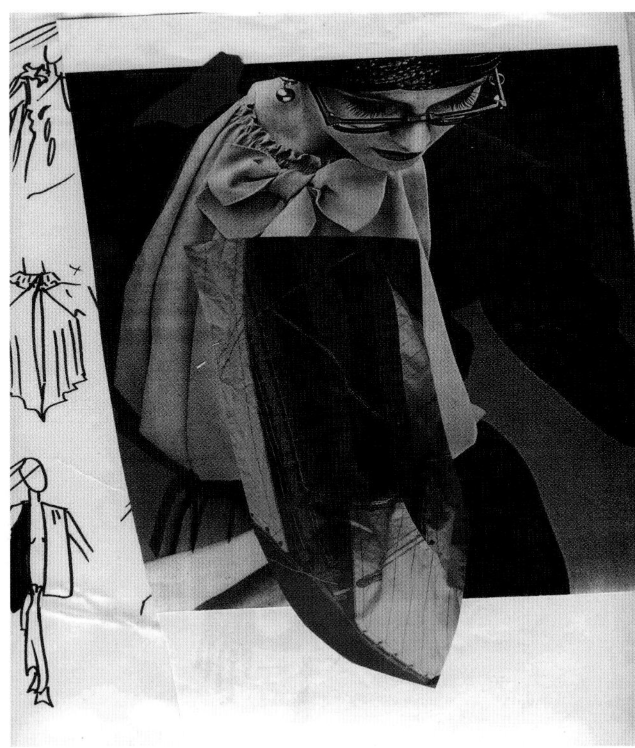

LOOK

This look comprises a two-piece classic blazer and skirt set. It features a strong retro-style geometric print. The cut of the double-breasted blazer, with two rows of three buttons and two flap pockets enhances its nautical feel even more. The outfit has a tailored London pop style. Elegance and sophistication are contrasted with the unisex duality with which Martin Lamothe always imbues its collections. When combined with simple accessories like these black covered platform pumps, the result is an outfit that is as chic as it is practical. This look is suitable for very different occasions and events, which is ideal for an *It*.

FAM IRVOLL

www.famirvoll.com

Fam Irvoll was born and raised in Oslo, Norway. She graduated from the ESMOD International Fashion School in 2005 and later from Central Saint Martins in 2008. Since then she has worked as an assistant to designers such as Vivienne Westwood, Gareth Pugh, and the Norwegian Peter Løchstøer. Her label is characterized by bright colors, 3D silhouettes, and cartoon elements, which were evident from her first collection. Fam Irvoll is inspired by *Alice in Wonderland*, cartoons, toys, and colored food like cakes and candy. Her label is different, positive, colorful, and exciting in terms of fabric use, sequins and beading, and 3D knitwear. Fam Irvoll has taken part in Oslo Fashion Week runway shows between 2006 and 2009, London Alternative Fashion Week in 2007, Two Rivals One Catwalk 2007 in London, and Nordic Look during Riga Fashion Week in 2008. In 2010 she won the Designer of the Year Award from Innovation Norway.

MY IT

My *It girl* would be a really colorful, creative, quirky fun girl. She is a city life girl who loves going out with her friends and having fun.

INSPIRATION

I have been hugely inspired by films such as *Alice in Wonderland*, *Peter Pan*, children's minds, toys, cartoons, food, cakes and candy. I'm very inspired by the 3D and cartoon side of making an outfit. This time I have combined all these things with a softer, more romantic touch by using pastel colors, silk lace and 3D sequin flowers and beads. About fabrics, I have used Indian silk lace, handmade sequin flowers, beads, silk jersey and cotton. The colors are nude, violet, pink, purple, turquoise and caramel.

CREATION

For me the design process starts by listening to music and working on the mannequin. My catwalk music is usually found before I even start the design process. Then I figure out a theme and name the collection. After this, I try to figure out color combinations and buy the fabrics. After that I start drawing my garments and work on the mannequin. As I am fond of using 3D elements, I do need to work a lot to make sure the garment is feasible. Here I have employed a meticulous disposition of the handmade flowers and the pearls so when they are finally sewed the effect is visually agreeable and it results in a comfortable garment for the person who will wear it.

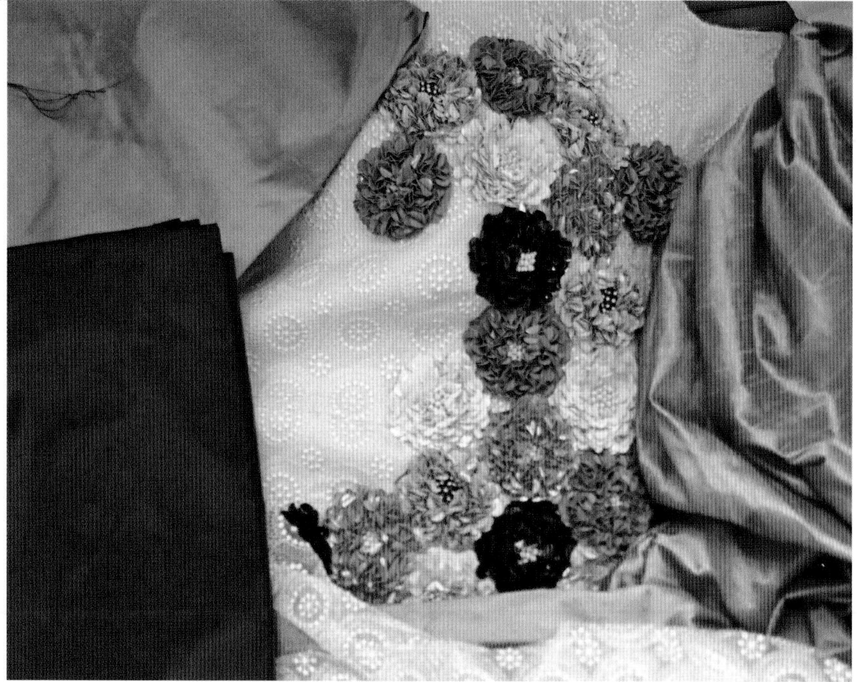

LOOK

The result is a fun outfit with predominantly bright colors, contrasting with pastel shades, like those on the Indian silk skirt. This combination of textures is also present in the contrasting fabrics, such as silk and cotton. By using 3D imagery, the designer has created a look that becomes a fun outfit, with volumes and relief that go from the skirt to the hat made with pearls. The model's hair color, strong makeup, and smile make this look unmistakably that of Fam Irvoll, and is immediately identified with her wonderful world.

Photography: Julia Grossi

FRANZIUS

www.franzius.eu

After an idyllic childhood in Berlin, Stephanie Franzius started out in the world of fashion in New York, where she worked for well-known companies in the sector like Adrienne Vittadini and Anne Klein. On her return to Berlin, she continued her fashion design studies at the University of Applied Sciences (FTHW), working for Robert Inestroza in Milan for a brief period before completing her education with a masters degree from the ArtEZ Fashion Institute Arnhem, in The Netherlands. Her degree show during the Paris Haute Couture Fashion Week in 2003 marked the end of her studies and would lead to the launching of her own label. After working as an assistant to Viktor & Rolf on their 2003/2004 fall/winter collection with Tilda Swinton, Stephanie returned to Berlin to begin exploring her own style and to work independently as a designer and stylist for other labels, tasks she would combine with teaching at different universities. The Franzius label brings together influences from many disciplines. Her collections have been presented at international trade shows in Berlin, Paris, Copenhagen, Seoul, New York, and Tokyo.

MY IT

She is a strong, self-confident woman, with an appealing elegance... who turned out to be none other than Paris Hilton! This is the story of how Paris Hilton became my *It girl*. As Stephanie Franzius and her team were asked to contribute some of their designs for a photo shooting with Paris Hilton on her next visit to Berlin, they were in the process of cutting the fabrics for the fall/winter 2008/09 season. The theme of the Snice collection played with the gossamer, figure-hugging fabrics worn by ice skaters – perfect for the American *It girl* and model. Inspired by the opportunity, the Franzius team set about designing a custom-made dress for the famous hotel heiress – a fluid, shimmering evening gown with a deep décolleté. At the shoot, Paris was so delighted with this elegant creation that she immediately bought it and wore it!

INSPIRATION

How would she dress? That was exactly the question going through Stephanie Franzius' mind when designing the outfit for the shooting with Paris Hilton. She wanted to portray the image of a girl growing up in the spotlight, to reveal her elegance and beauty through a subtle and luxurious allure, but without the distraction of catchy details. The Franzius look for Paris Hilton needed glamour and sex appeal, but it had to be cool and sophisticated at the same time. A design for a woman who is confident about her own physical attraction, like a mermaid – intriguing, but hard to catch, a beauty with a shimmery twist. The fabric for this piece had to be shiny, but understated, a toned-down luster with an icy sparkle, cool and sharp, but softly melting. The color inspiration was taken from the delicate silver gray palette of fish scales, a wet metallic look, with the surface quality of quicksilver.

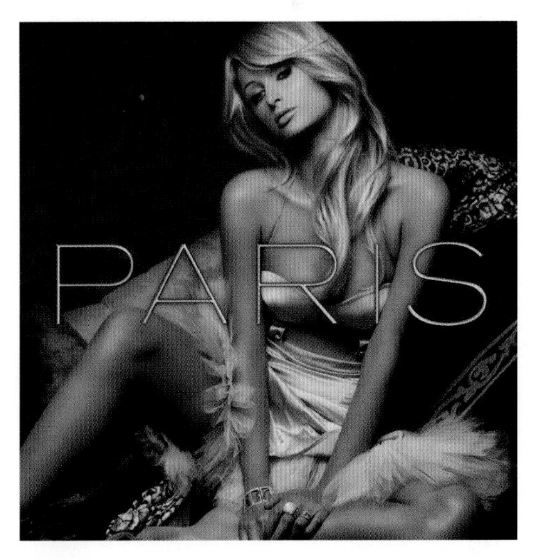

CREATION

The two basic features of this piece are the deep décolleté, balanced by its full floor length. The emphasis is on the waist, creating a slinky look with a refined sex appeal. Stephanie Franzius usually begins the tailoring process with high quality fabric and a dummy, preferring to drape rather than cut the material, allowing its natural flow to form the silhouette, which is then captured using minimal pattern cutting techniques. Franzius' working method is an intuitive and eclectic one, playfully combining influences from many design disciplines. Central to her approach is the concept of contradiction: strong meets soft, contrasting a casual attitude with an element of classic feminine elegance. With its associations of both power and fragility, this key piece reflects the typical Franzius style: unpretentious and laid back but always with a certain edge.

Photography: Piet Truhlar

Photography: Piet Truhlar

Photography: Piet Truhlar

LOOK

The final look has got the sensibility Stephanie Franzius is all about: a very elegant and sophisticated dress. The neckline and the cut of the chest accentuate the bust, giving it the touch of sensuality my *It girl* likes. In the image, Paris Hilton wears the garment smiling, and complementing it with a necklace and bracelet set. To the right, a model poses in the lookbook image.

Page 200 Photography: Michael Berger. **Page 201** Photography: Wiebke Bosse

FXDXV

www.fxdxv.com

FXDXV is a conceptual unisex project comprising the Scandinavian designers Felina Da Vida and Kim Jagua. Each collection is based on a concept, inspired by certain situations and events of interest occurring in the present. Felina graduated from Middlesex University, in North London, taking part in the 2002 London Graduate Fashion Week. In the winter of 2006 Felina and Kim (designer and movie stills photographer) founded FXDXV and had their debut at the Ideal Fashion Show in Berlin in January 2007. Since then their clothes have been stocked by such establishments as Galeries Lafayette in Paris, Best Shop in Berlin, Doshiburi in Barcelona, A Substitute for Love in Ibiza, and Delta in Tokyo, among others. In the summer of 2009, FXDXV set up I Love Tibet, a project to help Tibetan children exiled in Karnataka, India, which aims to support their education to become monks and to develop knowledge into human awareness. Felina and Kim's goal is to combine design and awareness in an environment that is both social and realistic. In 2010 FXDXV presented their pure and natural cosmetic range, Night by FXDXV, with chemical-free skincare products.

MY IT

My *It* is someone androgynous, indefinable, moving with and beyond time, reflecting beauty out of the box. Someone who dares to be present and chooses to be free. Someone who is aware of their approach to life and the appearance that directs energy in an environment.

INSPIRATION

To make casual elegant. As more and more diverse impressions are becoming moments of our everyday life, new combinations of cultures are our natural source of inspiration. We like to put our focus on the beauty of diversity and classical original production of garments, such as tailoring, hand-knitting and handcraft. Simple draped "outfits" from cultures such as Tibetan monks and African Masai inspire us to develop a different version of a most common Western garment. We have chosen natural fabrics for our three garments, such as baby merino wool yarn, wool and silk reverse (with a cotton interlining) and leather (with a silk interlining)—all in black color.

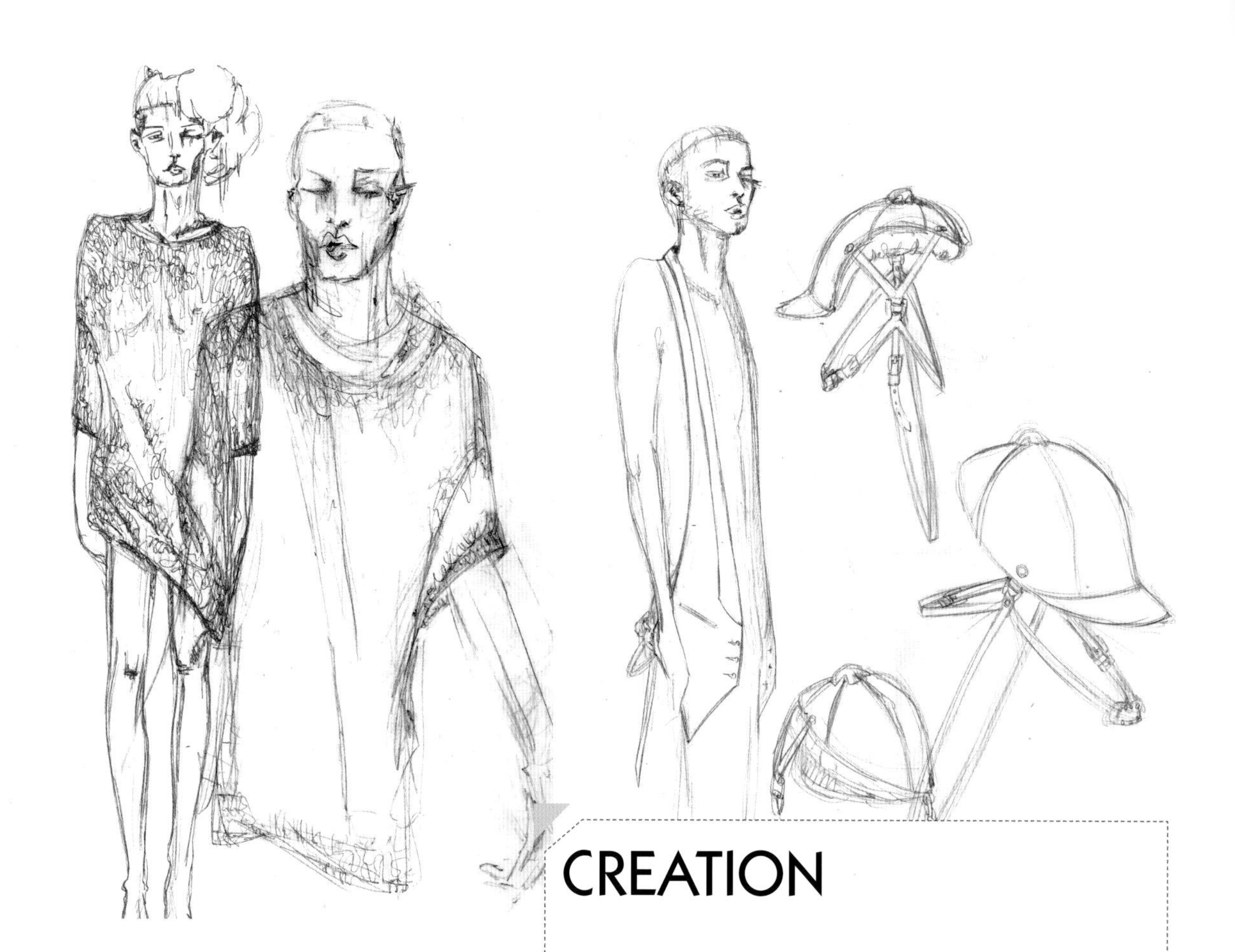

CREATION

The idea is to create a design that can be worn any day of the week, at any time and place. The combination of drape and knit as an oversized top is to make the piece, unisex, indefinable and adaptable to any occasion. The mix of classic tailoring, sports uniforms and a young street and club culture are the thoughts behind an oversized waistcoat and a riding helmet transformed into an asymmetric hat. We prefer that the making of garments be an evolutionary development, rather than a line production, as we believe the end result will take shape based on the energy put in to it. The combination of the light, soft yarn and the large stitches is a key to the desired outcome of an oversized knit. Regarding the waistcoat, the collar facing in silk is cut in one piece, and the two front pieces are held together by an adjustable silk-band on the back. The shape of a riding helmet, an asymmetric cut, leaves most of the back and one side open. The construction of the strap system plays an important role to keep the hat in place.

Photography: Kim Jagua

LOOK

The effect of the hand-knitted oversized top, is a draping and an alive piece that changes shape based on the body and position. The diversity of the piece makes it both cozy and elegant. The horse-riding helmet has been elevated to a hat, as a styling accessory, and the oversized waistcoat are unisex pieces (as are all FXDXV's garments).

Edition: Daniel Rull. Photography: J. M. Ferrater

Edition: Daniel Rull. Photography: J. M. Ferrater

GEORGINA VENDRELL

www.georginavendrell.com

Georgina Vendrell was born in Barcelona in 1983. Studies at the Catalan Fashion Insitute and an internship at Josep Font Haute Couture were the training grounds for this restless menswear revolutionary. Success and positive reviews have followed her since coming to the attention of the fashion world at the 2007 ModaFAD Awards. There she won the prize for best collection, enabling her to show her solitary collection at the following event, and which paved the way for her appearances at fashion shows such as El Ego at Cibeles, 080 Barcelona Fashion, and fashion weeks in Iceland and Valencia, where she was declared best designer. In the five collections she has presented to date, Georgina has been questioning conventional forms and patterns, leading to original results reminiscent of classic tailoring. Fabrics are very important in her creative process, becoming the actual inspiration for some of her collections. She considers herself to be a good observer of society and of what is happening around her. This condition feeds her need to interpret and respond to what the contemporary man requires.

MY IT

My *It boy* would be a young and dynamic boy who likes to feel good about himself and to express it through his attitudes, including fashion. He loves to travel and he identifies with the Northern European lifestyle. While a fan of the latest trends, he knows how to appreciate tradition. He's daring, but deep down is somewhat reserved, which makes him more interesting.

INSPIRATION

There are many sources for inspiration in the fashion world, but I think the real source is found in the street, with the mixture of cultures and daily life. To dress today's man, you need to be able to see all of those elements and know how to materialize them in a collection so that it is different but also coherent. Here my inspiration is the musician Patrick Wolf, an English singer-songwriter from South London. His music is known for its innovative combination of techno, rock, folk, and electro, and his looks are daring, studied, and surprising. The colors I'm going to work with are red and gray in different shades, and in cotton and gabardine fabrics.

Photography: Katie Corbet

CREATION

First I design the total look, keeping in mind the fabrics I'm going to use and my different sources of inspiration. I've drawn a very urban three-piece outfit made up of pants, a T-shirt, and a short sleeve jacket. It's a very urban style, based on classic patterns that have been updated with the fabrics and my interpretation of the shapes. I use the pattern for pleated pants but with a slim fit, low crotch, and jean rivets to break the classic look of this type of pants. I've designed two oversized cotton pieces to go on top in two different shades of gray: a short-sleeve T-shirt with a wide-neck, and a short-sleeve jacket in gray cotton with a tuxedo cut, wide lapels, and one button.

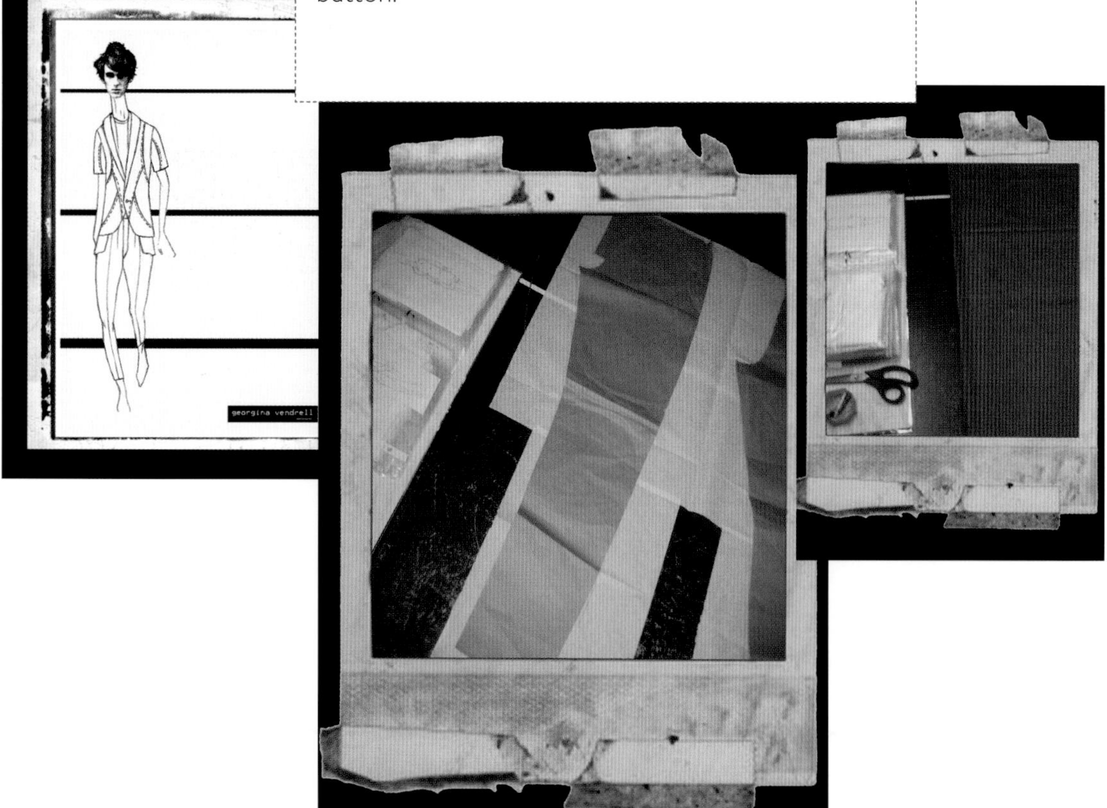

LON
DON

LOOK

This is a very current, casual look consisting of three pieces that can be worn at any time of day. The bright red pants contrast with the gray. However, the top pieces gain visual strength because of their original design. Comfort is a basic aspect of all of them. Depending on the accessories worn with them – shoes, glasses, hat, scarf, etc., you can achieve interesting combinations and very different effects. The model appearing in the photo, Alyosha Quoss, perfectly represents Georgina Vendrell's *It boy* profile; in fact, she has used him in all her lookbooks and runway shows since her very first collection.

GEORGY BARATASHVILI

www.georgybaratashvili.com

Georgy Baratashvili has Georgian roots, although he was born and raised in Moscow. Driven by his constant need for unrestrained expression, he demonstrated from a very early age a series of innate talents for drawing, painting, music, and, in particular, dance; in fact, he was a professional dancer for fifteen years. Baratashvili studied design and patternmaking in Moscow. He moved to London in 2003, where he finished his degree at the London College of Fashion and took an MA Fashion course at Central Saint Martins in 2008. During his time as a college student, he won several design prizes and collaborated with Preen in the design of pieces for their store. He also created a highly successful collection with Puma. In his degree show at Central Saint Martins, Baratashvili showed a different perception of current men's fashion, incorporating features and techniques that are not typically used in this field. He presented his eponymous menswear line at London Fashion Week in September 2009, which was a collection inspired by his past as a dancer, with a touch of dark romanticism. Georgy Baratashvili has become one of the most outstanding menswear designers on the current fashion scene.

MY IT

He is a young artist, a good friend of mine. We met in college many years ago. He has this effortless magnetism in combination with amazing personality, excellent taste, a great creativity and talent. After completing his art degree at Saint Martins, he went into the army, and now he is designing for a fashion company in Taiwan and continues working on his art projects. He has a very naturally toned body and unconventionally beautiful androgynous face.

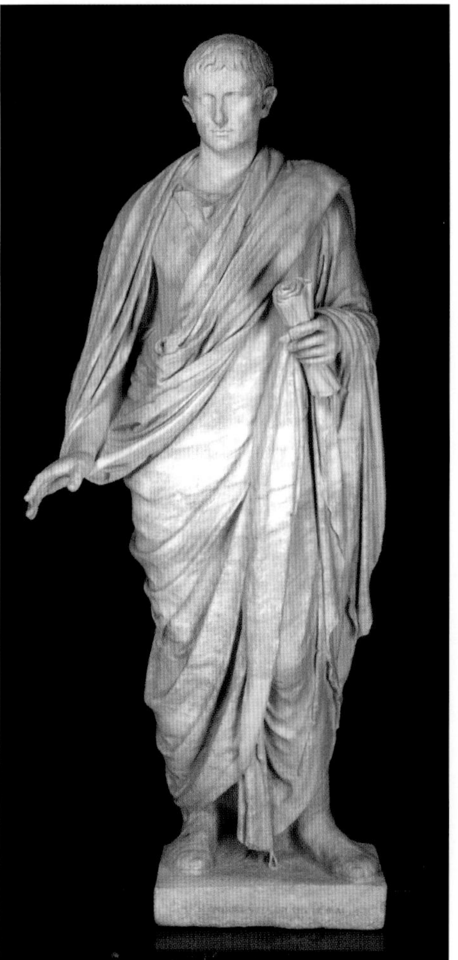

INSPIRATION

My *It boy* dresses very relaxed yet sophisticated, always looking modern without paying attention to fashion. I drew inspiration traveling through Italy. I thought about how everyday basic clothes change in response to time and the lifestyle of modern man. I tried to adopt draped clothes of Roman Empire citizens to the demands of contemporary urban life. Regarding the fabrics, it's a combination of treated distressed jersey and washed leather, always natural and good quality materials. I used very fine fabrics you would expect to see in women's wear and a predominantly dark palette: various shades of gray with some subtle color accents.

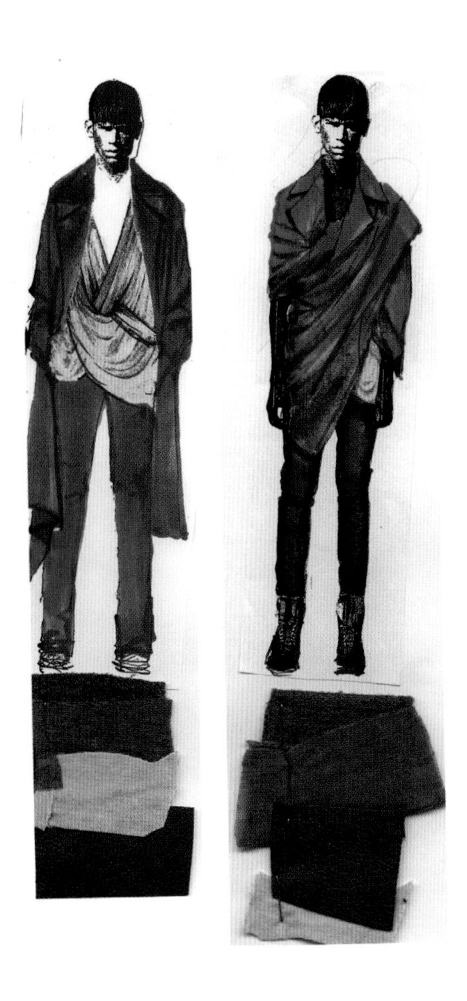

CREATION

Inspired by draped clothes of the Roman Empire, I transform basic pieces from the modern man's wardrobe, like slim fit jeans and a T-shirt and a jacket into leather trousers with a layer of superfine jersey over front panels, a draped T-shirt made of washed and aged silk jersey, and a cape made of washed wool jersey fused with superfine jersey over it. Before working with the definitive fabrics, the garments are made with basic fabrics to study the form. Then I make the fitting on a model to know if there is something to change and I do the modifications that are necessary. Finally, when I am sure that the pieces represent the original idea of the design, I move to the definitive fabrics.

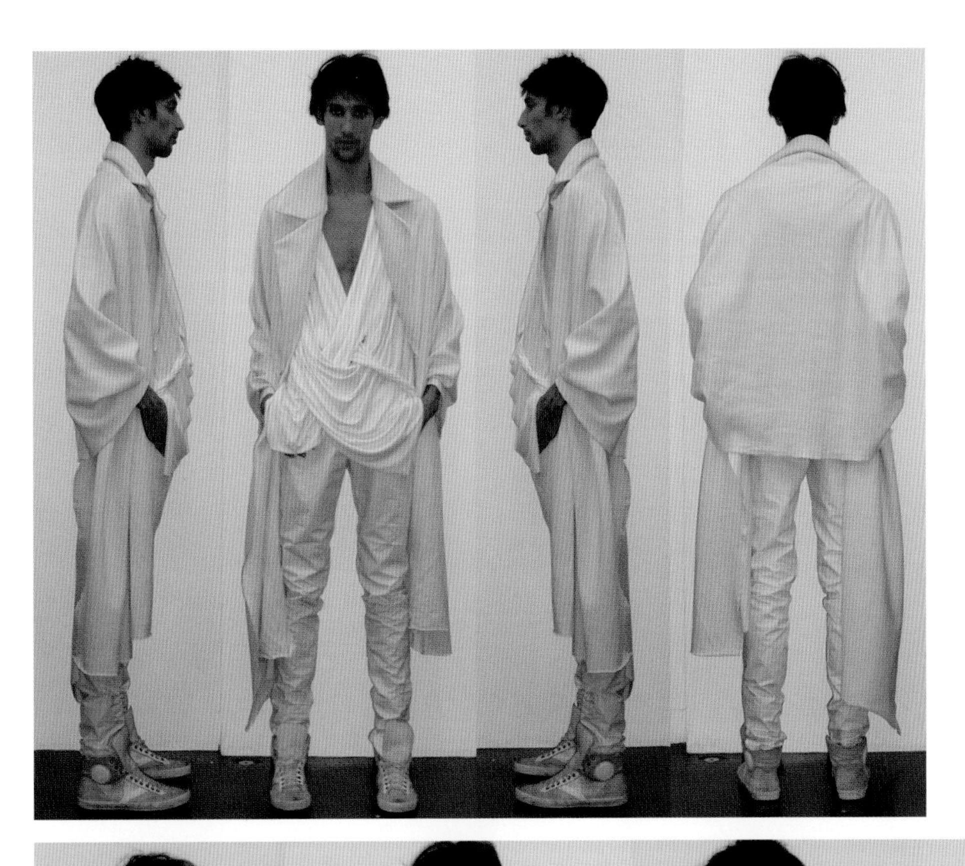

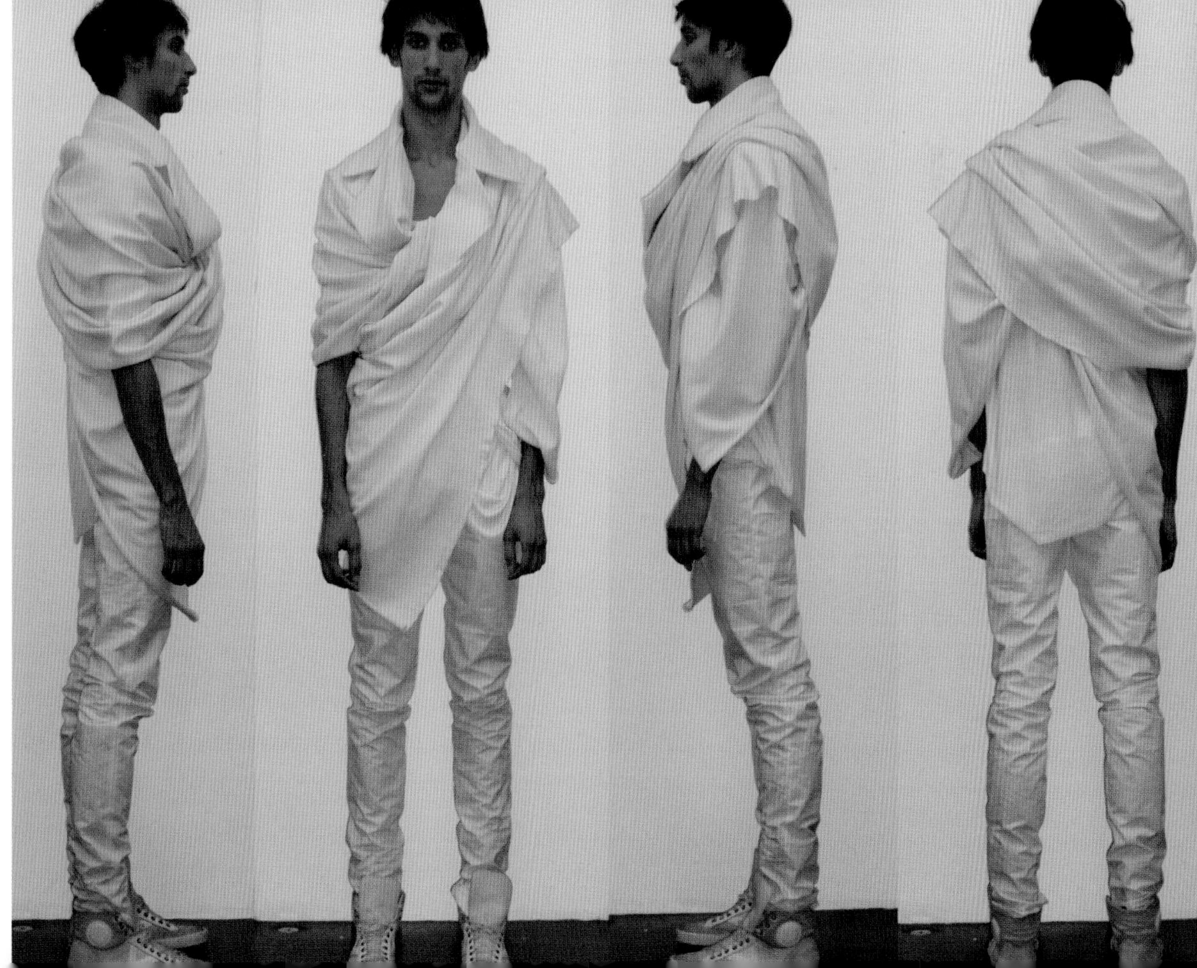

LOOK

The result is a very comfortable and romantic look composed by three pieces. The jacket can be worn as a cape. This way the outfit resembles a modern image of a Roman magistrate with the toga praetexta over a pleated tunic. The contrast of the leather with the wool and the silk creates a warm and elegant effect.

Photography: Brendan & Brendan

HANNA TER MEULEN

hannatermeulen.blogspot.com

Dutch menswear designer Hanna ter Meulen was born in Nijmegen in July 1985, growing up in the southern Netherlands, in the Maastricht region. She chose to study at the world-renowned ArtEZ Institute of the Arts, which has produced such illustrious alumni as Viktor & Rolf and Lucas Ossendrijver. She graduated in 2007 with the showing of her first menswear collection. Immediately after the event, she received an offer of employment from Ann-Sofie Back in London, where she went to work for a year as a studio and production manager. In 2008 she was accepted to do the prestigious MA fashion menswear course at the Royal College of Art, which has produced some of the most interesting menswear designers on the current scene, including Aitor Throup, James Long, Carolyn Massey, and Katie Eary. While at RCA, she was chosen as second runner-up in the IFF Fragrance Awards, Winner at the Conran Foundation Awards, and runner up in the ITS#NINE fashion competition in Italy. She graduated in June 2010 and is in the process of setting up her own label.

MY IT

My *It* is a gentleman who has a graceful flamboyance. He is a man of the world, eccentric but always stylish. He appreciates the new and innovative things, which may be in fashion, writing, electronics, architecture and food. He knows what his personal style is and he is very proud of it. He is a creative man who travels a lot and knows many people. He's the actor, the writer, the poet, the painter, the musician, the man that you pass in the street and then turn around to take another look at because of his striking personality and style.

P.221_Photography: Liam Aylott

INSPIRATION

The inspiration for this collection and outfit came in the first place from the film *American Psycho*. The clothes worn in the movie were the starting point for my research. In the late 1980s and early 1990s Armani and Versace were the key influences for silhouette and style. Next to that, the bases for any collection are first of all the fabrics and then the textile applications. In this case, weaving and smocking were the two techniques used. It became about the exploration of techniques shaping garment and making it mould to the male body, while enhancing it at the same time. All the fabrics for all my designs are always from the highest quality, so for this look there is no exception: high quality Scottish tweed, super fine wool, silk shirting, and mohair and cashmere knit. The luxury feeling that these materials give is essential in dressing my It boy. The color palette has been derived from the travels of the gentleman. I imagined him to have gone on an exploration trip to the North Pole, and the colors are then based on an old photograph I found from icy, eerie landscapes with lots of blues and grays.

CREATION

My sketch represents a very elegant look with a hint of the casual that is the feature of the twenty-first-century dandy. The outstanding piece in this look is a classic jacket made as several pieces in tweed. The original composition of the piece is designed with no seams at the armholes, achieving an original effect in which the garment fits comfortably around the shoulders. The pattern is worked out by interweaving different strips that will form a grid around the shoulder. This solution will give a more informal and modern aspect to a piece with references to classic tailoring. Mention should also be made of the shirt, which is made from a fabric with pale blue stripes, that is also made up in a traditional way, but with the addition of an interesting detail resulting from a combination of patches in the same fabric at the top.

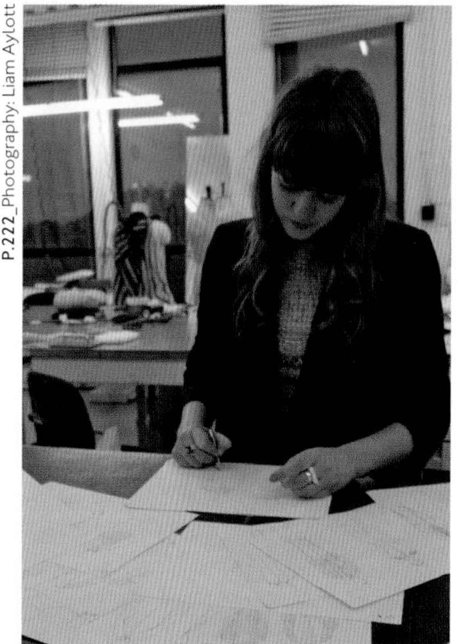

P.222_Photography: Liam Aylott

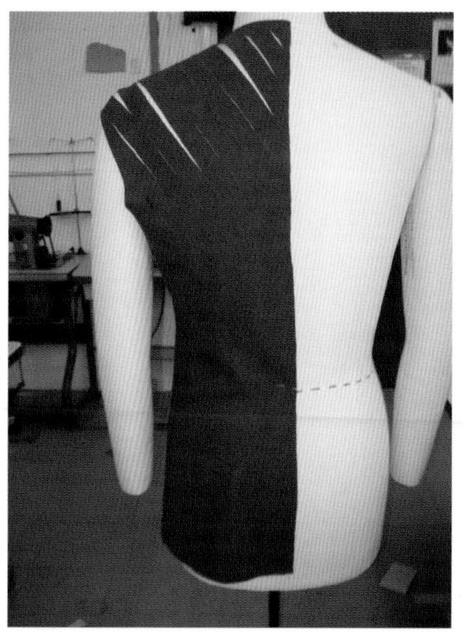

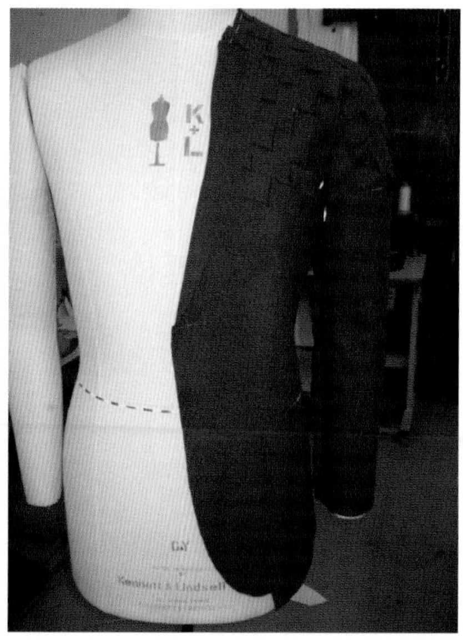

Photography: Liam Aylott

Photography: Liam Aylott

Photography: Liam Aylott

Pages 224+225 Photography: Brendan & Brendan. Styling: Will Westall. Hair styling: Michael Jones. Make-up: Martina Luisetti. Model: Jack Guinness, Models1

LOOK

In these images, the model is wearing the garments designed in combination with black pants, a two-tone jersey in black and gray and gray laced shoes, a look that conveys elegance and comfort with some sophistication. Jack Guinness, the model, is Hanna's *It*, or muse as she would rather prefer to call it. He is a Cambridge-educated actor, model, DJ, a contemporary Homo Universalis. He wears the clothes with such flair and ease that while we were having a break from shooting, people came up to him and asked where he got them. Now that is exactly what Hanna wants from her clothing and her muse. They make the perfect seamless combination.

H FREDRIKSSON

www.hfredriksson.com

The Swedish designer Helena Fredriksson lives and works in Brooklyn, where she puts together sophisticated collections that reflect the Scandinavian look mixed with the multicultural reality that is New York City. Her designs incorporate such concepts as modernity, nature, art, and sustainability, and they are inspired by the obscure psychology of Bergman movies and contemporary European painting. Added to this is a melancholy air that recalls the austere silhouette of the Nordic landscape. Her fashion outlook is influenced by her art studies, which is why her designs convey great knowledge of volume, color, form, etc. with pieces featuring contrast and juxtaposition. Her awareness of past and present are behind her use of both traditional crafts and new technologies, achieving a perfect combination of the two in her choice of fabrics. Fredriksson has presented her collections at New York Fashion Week for the last six seasons. She has also designed costumes for dance performances and for singers like Ana Matronic of Scissor Sisters. Likewise, she has worked with galleries and exhibitions in New York and Sweden. Her successfully consolidated label is currently sold in stores in the United States, Sweden, and Japan.

MY IT

My *It* is independent, creative, intellectual, open-minded, dynamic, vigorous, focused and grounded... with a free spirit and an ability to connect with people and culture around the globe. She is an inspiration and a model for an expansive mind and a way of life.

INSPIRATION

Inspiration is taken from the inner strength of women, from the courage to break boundaries and be independent. Fabrics are classic – tweed, herringbone twill, an open weave hemp cotton and original printed silk crepe, done in an innovative and sustainable way. As far as colors are concerned, they are dark and moody, with texture and print as a balancing force, a muted neutral classic palette that will stand the test of time and yet leave a footprint.

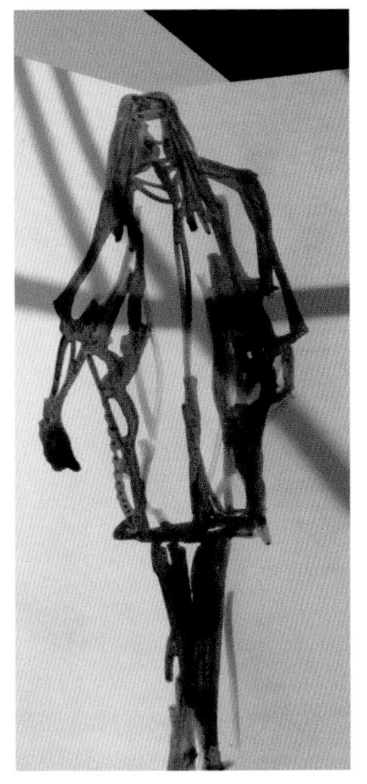

CREATION

This design consists of three pieces: a pencil skirt combined with a loose blouse with kimono sleeves and a cape. It's a mix of volumes that aims to lengthen the figure in order to project an image of elegance that is young and fun at the same time. The kimono sleeves are an extension of the piece, and their wide armholes make them more comfortable. This style of sleeve gives body to the silhouette and also moves elegantly with the wearer's movements. The black print over mustard transmits warmth and has a certain ethnic flavor. Ideally, this blouse should be combined with a very simple and body-hugging piece, as is the case of the pencil skirt in neutral herringbone twill (although it could also be combined with leggings or slim pants). Finally, kimono-sleeve blouses are often uncomfortable to wear with a coat, so a cape is the best way of completing the look.

LOOK

Helena always thinks up looks with volumes and silhouettes in mind. She designs with the aim of having the wearer feel enjoyment and comfort in her clothes. This page shows the result of the elegant skirt and blouse combination. An original bracelet creates an effect somewhere between bohemian and ethnic chic. In the photo on the right, the cape is closed with single button to give maximum comfort to the outfit. The high neck with a long gold necklace gives it an air of distinction. The combination of the three pieces, or the use of each one on its own, is perfect for an urban and feminine woman, and gives her a certain nostalgic, warm, and natural feel.

Pages 230+231 | Photography: Eli Schmidt

HILDA MAHA

www.hildamaha.com

Hilda Maha is a designer of fashion and printed fabrics who was born in Tirana, the capital of Albania, in 1979. She moved to Italy with her family in September 1990, where she lived until she departed for London in 2002 to study fashion design. She graduated with distinction from Central Saint Martins after specializing in fashion print design. Shortly after her graduation she won several competitions and a number of buyers became interested in her collection. While Hilda Maha was considering setting up her own company, she was chosen by the ITS agency as one of the winners of the PrintLab project, offered by Friulprint, a company she had collaborated with for a year as a print designer for different haute couture fabric collections sold around the world. She presented her personal collection for Friulprint at Première Vision in February and September 2009. She later decided to concentrate on her label, Hilda Maha, a task she shares with freelance work in fashion, textile design for interiors, and printed fabrics, and as a consultant to the clothing manufacturing industry.

MY IT

She has a multifaceted personality, which makes her quite chaotic but interesting and never boring. She is a fun-loving and hard-working woman who stands out in what she does. She doesn't like to waste a minute of life and fights for what she wants. Her values, family and loved ones are important to her. She has quite a high profile job and has a passionate and creative personality, though her intelligence keeps her grounded. She is strong but has a very romantic and fragile side. She is sexy but sweet.

INSPIRATION

Contrasts and juxtapositions inspire me. Craft and technology, heaviness and lightness, lots of colors, and black and white... Inspiration can come from everything, but creativity needs to be fed. As I am a print designer too, I start with making my prints and choosing the fabrics – touching and playing around with them inspires me. I asked myself: "What if metal was as fluid as silk satin? What would thick wool look like if it was as light and transparent as organza, or soft like velvet? What if warm soft wool that cocoons the body was encaged and trapped in cold and harsh metallic wires?" This was the starting point. Then I added a sexy and fun late-1970s and early-1980s inspiration, references to folk costume, Alabama Worley, Avatar, Helmut Newton and Moschino. As for the fabrics, their quality is extremely important to me. I'm constantly looking for the next best thing. Silk organza, silk velvet, silk satin and silk jersey play a huge part, sometime combined together in the same outfit, which creates depth and contrast. Then there is 100 percent wool, chenille and cotton. Fabrics are printed, black and white, or dyed to my exact color sample. I like colors, and with the 1970s inspiration along came an almost psychedelic feel to them. As this was a winter collection, I thought it would be nice for once to have color. I was bored with the usual sea of blues, grays and blacks so I thought I would take the risk and go with colors all the way, contrasting them with a little black or white, and a few outfits in block

CREATION

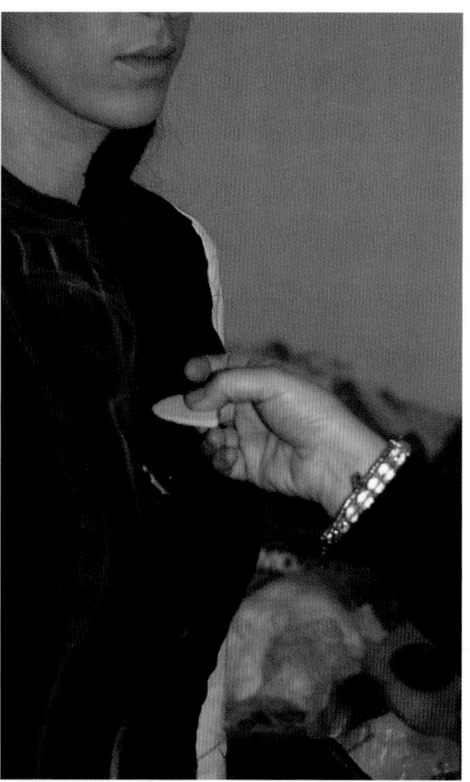

Keeping my moodboard in mind, I tend to do quite a lot of sketches, but I go back and forth to the dummy too. I've learned that sometimes it's better to leave the fabric do what it wants too, rather than force it, so sketches and fitting go often together, like a big work in progress. Waistlines and shoulders were the focus. I wanted to emphasize the waistline, so I raised it above the belly button, I accentuated the shoulders and I added skin-tight trousers. Backs are important too, bare or with sharp details. This coat is entirely lined in printed silk satin, the same fabric that follows on the outside in the details. The rest of it is in wool on the white one and in velvet on the black one. The proportions of the round details in the neck were changed too. I like to work with models on fitting. As much as I love my dummy, it's on the body where you see the garment come to life and where it needs changing. In this case the coat needed pulling in at the waist. I decided as well that the detachable sleeves weren't right so I changed them into normal sleeves.

CP14. 18/2
CP14. 18/21

LOOK

These images show two ways of combining the three pieces: the high-waisted pants with a matching jacket or with a white, high-necked coat with splashes of the same colors. These pieces are designed to fit the waist snugly in order to create flattering volumes on shoulders and hips: fun fall designs that enhance the angelical image of the model, Alek. Hilda Maha shows that besides her work as a fashion designer she is a fantastic print designer, which is why she always surprises with such original pieces.

Photography: Dizy Díaz

JUAN ANTONIO ÁVALOS

www.juanantonioavalos.net

Juan Antonio Ávalos is the young Spanish designer behind the eponymous ready-to-wear menswear label, founded in 2009. He studied fashion design at the Felicidad Duce School of Design and Fashion in Barcelona. During that time he collaborated with professionals from different spheres of the fashion world and won his first Tu Estilo, Tu Studio prize from L'Oréal Paris in Madrid. He finished his studies in 2007, graduating with the third prize for best collection, and started working for the Antonio Miró fashion house. With only two collections on the market, Juan Antonio Avós is already considered one of the promising talents of Spanish design; in fact, his first collection deservedly won the Premi Catalunya for emerging designers during the first edition of 080 Barcelona Fashion, which provided him a springboard to Paris, where he trained in 2008 with designers Bernhard Willhelm (developing printed fabrics for the 2009 spring/summer womenswear collection) and Thomas Engel Hart. He has also collaborated with companies like Converse and Superga, and with such photographers as Björn Tagemose and Daniel Riera. His designs have a transgressive, cosmopolitan, and dynamic style, for men looking for comfort in alternative clothes.

MY IT

He is full of life and wants to feel different from the rest. He doesn't want to be one of the crowd. He's drawn by the combination of colors, fabrics, and textures. He appreciates a practical dress sense, a studied design and conceptual work in a collection. He lives for fun and enjoying the moment.

INSPIRATION

We started off with ethnic concepts, music, and references from other artistic disciplines to create a new vision. The label style lies in the clash of styles and references. The use of color and combination of men's tailoring with sport are the unifying threads in all of our know-how. We like contrasting and combining textures of every kind. Our preference is for technical fabrics that can enhance colors and shine more intensely, but we don't look down on natural fabrics like wool, linen, and cotton. The inspiration for this project is the figure of Majinga Zetto, also known as Mazinger Z (Tranzor Z in the US), the famous manga by the Japanese artist Go Nagai and one of the precursors of the mecha genre: giant robots manipulated by humans. The color palette is a faithful reproduction of the character's colors.

CREATION

The design for the outfit is inspired by the manga character Majinga Zetto, and takes the structure of the robot as its reference, together with its colors. Four colors – red, black, gray, and blue – are used on the most visible parts, while the lining is yellow. The fabric is padded to represent the character's volume. The jacket is more developed because it will consist of several pieces, each with different padding designs. This required prior research into the design of the padded pieces and their ideal combination with each other. Despite faithfully reproducing a robot, the piece was intended to be practical and as wearable as possible.

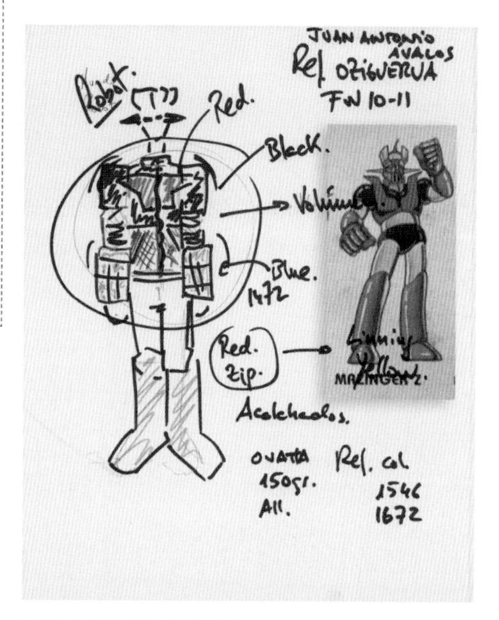

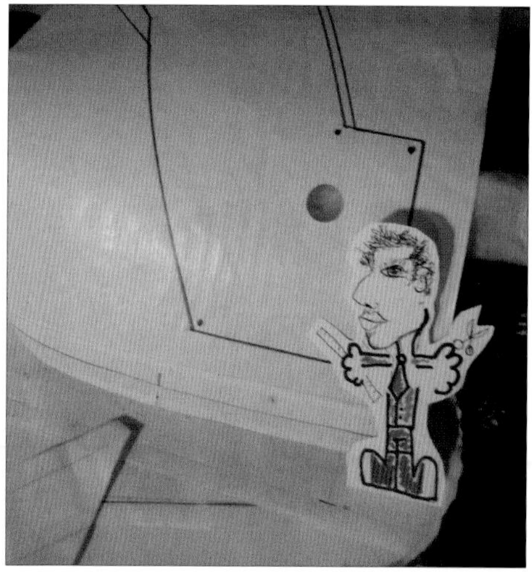

Ref. Ozigurva FW'11

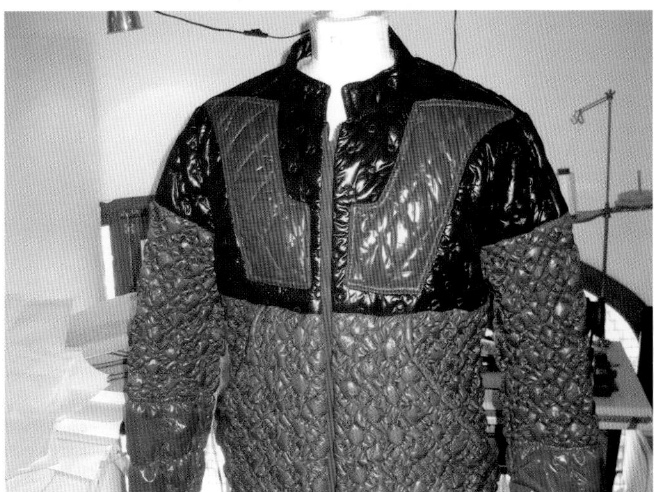

LOOK

The sum of a perfect study in design, volume and shape, together with the originality and creative ability of Juan Antonio Ávalos, has resulted in a very comfortable and urban outfit that conveys the strength of the manga character. The shiny fabric and the good choice of colors and details provide a sophisticated touch. The runway image shows a look completed with maxi headphones covered in the same padded fabric in black, makeup that gives a robot expression, and Converse Weapon basketball shoes – an authentic cosmopolitan cocktail.

WEAPON

JUAN VIDAL

www.juanvidal.net

When it came to deciding his college studies, Juan Vidal chose fine arts, which provided an important aesthetic base to his knowledge. However, owing to his interest in fashion and his family's long tailoring tradition, he reconsidered his career options and studied fashion design at the Felicidad Duce School of Design and Fashion in Barcelona. He came to the attention of the industry in 2005, during the ModaFAD Awards, where he won the prize for the best collection during that event. Since that time, his work has been acclaimed by many experts and followers. Juan Vidal has presented his collections at different shows in Spain, such as El Ego at Cibeles Madrid Fashion Week, 080 Barcelona Fashion, and Valencia Fashion Week, where he received the Revlon Award for his 2010 spring/summer collection. His designs show radical changes in style from season to season, but they always feature his very personal and recognizable mark, which conveys strength, elegance, and seductive femininity.

MY IT

The woman I design for is essentially a self-confident one for whom age is of no importance. One who sees herself as passionate, sensual, and impulsive. Feminism in a pure state is what interests me. These women have power. Seduction and fragility are their closest allies. They feel secure and enjoy the pleasures that shy women don't. They have character and perception, they appreciate the small details and they are aware that balance is their best weapon.

INSPIRATION

This dress has the femme fatale silhouette as its chief reference, but with a more contemporary focus. It's vital to have a feel for the past and know how to mix it with a touch of the suggestiveness to create something new. At the same time, I believe it's interesting when handwork is added because it brings delicateness to a dress. In my opinion, "too much" is excessive, but it stops being excessive if I contrast it with something formal. And something "informal" becomes interesting when you can appreciate its structure. That's why I consider the study of volumes and shapes to be important. Color is essential. It's expression. An eccentric piece can be just as interesting as an austere one if you continue to see the woman and not only the dress. This time I've chosen red because its attributes are almost all superlative. It's the color with the greatest emotional impact. Its physical effects are said to be so strong that prolonged exposure increases the average heart rate, encouraging the flow of adrenaline in the blood and bringing on a kind of flush. It's a turgid color. It takes attention away from everything else, outshining all other colors around it.

CREATION

There are designs that start off as experiments, from the feel of the fabric. You have a basic idea of what you want but you let the fabric itself breathe life into the dress. When making a dress, you have to know what to show and what to hide, where to make it fall from the body, and where to take it in to create a silhouette that a woman feels comfortable in. My way of working has a traditional base, using hands I know and can direct. They work steadily and follow the guidelines I set previously in more personal designs.

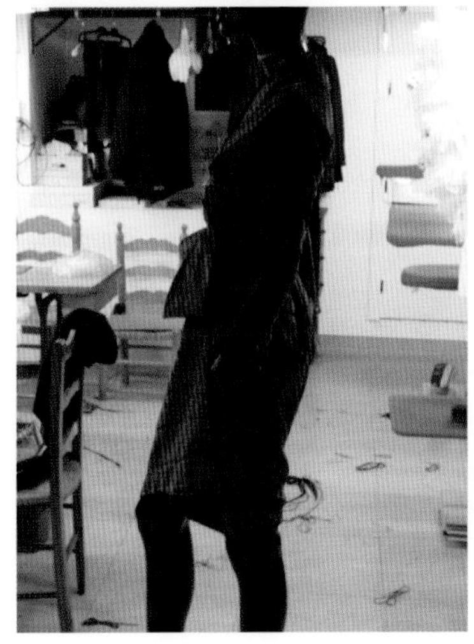

LOOK

The result of this work is a dress that envelops a woman's femininity. Instead of taking prominence away from her, she becomes the focus of attention. The overlapped layers and folds are gathered at the waist to spread the volume between the bust and the hips, emphasizing the thinness of the waist, arms, and legs. The result is elegant, sensual, and very feminine.

Pages 248+249 Photography: Ferran Casanova/Blue Studio

KILIAN KERNER

www.kiliankerner.de

Kilian Kerner works with his feelings. This designer was born and raised in Cologne, Germany, and studied theater in his hometown and in Berlin between 2000 and 2003. He later decided to make a career for himself in fashion, driven by his passion for dressing and because he had the feeling that devoting himself to design would be right for him. What sets Kilian apart is the great emotional quality he gives to each of his designs. With the design of his first collection, Überhaupt und Du, he already demonstrated his absolute trust in his intuition. The brand is currently celebrating its first minor jubilee after its tenth collection, and can now boast of its mastery of the technical concepts and know-how. Kilian participated in the Mercedes-Benz Berlin Fashion Week for the first time in the summer of 2008, and he has now been showing there for the last five consecutive seasons. This is why the brand has become a firm feature of the German fashion industry, and it is now a must to have Kerner as a fixture of the German capital's fashion show calendar.

MY IT

She is a self-confident, career-focused woman who is ambitious and independent and at a high point in her life. She has an innate awareness of fashion and places great importance on her appearance. She demands a lot from her wardrobe, which should emphasize her character and reflect her personality. She is set apart from the rest and dresses in a timeless and minimal fashion, confident of her style.

INSPIRATION

My designs take their strength and originality from the elements that have had a decisive impact on the creation and development of the Kilian Kerner label. The story of how the label was established began with my main source of inspiration: my enthusiasm for music and the feeling of weightlessness you experience at a concert. I've been bringing to my label the energy that comes from the power of that moment, and its dynamism and emotional load. I see fashion as the interpretation of moments and the meaning of life associated with those instances. Using this base, and in a way that I've worked out for myself, I've always managed to create a new language without placing restrictions on style or genre. There is a story behind each one of my collections. The designs are presented every season on the runways accompanied by live music, thanks to the collaboration of bands that compose songs for every collection, and who make it possible for the sparks of inspiration behind my work to be felt. Splinter X and Mor La Peach are some of the bands that have taken part in my shows.

CREATION

First the collection is studied by using test fabrics to obtain the best possible results and for the dress to fit perfectly and caress the body, creating a sensation of self-confidence in the wearer. Sometimes it is necessary to redo the test piece three times until all of the details finally come together. The dress was designed entirely in red. The combination of materials allows the different shades to be distinguished – the red of the cotton, the red of the chiffon, and the bright red of the silk – to create a harmonious fusion that provides the dress with its elegance. The upper layer of the dress is made in polyester, and the intermediate layers and the sleeves are 100 percent silk. Added to these are the bustier, the straps, the neck strap, and the lower part, made in virgin cotton. The bustier is lined in 100 percent silk.

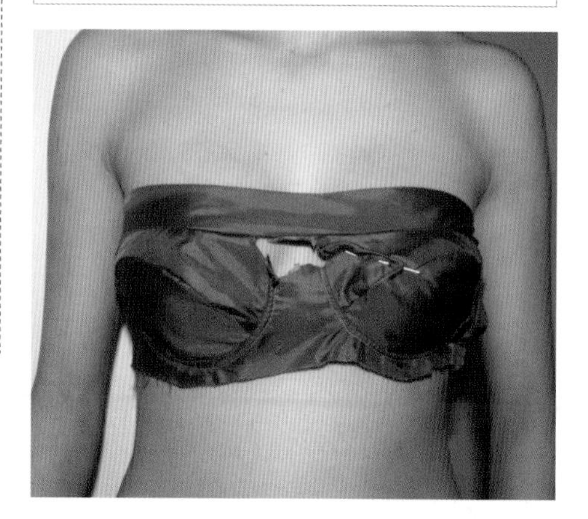

ARCELLO RUBINI 2010

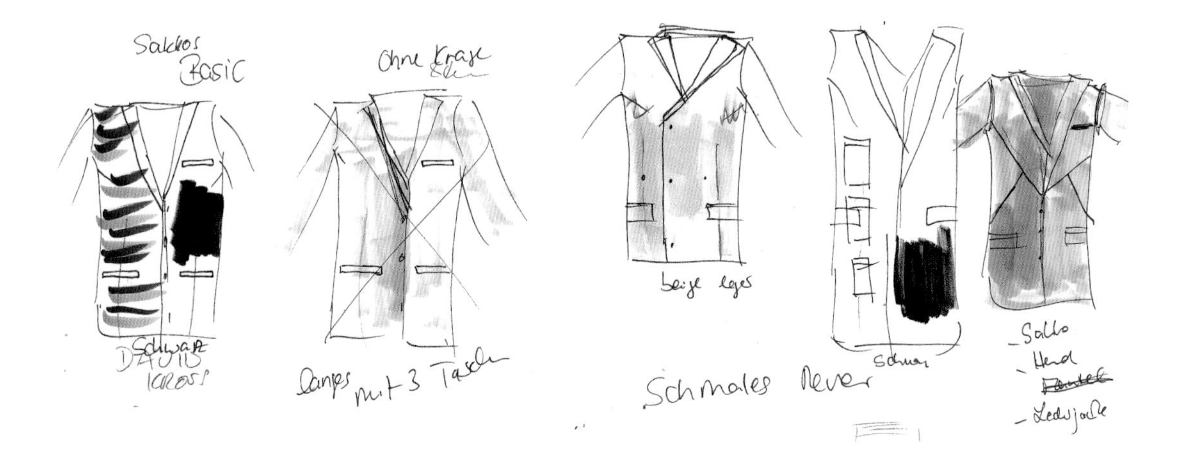

CREATION

The jacket makes use of a single color, navy blue, although different shades can be distinguished, because one of them is navy blue wool and the other is bright blue silk. The combination of materials makes this color distinction possible and turns the jacket into a truly special garment. The fusion of both shades creates a unique harmony.

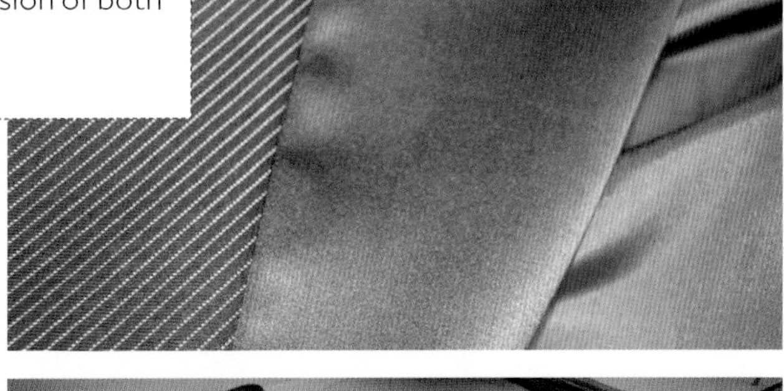

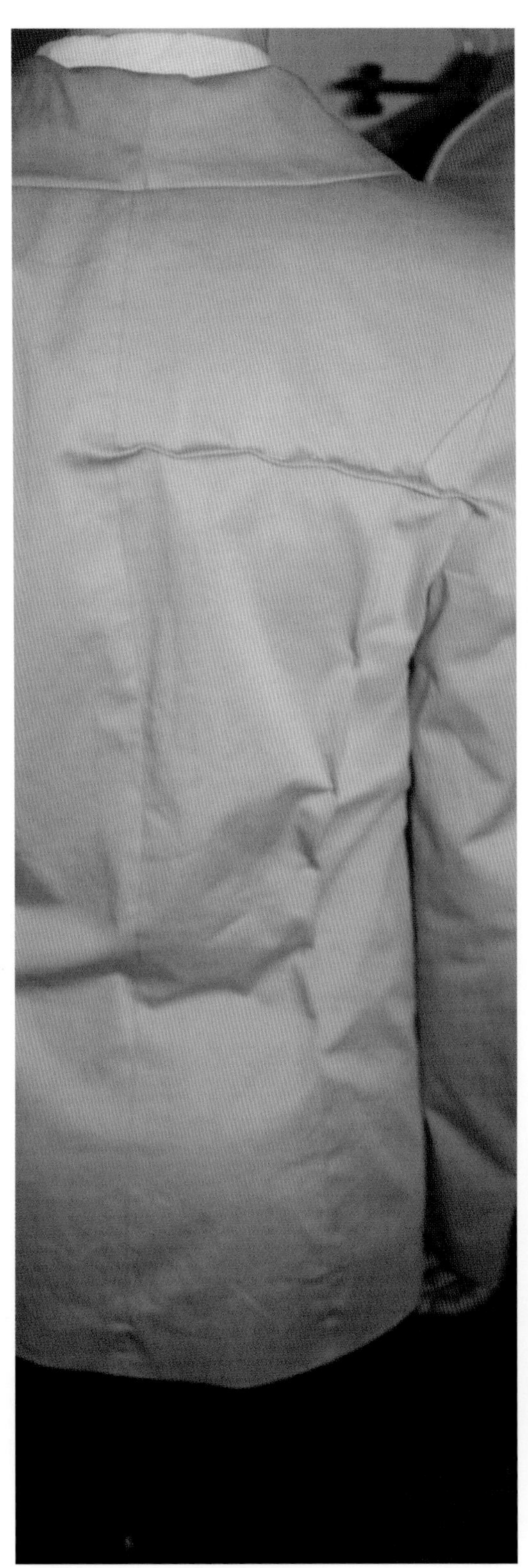

LOOK

Both looks embody the essence of the label. They are pieces with a young and romantic spirit. She wears a spectacular and very elegant and dynamic design, which features sheerness, contrasting fabrics and nuances. The bright red turns the model into a genuine, feminine and updated Gilda.

LOOK

The look presented for the man features a jacket with clear reminiscences of classic tailoring, and small details like exclusive buttons and a combination of fabrics that give it a unique feel. Accessorized by a neck scarf and a striped sweater, the result is very elegant.

LA AGUJA EN EL DEDO

laagujaeneldedo.blogspot.com

Ismael Gómez Figueroa studied advertising and public relations and audiovisual communication at the University of Seville before becoming interested in the mysteries surrounding clothing design. His first forays into the world of fashion were self-taught, until he acquired the necessary experience to found La Aguja en el Dedo in 2004 and open his own store in Seville, Spain. He presented his first runway collection at the Andalucía Moda fashion show in March 2008. The following June he launched his second, Geometría sp. para Septiembre, at Mustang Fashion Week, an event programmed as part of the Benicàssim International Festival. The same year he also took part in the El Ego de Cibeles showroom as an exhibitor. For the label's third collection, he became partners with Javier Bartel, a young Sevillan designer and patternmaker. Javier Bartel studied fashion design at the Metrópolis School in Seville, combining it with patternmaking and computerized patternmaking studies at the Imagen School in the same city. Ismael and Javier currently work closely on the design of their collections with their 2010/2011 fall/winter collection being the first and successful fruit of their collaboration, presented at the South 36-32N fashion show in Cadiz, Spain, in June 2010.

MY IT

La Aguja en el Dedo receives its energy from daily life. Our *Its* stand out from the crowd by their natural look and their way of dressing, which is the mark of their identity. They transmit their spontaneity to us and we love their more innocent side, without overlooking their elegance and style.

INSPIRATION

We normally work with the chaos of thousands of ideas, which start to emerge from the initial excess. They are filtered to eliminate the unsuitable alternatives until the perfect solution is found for each garment. The inspiration for this look comes from everything that forms part of our surroundings. We appreciate spontaneity and naturalness, which is why we want our creations to capture this spirit. We enhance the feeling of individual freedom through fullness and prints in our clothes. Loose and comfortable shapes and pleats are interpretations of innocence. Childishness and a carefree spirit are reflected in the prints and how we use them on stockings, and finally, the awareness side and the road to take are represented through the belted jacket. The fabrics we combine are tweed, faux suede, silk, and cotton. The colors we chose are ocher, mustard, sky blue, and stone gray... earthy, natural, and romantic colors; the combination of all of them takes us to the center of the earth, to its bowels, where we can feel totally involved in this world that gave us life and which we form a part of. The navy blue gives rigidity to the prints, settling them and defining the darkness that is also a part of everything that has light.

CREATION

We started with sketches as our reference, although they were changed and developed all the time, with the making of the prototype. As we work together on the total development of the piece, it's easy for us to make the necessary changes as we go. We mark any changes we make on the sketch throughout the creation process. We try to be meticulous and pay attention to detail during the cutting and making up of the garment. This look was quite clear from the start and we didn't have any problems while we were putting it together, except with the jacket, which started out as a cape (we finally had to cut the pattern out twice). We wanted to give the skirt a lot of volume by making it in layers. The stiffness came from the gum treatment of the interlining fabric. We emphasized the waist area as far as the hip to enhance the feminine curves, while trying not to restrict movement and comfort. We used the same fabrics and colors in the different pieces making up this look, which was designed for total continuity over the body so that it had the appearance of a dress.

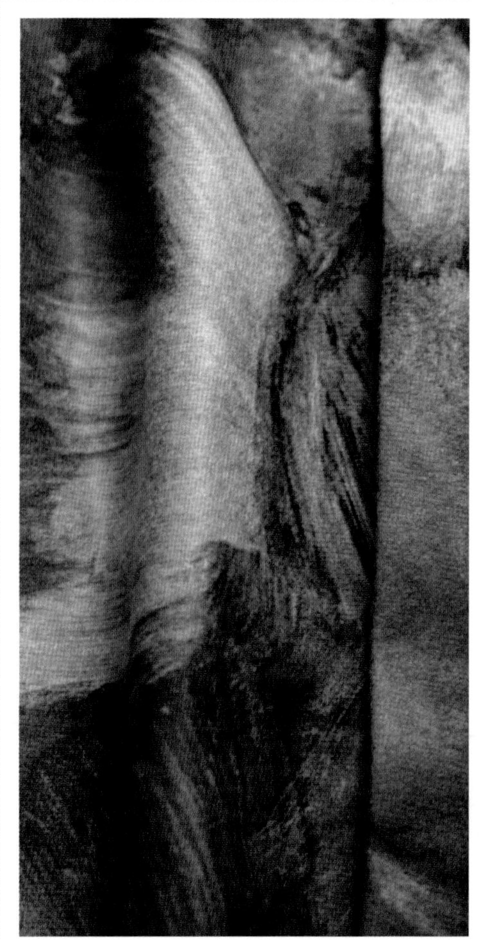

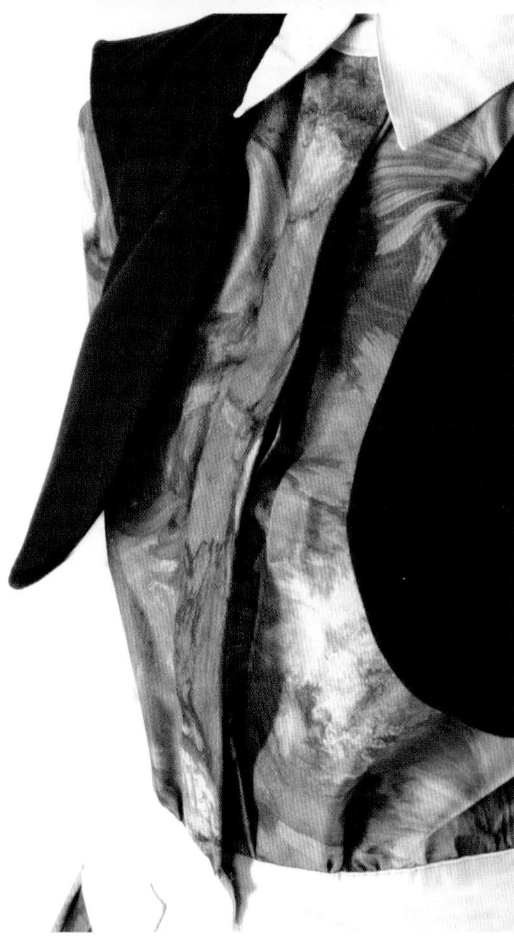

LOOK

This is a very comfortable look. Although it has a certain aspect of a uniform, it eschews all of the connotations that come with that type of clothing. The different pieces are adaptable to any situation. They combine easily with other basics to provide personality and an exclusive charm. The original cut of the skirt makes it ideal for cocktail parties, and that of the blouse makes it an essential piece of workwear or daywear. The jacket complements any kind of garment.

LESLEY MOBO

www.lesleymobo.com

Lesley Mobo is a London-based Filipino designer. After earning a fashion design degree and MA, topping his class in both at the prestigious Central Saint Martins College of Art and Design, the designer won acclaim from such established figures in the world of fashion as Renzo Rosso from Diesel, Ennio Capasa from Costume National, Antonio Marras from Kenzo, and Raf Simons when he won the Diesel Award during the third edition of International Talent Support in Italy. The winning collection was inspired by the struggle for survival in extreme conditions and was titled Obesity in the North Pole. Besides the capsule collection he created for Diesel – which sold out in New York, Berlin, Paris, Antwerp, London, Milan, and Tokyo – Lesley Mobo's designs are familiar to a significant number of experts and to *Vogue*, *iD*, *Dazed and Confused*, *Self-Service*, and *Purple Magazine*, among other fashion publications. Mobo's signature designs explore forms, combinations of textures, and studied patterns. His designs have graced such celebrities as Daisy Lowe and the top model Caroline Trentini, and they have been photographed by such masters of the camera as Mario Sorrenti, Richard Bush, and Rankin.

MY IT

The brand focuses on the personality and character of the individual woman wearing the clothing, giving her contemporary clothing with haute couture renewal in terms of feel and look. She has a modern lifestyle with a classical femininity, striking the right balance between masculine and feminine elements with the correct amount of nonchalance. It is like Versace meeting Yamamoto in woodland! It is about being sensual without being drenched in sex; What makes a woman today a modern woman.

INSPIRATION

Inspiration comes from the village of Matavenero, gathering the possibilities of adaptation and cultural isolation in physical, social and physiological terms. There are certain influences working through the culture that form and steer the concept of modern femininity. This was an experimentation of subtle glamour mixed with giant insect-like raw wool creations showing both the conventional and unconventional form (and figure) of the human body. The message was not just about containing the body but also about extending it.

CREATION

This process is the most exciting stage in design – the ultimate expression. On a day-to-day basis a designer relishes the challenge of turning his ideas into reality. Even if the main source of inspiration is not conceptual or intellectual, they are multi-leveled in terms of problem solving. Working through fabrics, patterns and finishings, and finding solutions in constructing them, is part of the main experiment. It can be interesting to see how the first input of a designer's idea can alter the direction of the final product. Designing a garment sometimes is like studying anatomy – the designer needs to be familiar with the basic human body structure, how the tendons and muscles are attached to the skeletal system and how they move in frame. These are the underlying forms that will dictate how a fabric moves and fits in harmony or deviates with the body. This garment has been developed partly out of traditional patterns of a male coat. Many of its details are also derivatives of functional apparel associated with labor and the military. The simultaneous requirements of protection and mobility result in an interpretation of the body that is specific and non-negotiable in parts (as in positioning of arms) but open to generalization and abstraction in others (the contours of the shoulders, hips and chest).

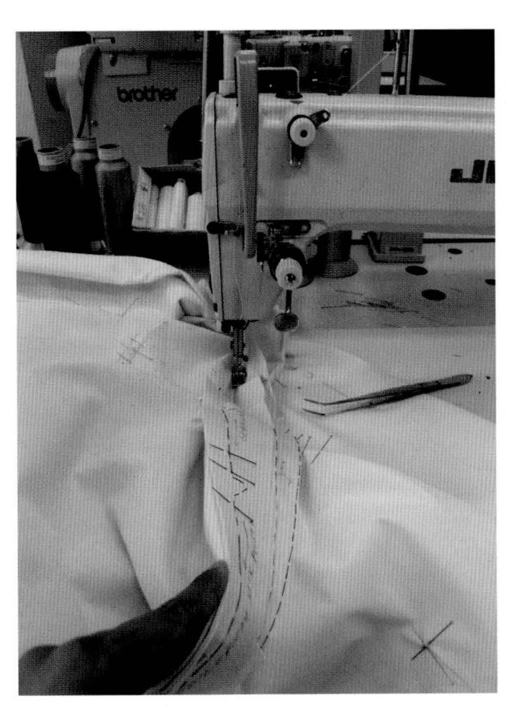
brother

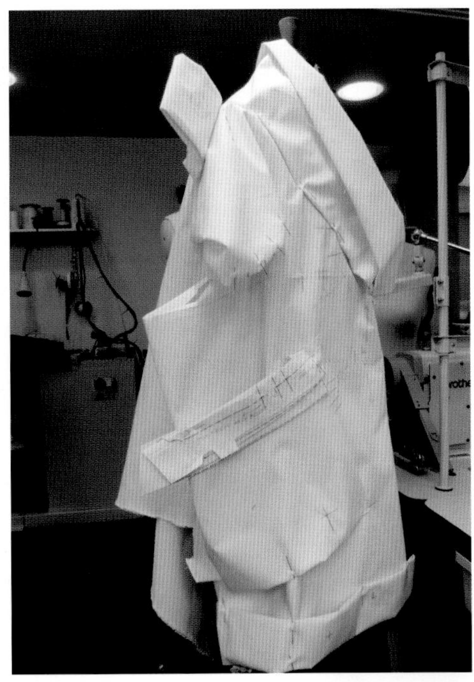

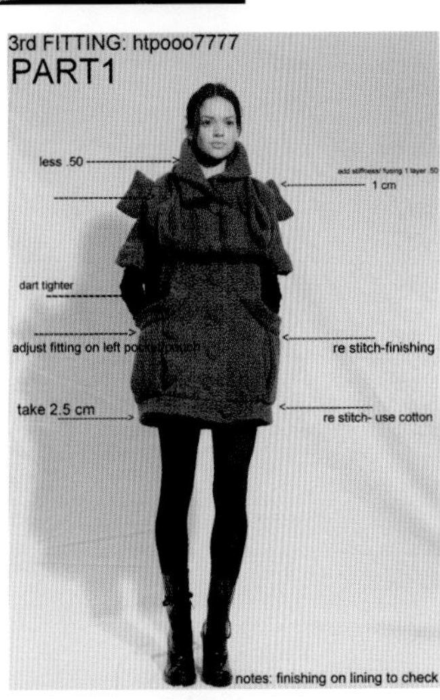
3rd FITTING: htpooo7777
PART1
less .50
add stiffness/ fusing 1 layer .50
1 cm
dart tighter
adjust fitting on left po
re stitch-finishing
take 2.5 cm
re stitch- use cotton
notes: finishing on lining to check

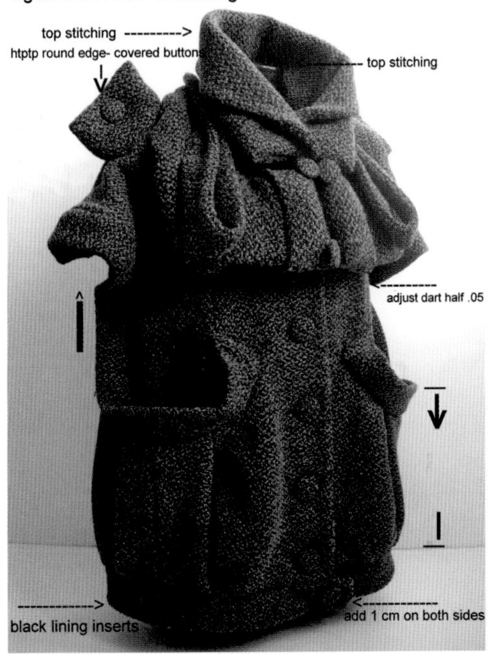
figure # 077789- first fitting
top stitching
htptp round edge- covered buttons
top stitching
adjust dart half .05
black lining inserts
add 1 cm on both sides

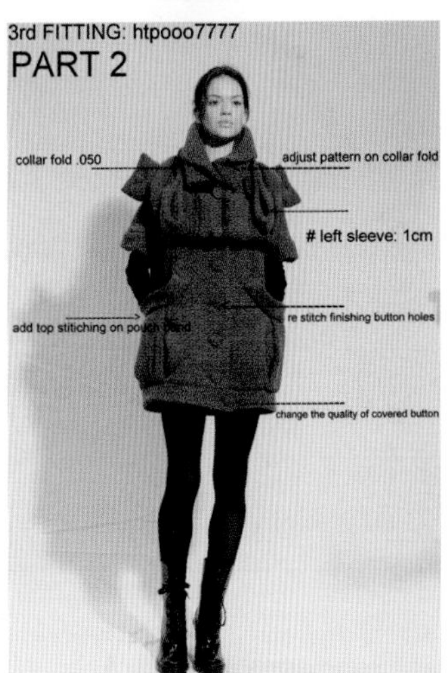
3rd FITTING: htpooo7777
PART 2
collar fold .050
adjust pattern on collar fold
left sleeve: 1cm
add top stitiching on po
re stitch finishing button holes
change the quality of covered button

LOOK

This is an extraordinary look, featuring a woolen coat that is distinguished by its adaptability and the ease with which it can be transformed. This is made possible by the detachable pieces, the shape of the shoulders, the open pleats, the large neck, and the oversized pockets. The references are to men's tailoring. The look is accessorized with a black sweater and panty hose, patent leather military-style boots in the same color with sumptuous golden embellishments. Even the hairstyle is an integral part of this outfit designed and overseen by Lesley Mobo. It is an ideal look for a modern, fun-loving girl with loads of personality who likes to dress naturally with style.

MANUEL BOLAÑO

myspace.com/manuelbolanho

Manuel Bolaño Gómez was born in Barcelona, Spain, in 1984, although he lived in Lugo until his teens. He returned to Barcelona to study fashion design at the prestigious Felicidad Duce School of Design and Fashion. While studying, Bolaño worked as an assistant for designers Arturo Guillén and Gabriel Torres in the patternmaking department of Y Can Fuck W. After graduating, he joined the design team of the international Spanish company Mango, an experience that ended when he was selected to take part in the Catalan government's Projecte Bressol, which supported the development of his own label over a span of three years. He has taken part in a number of local fashion shows, including the Pasarela Abierta in Murcia and 080 Barcelona Fashion. His collections have also received a number of first prizes, including that of Madrid Young Designers and the Young Talent Prize 07 at the Bread & Butter trade show, and he has been a finalist at many other contests. Manuel Bolaño's work has been highly praised by experts since his beginnings, and has been cataloged as part of the solid and renewed heritage of Spanish haute couture. His collections are very different from one season to another. However, there are always common denominators such as the fine detailing, dazzling creativity, and marked and very well studied references.

MY IT

My *It girl* is a woman who steers clear of conforming to trends. She has an active social life. She looks for one-off, exclusive pieces because she thinks they enhance her personality even more.

INSPIRATION

My inspiration comes from a visit I made with my mother to the Celtic hill forts in Galicia (*castros*). The volumes spring from the image we have of our childhood, when our mothers put our raincoats on us over our schoolbags. The teddy bear is incorporated into the clothes as a reminder of our toys, in my case to remember the teddy bear I took everywhere with me. The fabrics are silks and wools mixed with cotton, creating evocative shapes and textures. The softness of the hand-woven mohair recreates the stones of the hill forts. The shades of gray reflect the stone and the cold climate of Galicia; the camel conveys protection and affection.

CREATION

The drawing of the design is my attempt to represent as faithfully as possible how the finished piece will look. In turn, it helps me to imagine the patterns for the pieces. This is a jumpsuit with a fitted, elasticized waist featuring the original detail of four teddy bear heads surrounding the torso. The pattern for the heads is complex. Fitting the heads onto the jumpsuit so that they can be integrated is even more complex. Several trials will have to be made to know if the garment is stable and comfortable, and to make sure the heads stay put. This way any problems that arise can be solved when it's fitted on a person, and we'll make the piece as comfortable as possible.

Courtesy of TrendsLab BCN

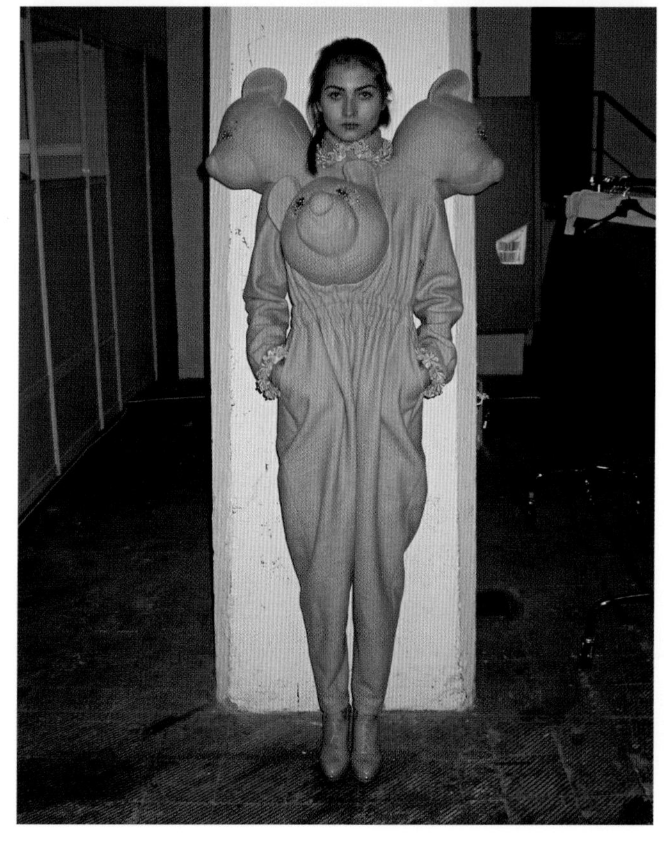

LOOK

The mixture of different fabrics can achieve new textures and interesting effects.The volumes distort the woman's body; however, the tight-waisted silhouette insinuates feminine curves.The amazing platform boots with a wood finish combine perfectly with the outfit.The details and embellishments, together with the styling work, complete the look to bring about a visual explosion, an image that seems to have come out of a cool tale.You can also see on this page another outfit in camel designed along the same lines and from the same collection.

MARTIN HAVEL

www.myspace.com/martinhavel

Martin Havel was born in 1979 in Pelhřimov, Czech Republic. In 2005 he finished his studies in textile and fashion design at the Technical University of Liberec (Faculty of Textile Engineering), although he had previously received training in clothing technology, specializing in men's tailoring in high school. He is currently finishing his fashion design studies at the Academy of Arts, Architecture and Design in Prague. This designer has been involved in a large number of exhibitions and events in his country and abroad, including the European Design exhibition in Nantes, France, and Design Match CZE:SVK, held at the National Gallery in Prague. He has taken part in Prague Fashion Week on several occasions, where he received the Talent of the Season prize. He has also been shortlisted for the annual Czech Academy of Design awards in the designer of the year category. For Martin Havel, clothes are as practical as they are pragmatic, expressing the life philosophy of whoever wears them. His designs have appeared in such publications as *Elle*, *Woman*, and *Star*.

MY IT

I suggest the woman who is confident. She is a woman who can appreciate the exceptionality and singularity of the moment spinal cords models. Intellectual above all, she knows what she wants in life, and she also retains her feminine freshness. She is a woman who is not afraid to be different and has her say.

INSPIRATION

My inspiration is life. I am inspired by the environment that surrounds me, by history and presence, by people I have met, by things I have seen and by music I have listened to. Everything I am experiencing and I do has an impact on me. That is naturally reflected in my work. In my work, I deal with social subjects in the world. In previous collections I worked with subjects like social networking portals, media, consumerism, anorexia, and cheap Asian textile. The look I am presenting here is from the collection that I am just finishing. The collection is about an elegant way to balance on the edge of abyss of gender. It is a collection about reality and dreams in which I examine the definition of my design style. The mood of the collection is influenced by thoughts of Sigmund Freud and by René Magritte's surreal paintings.

CREATION

From the beginning, I should know what I want to tell people. Then I create a concept of the collection, the sense of my new work. Like a director in the theater, I create a plot for the new collection, and also the beginning and the end of the collection. I don't like illustrative and complicated things. The aim is to motivate people to think about themselves in a dressing context. When I have a clear idea on the subject, materials, colors, shapes and the goal I want to reach, I begin to create. The look I will show here is based on a classic men's suit, which emphasizes my education in the field of men's tailoring. The jacket, inspired by the male silhouette, is looser, with deep-shaped lapels placed at the chest. The jacket and the trousers are made of fine wool with an addition of elastane. The top has a layered impression of a black shirt over a white sweater with a V-neck. But it is actually a one-piece shirt, made of the same cotton shirting fabric in different colors: black and white.

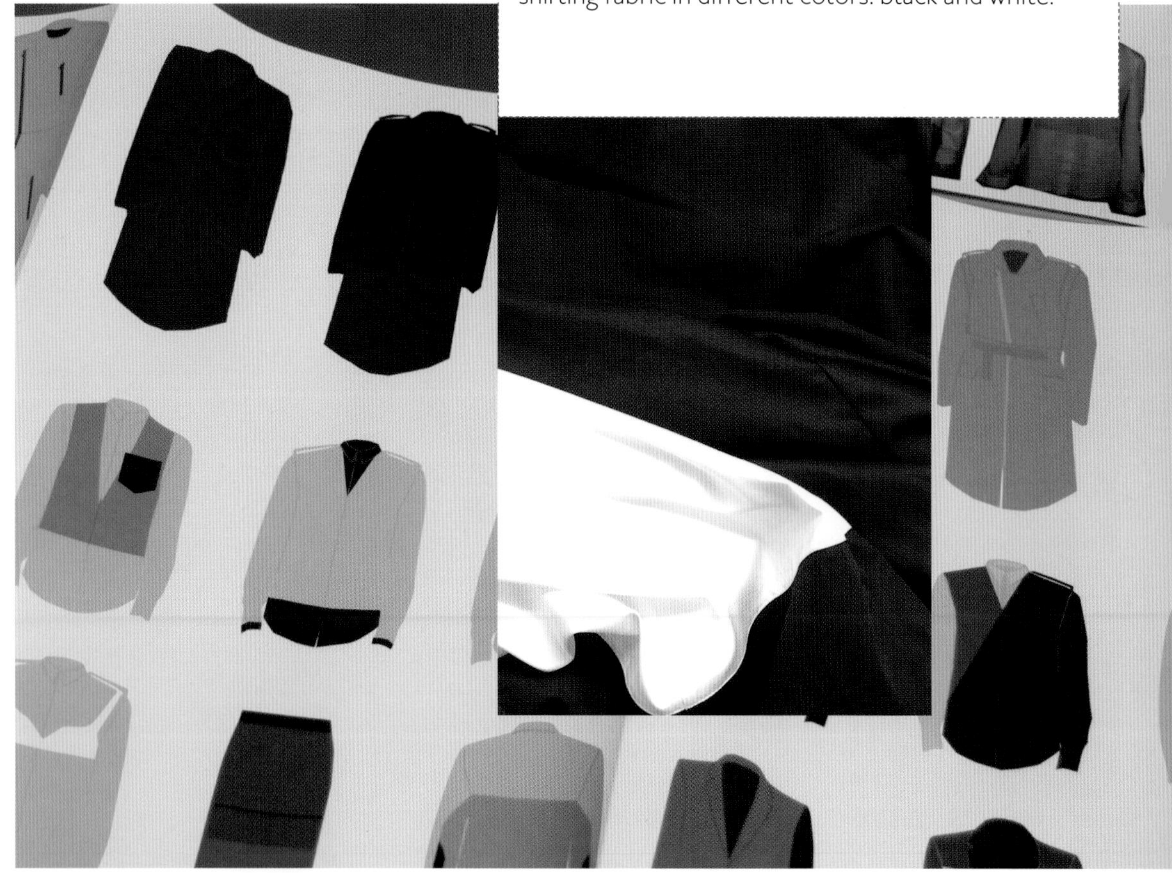

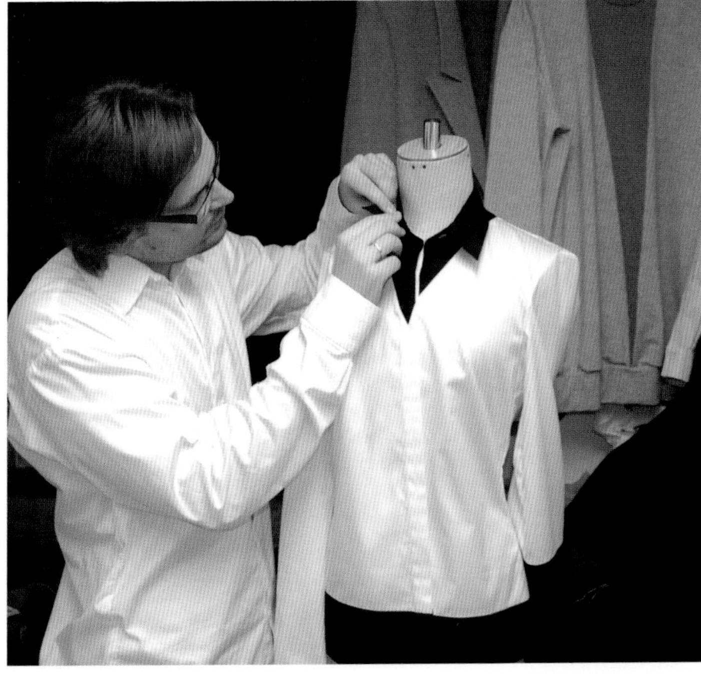

MARTIN HAVEL

LOOK

This look is created using a double superimposed effect: one formed by narrow-legged pants under shorts, and another consisting of a black V-collar over a white shirt, together with a jacket strongly inspired by men's tailoring. The combination of black and white is always elegant and austere at the same time. However, the double pants and the collar effect add a modern and singular feel to the outfit. With high heel sandals, court shoes, or lace-ups, this outfit can be jazzed up without losing its characteristic elegance. The model conveys the confidence and strength Martin Havel looks for in his *It*.

MASON JUNG

www.masonjung.com

Mason Jung was born in Seoul, South Korea, in May 1977. He graduated with a degree in clothing and textiles from the Kyung Hee University in his hometown in 2007. During his years as a university student, Mason served in the South Korean Army for twenty-six months, where he experienced the discipline of military life. That experience led him to reflect profoundly on this regimentation, something he reflects in his designs. After graduating, Jung worked for a number of commercial clothing brands in his country. In 2007 he moved to London in order to present his work to a broader public. He earned an MA at the Royal College of Art in the British capital, where he learned new methods and explored alternative forms of creating fashion. In his final year at university, Jung took part in the International Talent Support (ITS) fashion competition, where he won the prize for Fashion Collection of the Year. In 2010 Mason worked for Maison Martin Margiela in Paris and at his alma mater in London as a visiting professor. His designs are exciting and features include the exquisite patternmaking involved in the pieces and the way he develops a concept from beginning to end.

MY IT

People who appreciate unconventional opinions. In a broader sense, it includes all of those within the culture who want to see more diversity and possibility. Fashion is largely dominated by images and final looks because of its commercial system. In such environment, pure creative work and subtlety are less considered. More and more people are becoming inclined to experience different things, and new ways of fashion consumption will be needed.

INSPIRATION

This work is a reaction against the enforced uniformity of my upbringing and a celebration of individuality. Life back in Korea has largely influenced my work. The country has elements of totalitarianism and regulation in its national identity and I questioned what makes people embrace such a concept. Likewise, I found those attributes in clothing as well, especially in menswear. My designs are mainly focused on “ordinary looking garments” that sometimes show drastic transformation and have unique construction behind the visual. The choice of fabric is also made to make the garment look “normal.” I use representative fabrics for each kind of garment, such as standard wool for jackets and white cotton for shirts, which also act as a device for sartorial deception.

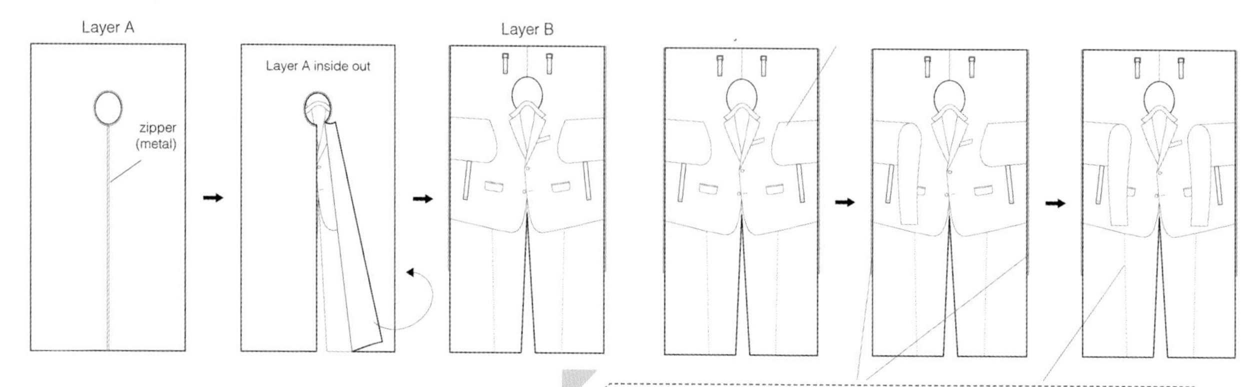

CREATION

The design starts from the idea itself, not from visual reference. My design process is realizing a conceptual idea into physical forms. As seen in the Sleeping Suit and the Blanket Suit, I try to develop new methods to construct garments. It usually takes far more time than it would to create nice silhouettes and details because it's not something directly visible. It's hard to tell which direction I need to go. Sometimes I don't even know if it's really possible. It is like problem solving: the process of finding the solution itself is a big challenge, and that's where my focus is.

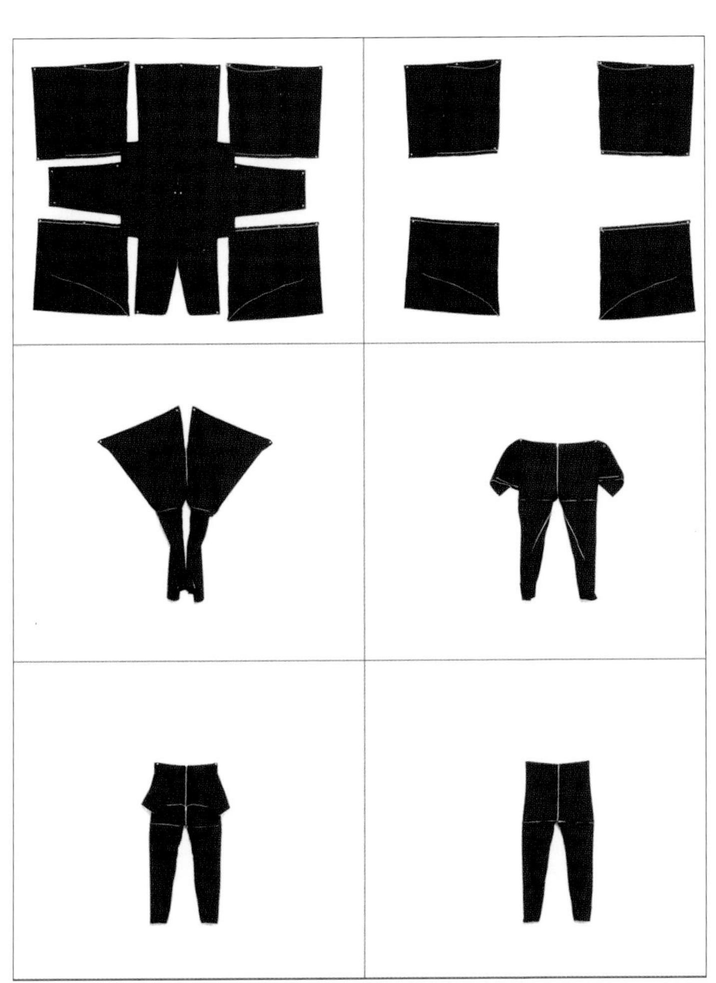

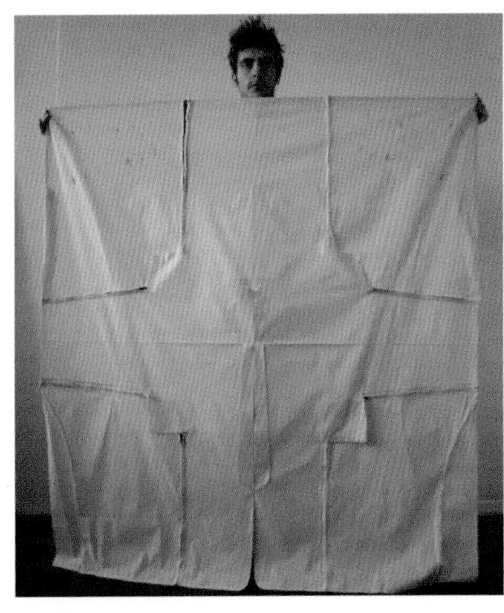

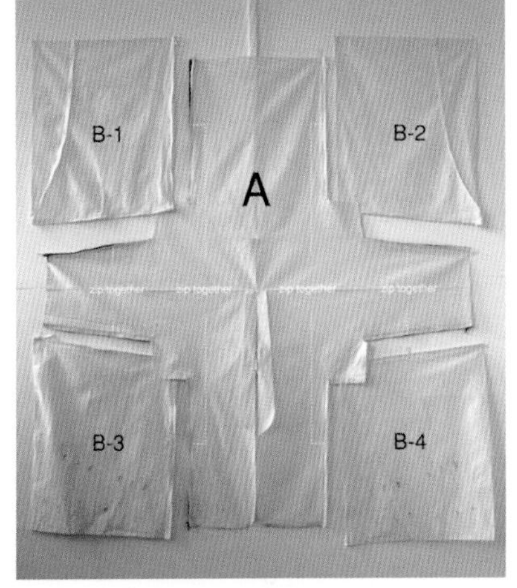
B-1
B-2
A
B-3
B-4

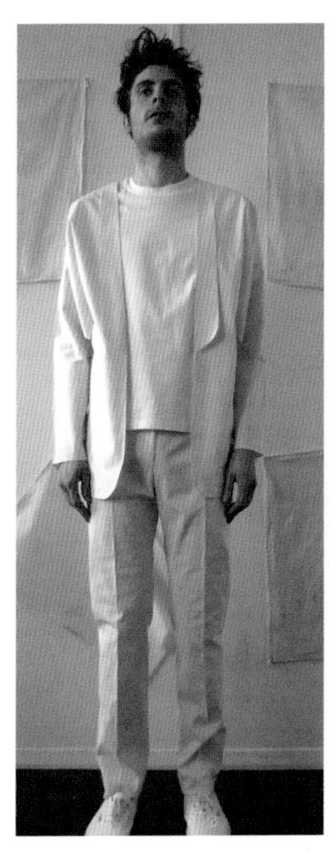

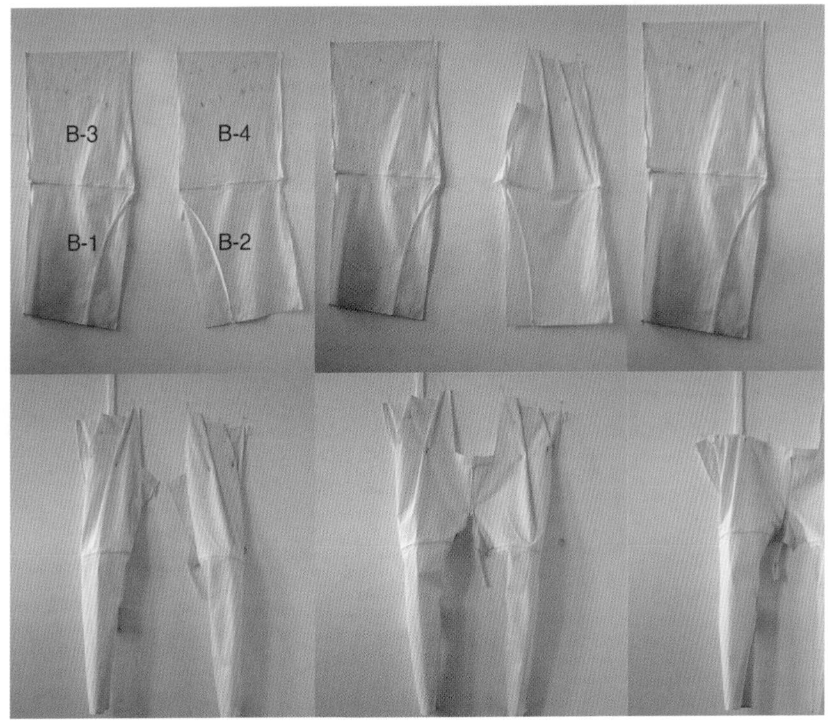
B-3
B-4
B-1
B-2

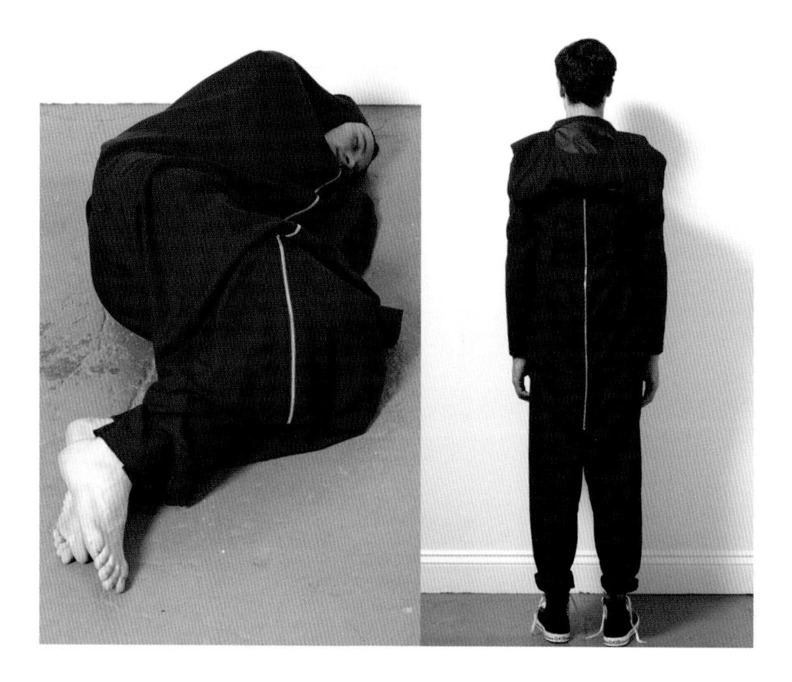

LOOK

Mason Jung's work is not only admirable for the way he makes his clothes, but also for the philosophy inherent in each of his designs. He imagines, visualizes, and designs, in a process where the creative stage is as important as the final outfit. The image on the right perfectly reflects this process and how the piece is developed from a sleeping bag to become a suit. The outfit is comfortable, dynamic, and perfectly adapted. It is a singular project for guys who want new experiences in fashion.

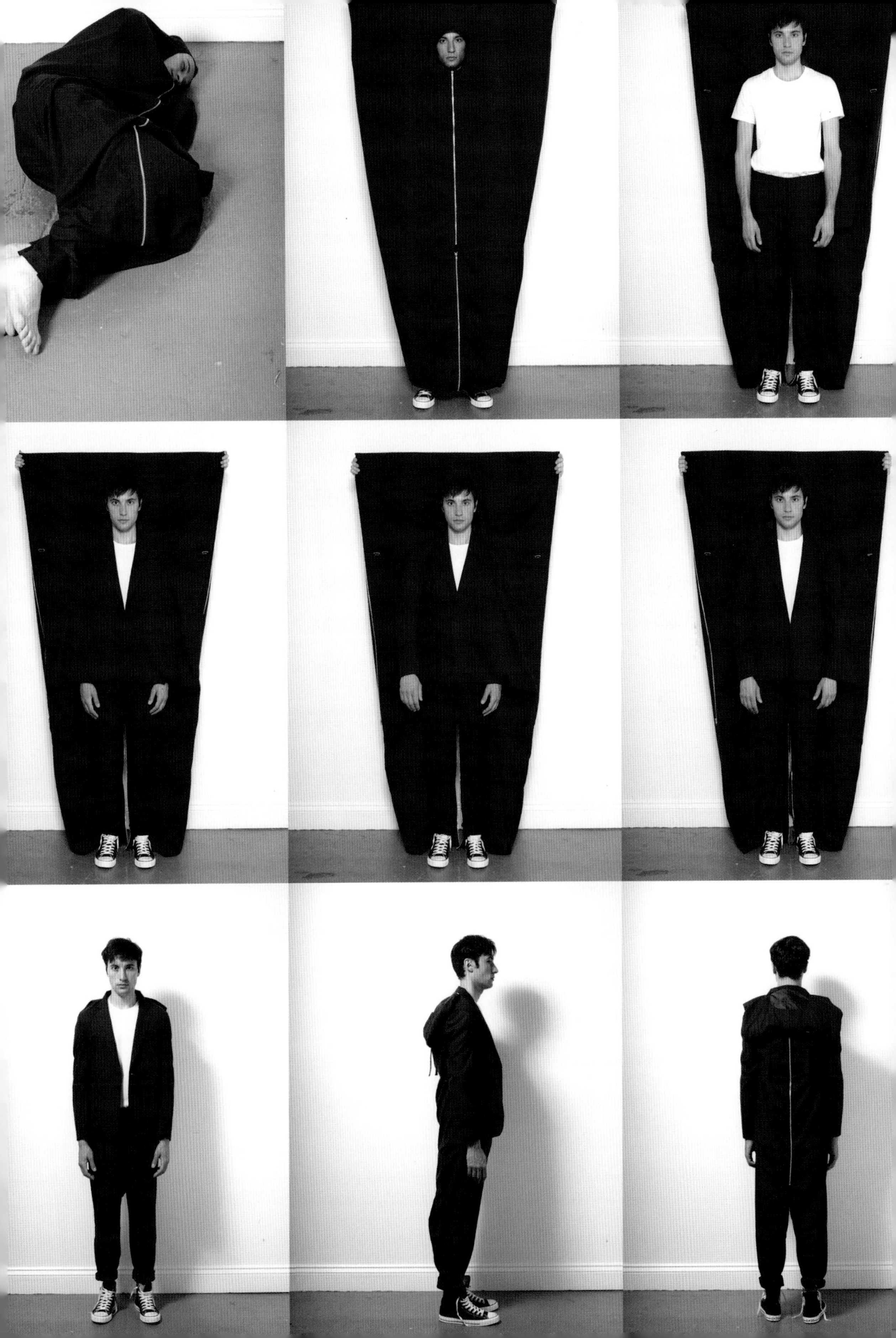

MAYA HANSEN

www.mayahansen.com

Maya Hansen was born in Madrid in 1978. She graduated with distinction from the Madrid Fashion Design College (CSDMM) in 2002. She had already begun to receive her first acknowledgements, such as the 2000 Porto Fashion Awards, given by the Portuguese Institute for Trade, Investment, and Tourism, with her Interacción collection, bringing together contemporary architecture and fashion and based on the work of Valencian architect Santiago Calatrava; the second prize at the Smirnoff Fashion Awards; and the Silver Thimble at the Paços de Ferreira International Competition in 2001. The Smirnoff Fashion Award shortlisting led to her presence at Pasarela Gaudí in February 2002. After her internship at Javier Larraínzar's atelier, the designer founded her eponymous label in 2004, and has been specializing in corsetry since 2006. She has spent years researching this type of garment and compiling very old information and patterns in order to reinterpret them. Her label is present today in countries like Spain, Britain, the US, Japan, and Switzerland, among others. Maya has presented her collections at trade shows such as Erotica UK, which brings together the world's best corsetmakers. Her designs have also been exhibited in festivals like Wave-Gotik-Treffen and Festimad. In 2009 she presented Mint-Chocolate at Valencia Fashion Week, and in 2010 exhibited the Steampunk: Lost in Prague collection in Valencia and the Heavy Metal Couture collection at El Ego de Cibeles inside Madrid Fashion Week.

MY IT

The figure of my *It girl* would correspond to girls with a special character, like the singer and burlesque performer Vinila von Bismark. Known for mixing musical styles as varied as new wave, rockabilly, or electronic, her image is a faithful reproduction of the 1940s pin-up girls. Vinila took part in the opening of the Mint-Chocolate runway show, posing on a hoop, swing, and trapeze decorated with roses. She demonstrated how a corset can be used in a gentle, fun, and elegant way.

INSPIRATION

Cakes. Cake colors. Cupcakes. The flavor and appearance of British cupcakes. Strawberry and cream. Vanilla and Chocolate. Banana and hazelnut. Vanilla and cherry. Custard and chocolate truffle. Dark chocolate. Mint and chocolate. Desserts. Marshmallow. Candies. Cotton candy. Marie Antoinette. Laughter. Roses. Birds. Green leaves. Spring. With fabrics, there is a predominantly decadent retro feel with luxurious fabrics such as faux suede, satin, taffeta, and organza, mixed with futuristic plastics such as latex or imitation leather in accessories. The interior structure of the corsets is in serge. Cool colors like lime green, grass green, bubble-gum pink, and cherry red, mixed with muted and delicate tones like pastel pink, aquamarine, vanilla, or flesh tone, and finishing in restrained colors like chocolate brown and black. Music. Birdsong. The 80s. Sweet/fetishist.

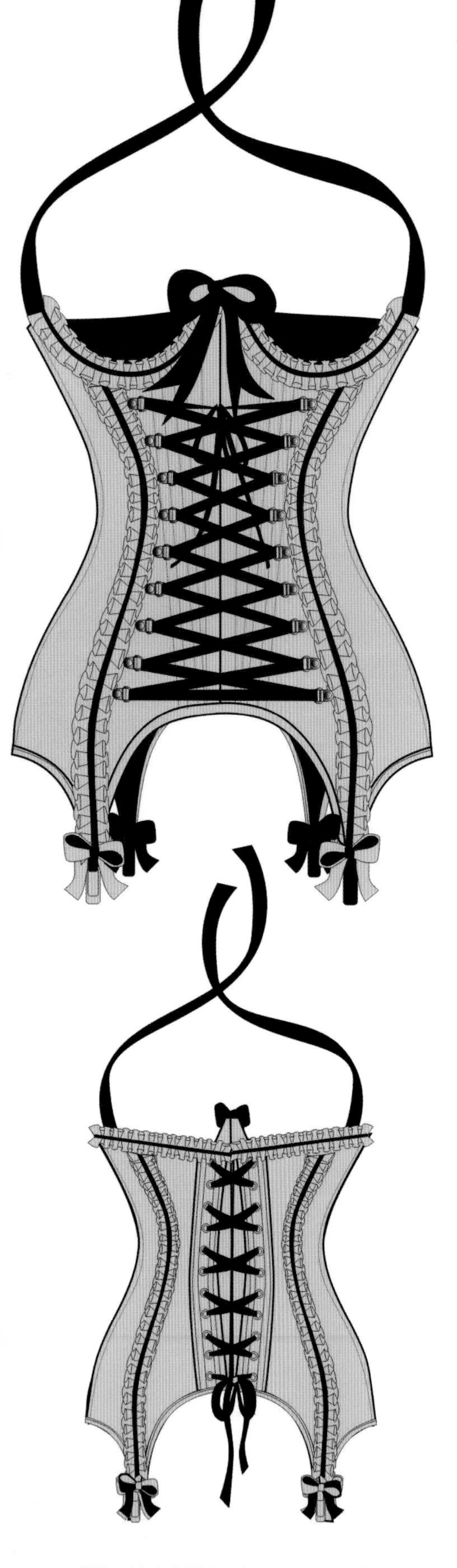

CREATION

We don't like to do illustrations. We find there is no better technique than designing directly on the cutting table, with the fabrics, interlinings, trimmings, and embellishments in you hands. Although we have color guidelines, they are sometimes modified when we see that a fabric matches another perfectly and gives a fabulous result in a specific color combination. We normally create a beautiful chaos on the cutting table where everything is important. It's our decision to sort it out and combine it in a corset. Our base is the corset and we can't stray from that. It's vital to know the strict technique required by this garment before putting together a collection. A fabric can be changed or ruled out because it doesn't meet our expectations for corset making. Sometimes the next step is customizing fabrics with all kinds of embellishments and trimming. Other times the actual pattern is what challenges the corset to break rules. I try on most of the designs myself in the workshop. It's important to know how one type of corset or another feels when you wear it. I usually do this alone when there is a moment of peace in the workshop, because only I know how to detect a flaw, when a color can be improved, when a pattern has to be changed and when the idea I wanted to convey with the design is not clear enough. Afterwards we grade it down two sizes for the runway. Sometimes a skirt can transmit the feeling of flying, while another can be so stiff you can't walk in it. The same thing happens with corsets, which can be as sweet as they can be transgressive.

brother

LOOK

These amazing images seem to have been taken a long time ago. It is actually a sample of what Maya Hansen is capable of saying through her language and way of expressing herself: the corset. In this case a single image can convey all the inspiration and references that influence the design of the collection. It features plenty of details, like pleated trims, appliqué, and flowers. Meticulous construction, perfect finishes, waist-reducing cake corsets, ultrasexy silhouettes but sweet, sophisticated, and modern at the same time. Decadence and order. Between lingerie and prêt-à-porter. A hyperfeminine universe for self-confident women.

Pages 294+295 Photography: Carlos Luque

MOISÉS NIETO

Moisés Nieto Narváez was born in Úbeda, Spain, in 1984. His furniture design and advertising and graphic design studies helped him to find his aesthetic base. He later enrolled in a clothing and patternmaking course, paving the way for his move to fashion design. In 2010 he finished his fashion studies at the Istituto Europeo di Design in Madrid. The school gave him the opportunity to work at close quarters with designers from Klavers van Engelen at the Arnhem Fashion Biennale in the Netherlands. During the five years of his degree course, Moisés worked on parallel projects as an illustrator; he worked as an assistant to Antonio Alvarado for his collections presented during Madrid Fashion Week; and he created his own designs, presented at Spanish runway shows such as the Andalusian South 36-32N. The designer has also won competitions like Una Novia de Impresión, organized by Canon España and Lorenzo Caprile in 2008, and has been a finalist in a number of others, such as the Triumph International Awards in 2009.

MY IT

I take into account the essence of a woman, where she's going, and where she's been. It's impossible to resist a strong, spirited woman. The muses in the world of Julio Romero de Torres (a nineteenth-century Spanish painter) are my inspiration when defining a woman's personality. Their mysterious gaze and the sensation you get from anonymous women who have been unfairly consigned to oblivion drive me to create clothes with the same spirit. That kind of woman will not accept just any material. She is far beyond a standard gray. The nineteenth century revealed female minds capable of revolutionizing the street with their austere, simple and emphatic luxury. The perfect *It*!

INSPIRATION

The history of Spain and its clothes is the main source of inspiration for my collection. The social differences and sumptuary laws of the time revealed to me the qualities of rigorous black and traditional crafting. I use a hyperbole of the sixteenth and seventeenth centuries in Spain and revisit shapes and volumes of the time, which I adapt to the present. It's the essence of luxury, understood as a trend, and a defense of what we wrongly understand as folklore. Austere shapes with complex construction. Forgotten volumes and a new take on small details in finishes and embellishments. I look for innovation in the combinations of materials. Neoprene and the color black are the bases of this collection. I used resistant and waterproof materials with body to remove restrictions to volume. I mixed technical fabrics with organic ones, such as fur, boiled wool, knits, and silk chiffon. For the high end of the collection, I reconstructed old fur coats rescued from Berlin markets (fox, rabbit, astrakhan...) and I changed their design and shape radically by shaving part of the fur to create new effects. The accessories are made with plant fibers, such as traditionally processed esparto grass (a popular art in my hometown), to give the pieces a new sense of austere luxury. I use austerity as the base of my inspiration. Austerity is also present with colors, but there is richness in the materials and textures, which stand out for their shapes and reaction to light.

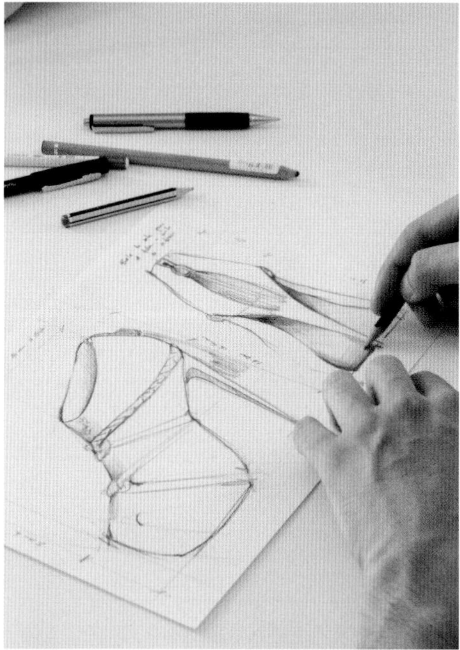

Pages 296+297 Photography: Carlos Luque

CREATION

The creation process for any of my collections begins with a previously considered idea. Here is where I begin to create volumes directly with the raw material and support. Modeling is the fundamental part of my pieces. They're all modeled on the dummy first. Viewing the piece on the body and working on it is the best way to define my style. I always sketch and illustrate the pieces once they're finished. In this case, both pieces are modeled on the dummy to obtain the shapes I have in mind. From this point on, the creation process is mechanical: technical specs, patterns, cutting and sewing. I enjoy my work most when I'm making up the pieces. The lamb napa top is modeled so that there are no seams on the bust darts, giving it a special volume. The skirt also follows the same process, and is seamless. These are two pieces that contrast in fabric and shape, yet they come together perfectly.

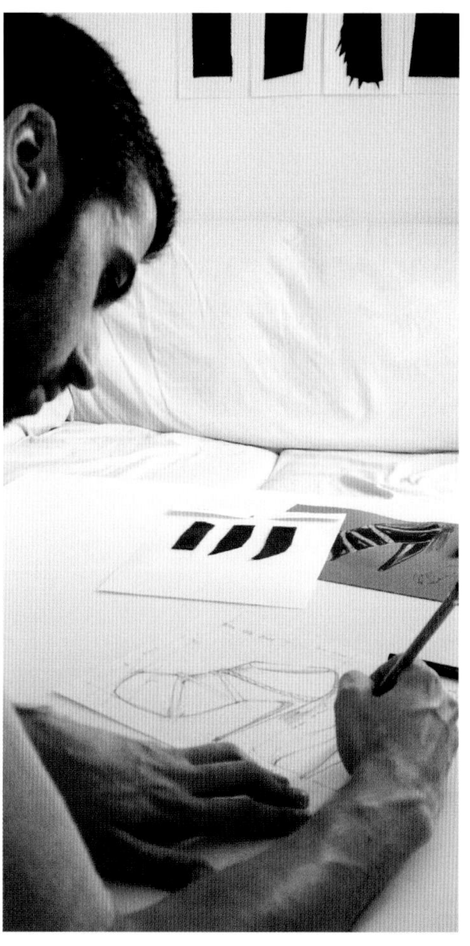

Pages 298+299 Photography: Carlos Luque

LOOK

This look is an interpretation of the austerity of the sixteenth and seventeenth centuries with a contemporary spirit. Organic fabrics like lamb napa and technical fabrics like white neoprene make a unique combination. The skirt has a smooth, symmetrical shape that conveys an impression of weightlessness and austerity. The top is structured to give the shoulders volume and to enhance the feminine bust curves. The accessories are also one-off pieces. The shoes are in lamb napa and esparto -grass cord made in the tradition of southern Spain. The hat is made from hand-braided esparto grass with very fine gold chains.

NEREA LURGAIN

www.nerealurgain.com

Nerea Lurgain was born in San Sebastian, Spain. She earned a degree in fine arts at the University of the Basque Country in Leoia. Later, her passion for fashion led her to move to Barcelona to study fashion design at the IDEP Image and Design School. In addition to her academic background, Nerea moves in different areas of design and art in general, which provides her with ideas, sources of inspiration, work methods, and design mechanisms that go towards her unique and very personal way of designing garments. Her great talent and and perception of fashion were the values that the Catalan government used to select her to take part in Projecte Bressol, one of that institution's most ambitious fashion projects. She has participated in the competition organized by ModaFAD and in the 080 Circuit fashion show, both in 2007, in exhibitions including the ones held at the Suspect Club and at CCCB, the Center for Contemporary Culture, both in Barcelona, and in trade shows like Bread & Butter, held in the same city. Nerea has also presented her designs at shows and in showrooms within Spain and abroad, including 080 Barcelona Fashion, Andalucía de Moda, the Dalian International Show in China, Fashion Freak in Barcelona, Madrid Fashion Week, and China International Garment & Textile.

MY IT

My *It girl* lives uptown and has had a very deep relationship with the artistic world since childhood, and that love flows from work to leisure time. She doesn't let her life become too full of rules or traditions, although she has a sensitive link to all her origins. When it comes to dress up, she likes comfortable, exclusive and timeless garments that can perfectly match with her magnetic personality and charisma.

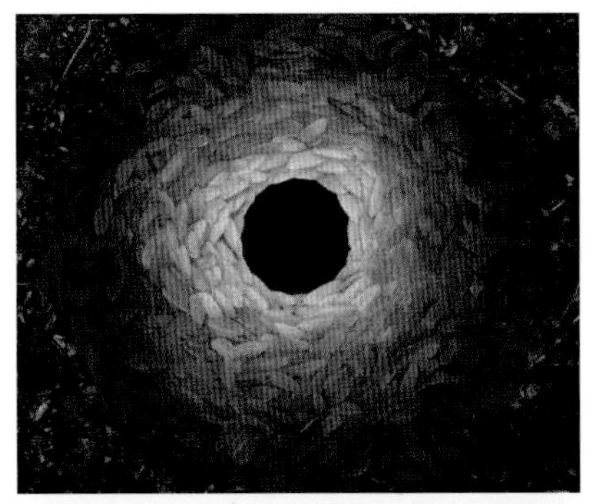

INSPIRATION

Inspiration always comes from artistic movements or works made in another art disciplines, but it is especially based on her personal experiences. One sample of her concepts and ideas is her new collection, which was inspired on earth as an element of nature. Every season there is an invited artist who takes part in the creative process or enriches the collection in some way. A musician, a sculptor, a silk-screen printer and a land artist already joined the brand. As far as fabrics is concerned, natural fibers, such as cotton, bamboo, line and wool, are used to make comfortable and quality garments. All printings are exclusive, and sometimes even unique, because of the artisan way they are elaborated. Silkscreens walk together with digital printings, embroidery, creases and delicate details, combined with colors of the earth, stones and minerals, such as red, gray and black.

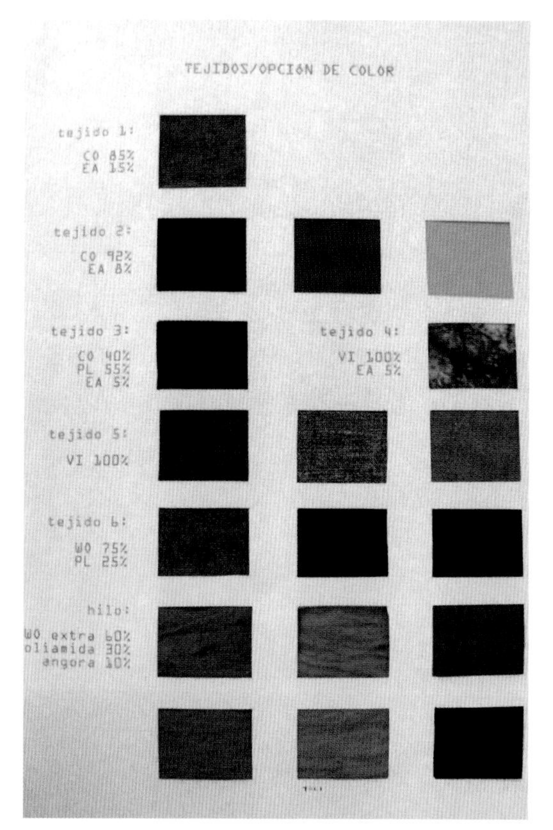

CREATION

It is important for me to know which fabrics I am going to use. In this case the fabrics represent the warmth of the earth, so all of them will be natural fibers. As you can see in the photos, the circular forms are very associated with the elements of nature and perfection. For this reason, I decided to work the fabrics in circular knitting and tricot. We hardly work on the fitting process to give birth of our ideas. It takes many proofs, first over the mannequin and then over the model, just to find the desirable volume and silhouette.

LOOK

Esther is wearing leggings and a shirt with dolman sleeves covered with a red scarf that acts like a bolero, and Pauline is wearing a large-sleeve jumpsuit with central printed buttons and a red jersey with a knotted scarf that reveals the nude of her neck. The printings were based on trees painted by an invited artist. The result is a dynamic look where there is a play of movements among the models. The garments match the colors and shapes as if they were trees over the earth.

OMER ASIM

www.blow.co.uk/omer

Sudanese-born designer Omer Asim studied architecture at the Bartlett Faculty at University College London before going on to study a postgraduate course in organizational and social psychology at the London School of Economics and Political Sciences. He was an intern for a time with the United Nations Development Programme and was a step away from becoming a psychoanalyst when he decided his place was in fashion. It is precisely the influence of the social and sentimental aspects he explored through his experience with the UN and to his background, studies and knowledge of architecture that he combines in a cocktail reflected in his designs. Those designs are characterized by great sensitivity, and with an undercurrent of social criticism and detailed patternmaking that approaches architecture. This allows him to achieve highly sculptural pieces with great significance. Among his experiences in the world of fashion, Omer has worked for Vivienne Westwood for approximately one year, and as a wardrobe assistant for the movie saga *Harry Potter*. In 2009 Omer presented his first collection at the independent On|Off show, which is held each season to coincide with London Fashion Week. His first designs have been very well received by fashion experts and the fashion press.

MY IT

She is the other *It*: comfortable and self-confident. She knows what suits her and she is happy to try new things. She takes fashion with a pinch of salt and she is suspicious of fleeting trends. The other *It* is self-styled and doesn't need a friend's opinion to buy a frock. She's a natural. She is generally concerned about buying ethical green fashion, but she doesn't do it as a matter of fashion. Quality, craftsmanship and deflected luxury are high on her list. Most importantly, she doesn't rub it in everyone's face. She's dignified and cool about it.

INSPIRATION

I am very interested in pre-modern forms of dress. I find it fascinatingly simple and complex. However, the pleated corset was conceptualized from a photograph captured by Kevin Carter (*The Child and the Vulture*) during the Sudan civil war in 1993. The photograph won Carter the Pulitzer, and arguably it drove him to take his life. I don't think you can forget that image if you see it. I wanted to pivot my first collection on a strong memory, and I found it much easier to look at that photograph afterwards. I found the inverse of Carter's photograph in another set of photographs taken by Sipke Visser (*At last, the chickens!*). I created the corset as a bird of prey – a vulture. I wanted it to usher in death as well as mercy and relief. I tried to express that by blending in beauty with an aggressive instinctual feel. About fabrics, I generally gravitate towards extremes, either stiff, such as cotton organdy, paper silk, satin organza and gazar, or soft, such as washed cotton, mat jersey, cotton voile, chiffon and tulle. Stiff or soft, they have to be natural fibers, but I have come across a few great synthetics. In this instance, I relied on the stiffness of paper silk to create the 3D pleating and on the heavy cottons to create the base. Muted colors work best with my cuts, but every now and then I splash in a strong color, depending on the mood. A few years ago I saw everything in black. Now I'm seeing a lot of white, and occasionally grass green and yellow. I also find a particular shade of peach-pink very useful.

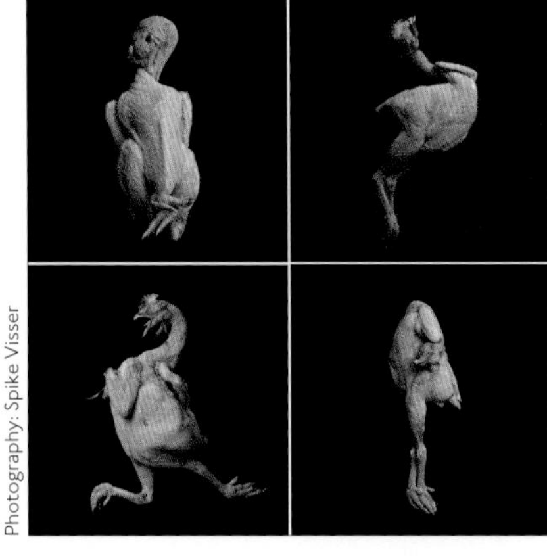

Photography: Spike Visser

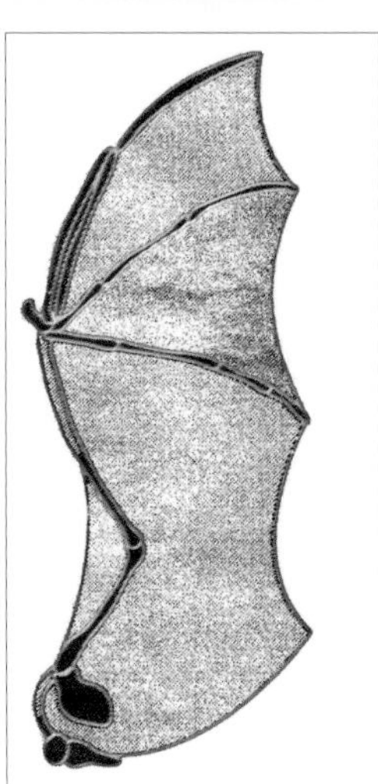

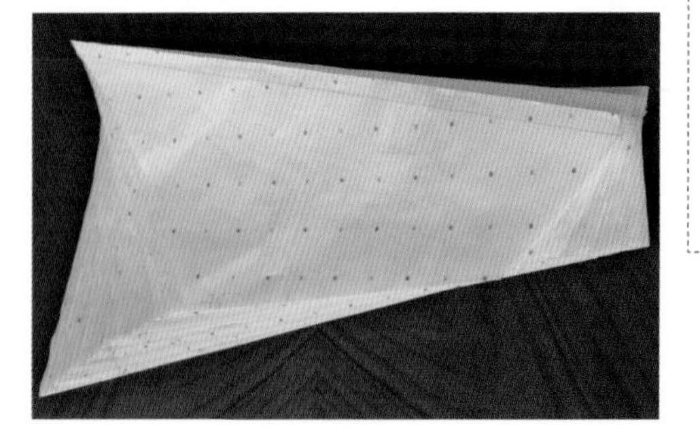

CREATION

A great deal of my design is in the making process itself. I resent sketching. It rules out all the beautiful mistakes and accidents. I work on the half-scale dummy before moving onto the full-scale. It usually helps me to solidify my ideas. Primarily, I design through the concept of the cut. I developed the pleated corset from a circle to echo the traverse of carrion around its prey. I worked backwards by developing graduated 3D circular pleats with a sliced-through effect to add to their perspective. The torso was sectioned accordingly while imaging how the pleats will diffuse away and into each other to create a light wing-like structure. I visualized and worked the seaming on the stand without the aid of a sketch. This gives me a realistic proportion that I can manipulate to achieve the effect I'm after. The severity of the aesthetic lies in the sharp edges that jut out where the lines usually lie straight. A pleat pattern was developed for each of the ten pairs of segments of the corset, graduating from 10mm (0.4 in) at the locus and diffusing away into 40mm (1.6 in). This created a puzzle of hand-pleated patterns that sits precisely within the corresponding segment. The skirt was created from the same circular pleating principle. Pleats were oversized, sliced-through and graduated by 5mm (0.2 in) from back to front. The skirt can also be slung into an oversized bib to recall the child in Carter's photograph. All the pleating was done by hand, and each pleat was secured to a base at the measured distance by a looped stitch. The pleated segments were appliquéd on to a softly boned base made from two layers of cotton drill and calico. The base was molded closely to the body, with the pleated segments echoing the seaming. Flattening out the seam thickness demanded a great deal of craftsmanship when more than two seams converged to a point. The same method was applied to the skirt/bib.

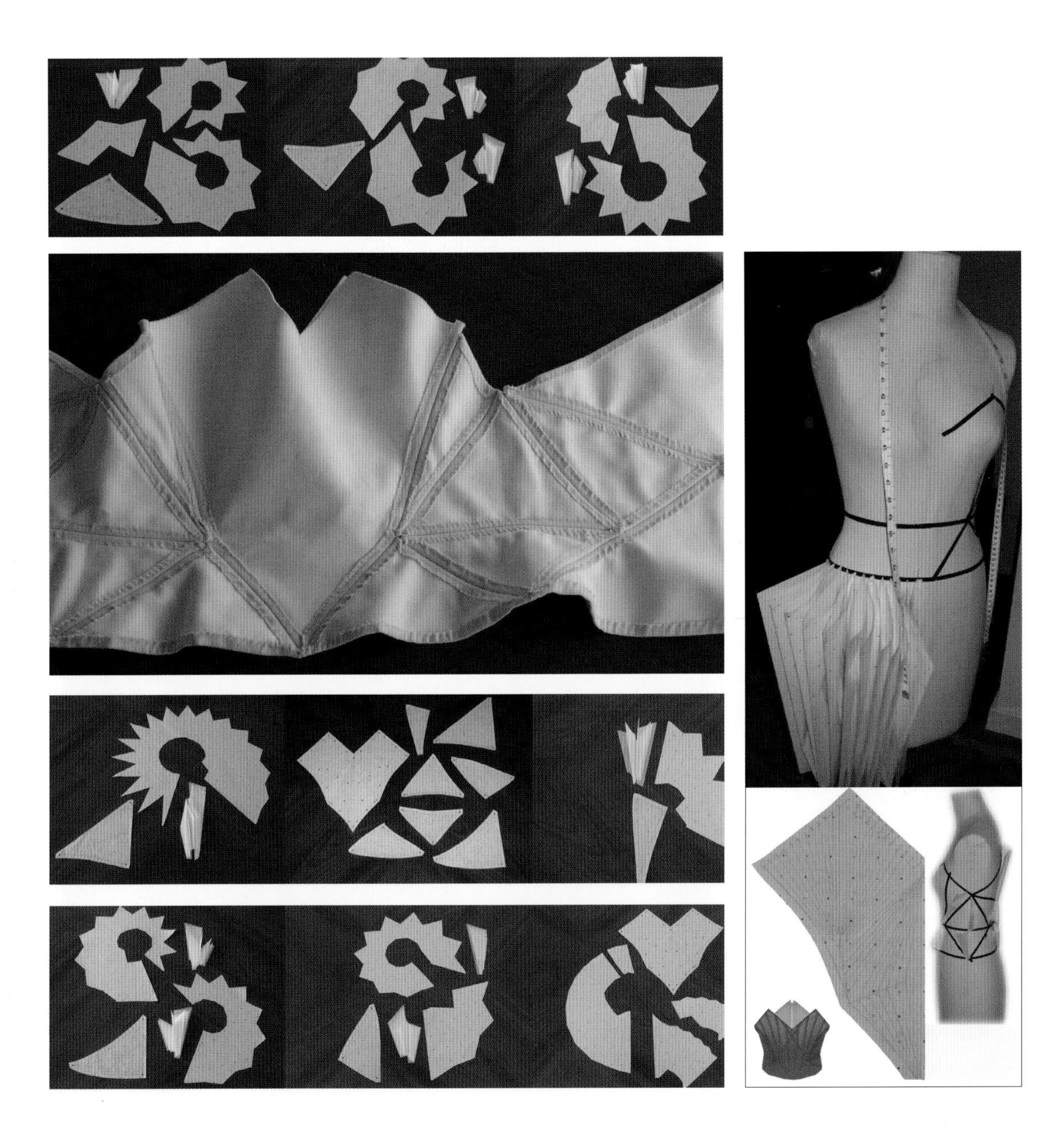

LOOK

These three images, taken by friend and photographer Sipke Visser (author of the *At last, the chickens!* photo), show Omer Asim's great sensitivity, naturalness, and meticulous technique – halfway between fashion and architecture – with an outfit made up of a perfectly-structured skirt and top that conveys lightness, elegance, and sophistication.

Pages 310+311 Photography: Spike Visser

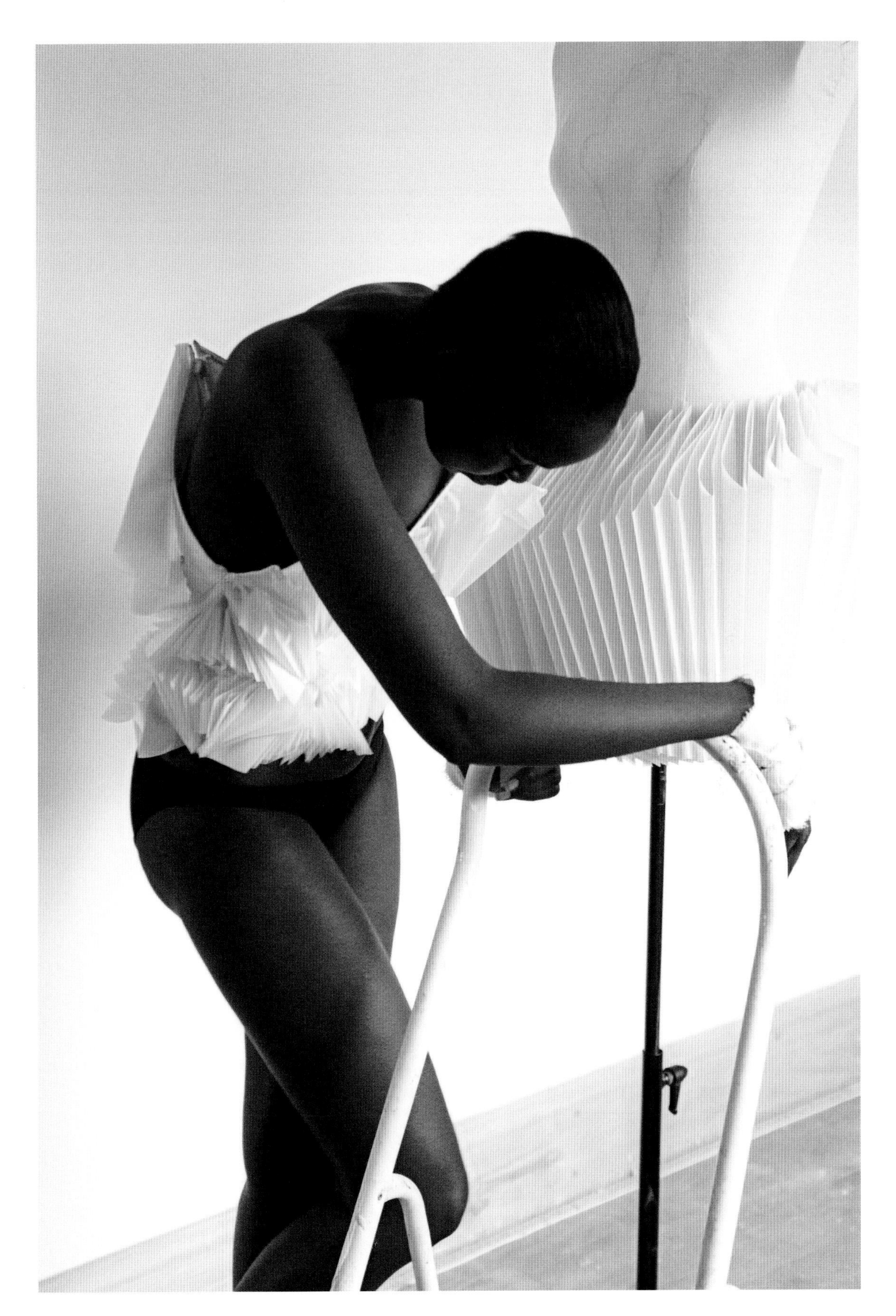

OSTWALD HELGASON

www.ostwaldhelgason.com

The Ostwald Helgason label was created in 2006 by Susanne Ostwald and Ingvar Helgason. Susanne Ostwald was born in Leipzig, Germany, in 1979, and she graduated with a master's degree in fashion design from the Burg Giebichenstein University of Art and Design in Halle. Ingvar Helgason was born in Reykjavik, Iceland, in 1980. He studied fashion design in Copenhagen and worked as a tailor in his home country before studying fashion management in London. These two designers met while working in a design studio in the British capital. After receiving two design grants from the German government, they were invited to present their first collection at the German embassy during Paris Fashion Week, and later, in 2008, during Berlin Fashion Week as part of the young talent program. Their pieces are a mix of tailoring and draping that go to creating a gentle architecture, structured pieces that have become the label's signature. Their method involves both designers being responsible for the concept and general look of each collection; however, Ostwald concentrates on the palette of colors and print designs, while Helgason centers on the forms. By using exclusive prints, strong colors, and a modern interpretation of couture, they have gained the attention of figures renowned for their honed sense of style, such as Daphe Guinness and Rihanna.

MY IT

According to the mood of each season, Ostwald Helgason has in mind a different girl that embodies their ideals. This season it was a very active woman who spends her free time doing sports like swimming, boxing and fencing, but in the evening she goes out to hang out with friends and socialize. In order to achieve a look that is rich in references and textures, they try to combine impossible opposites, which in this case was ladies who lunch and boxers.

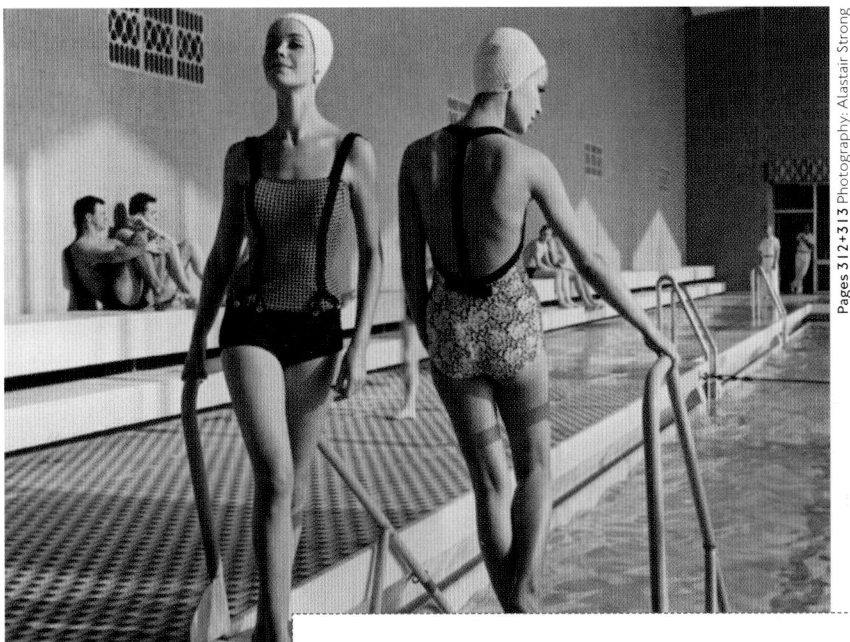

Pages 312+313 Photography: Alastair Strong

INSPIRATION

The collection also references Japanese interiors – lacquered surfaces, bamboo, woven straw mats and ikebana (Japanese flower arrangements) – mixed with sportswear, graphical patterns, clean lines and the high contrast found in old photographs. Ostwald Helgason continues to work with its signature: photorealistic replicas of existing items that through subtle manipulation of color and form create new surfaces. Haptic richness of textures ranges from soft liquid silk satins and polished leather to high shine Italian double woven wool and thick, soft mohair knits. Stretch net trimmed with soft napa leather is then mixed in to bring lightness to the collection. The colors of this collection are a subtle mixture of charcoal, steel gray, off-white, beige and black combined with rich hues of ice blue, frosty green, orange and dusty pink.

P.314+315_Photography: Alastair Strong

CREATION

We work hard sketching and studying the fabrics, textures and prints that we will use in the garments. The sketch of the final outfit is shown in the above photo. It is actually a collage but that is how we build a lot of our designs. We like the contrasts. For this reason we mix transparencies, wools and leather, which transmit different sensations. In those pages we show some outfits that are being matched up with the right fabrics, prints and colors for the sampling edit. For the look that we will show here, we have chosen four pieces: a white jacket combined with a black shorts, a transparent top and napa gloves. The jacket needs a special care in its construction in order that all the lines stay impeccable and very structured, as we like it. Here we show the jacket toile in its final stages of fitting while the collar length is being adjusted.

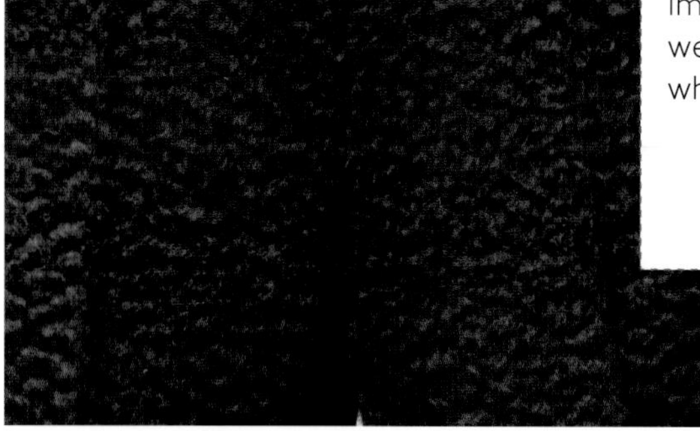

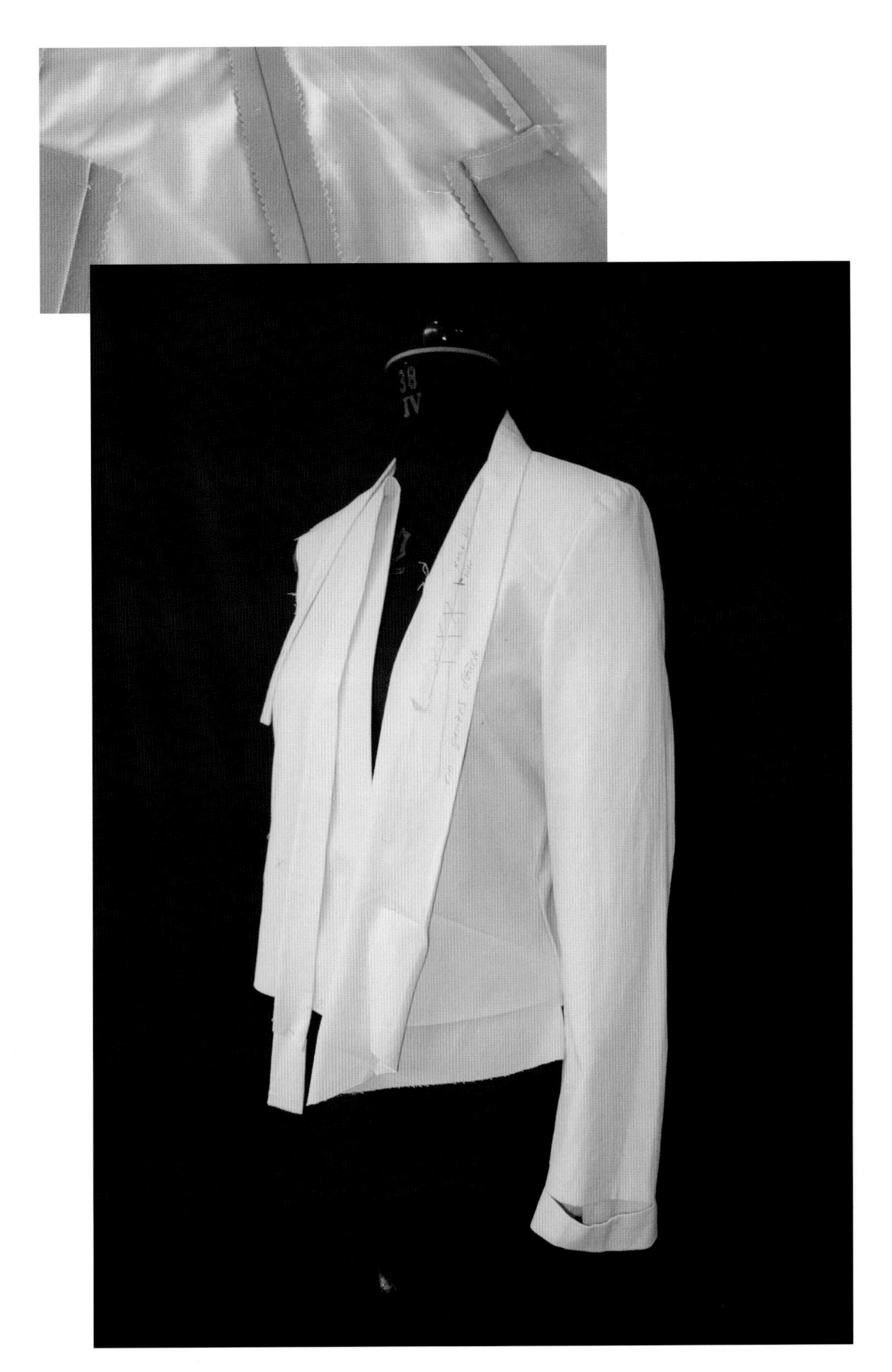

P.316+317_Photography: Alastair Strong

LOOK

The result is a sensual look for a very active woman who seeks a touch of sport lines in her garments (according with her life style) but at the same time likes to feel comfortable and sophisticated. To add contrast, the light tailored wool jacket is styled with a pair of mohair shorts that are knitted to resemble astrakhan fur and accessorized with shiny napa leather gloves, a sheer sporty hooded top and a pair of knee high boots in black leather.

RACHEL FREIRE

www.rachelfreire.com

Rachel Freire is a London-based fashion designer with a background in fine arts who debuted at On|Off during London Fashion Week in February 2009 at the Science Museum. Her work appears in such publications as *Tank, Dazed and Confused, AnOther, Zink, Issue One, Sublime, Timeout*, y en prensa artística como *Flux, Juxtapoz*, and *The Illustrated Ape*. She has designed special pieces for Beth Ditto, Christina Aguilera, and Rihanna, and her work is admired by Courtney Love, Saint Saviour, and many others. Graduating from Central Saint Martins in 2006 with a degree in design for performance, Rachel is self-taught in patternmaking and tailoring, and has never studied fashion. Her influences come from the passion for historical costume and futuristic imagery. In a world obsessed with androgyny, Rachel Freire's challenge is the fusion of the ultra-feminine with the ultra-masculine. Behind the dramatic silhouettes and decadent embellishments, her clothes are designed to be wearable, durable, feminine, and very flattering.

MY IT

The woman who wants to look amazing and yet not worry about ripping a seam. She is a woman who is comfortable both in a big dirty city and in a deserted plain and wants her clothes to protect her, yet remain feminine and beautiful. She sees clothing as a walking wearable art and she is not afraid to express herself through her second skin. To be at one with an outlandish garment demands a strong character and resolve in who you are as a person beneath it. An awareness of the ethics does not have to mean dull cotton garments. It can be upheld by investing in pieces that come from a house that respects the process of producing for those who do not have the time to consider these things in the whirlwind of life.

INSPIRATION

Androgyny is such a prevalent influence in modern fashion, blurring the boundaries between the sexes. I am interested in the equal and the opposite: the ultra-feminine and ultra-masculine in a harmonious combination which uses both elements seamlessly. Decadent and detailed pieces require a handmade attention which would never be possible in a factory, and to own one piece would supersede the idea of having many. Clothing should be akin to a uniform, which empowers the wearer, something timeless and universal. It should be inspired by characters from one of many possible futures that only exist in our minds, in stories, on celluloid; now brought to life, drawing their inspiration from all the elements that make up our amazing history and culture. Modern technological fabrics should be combined with delicate yet powerful fabrics, and you should always use the best materials, the ones that have stood the test of time, such as leather of the highest possible quality. The throwaway generation needs to be slowly pushed out of our culture in favor of quality and longevity and respect for garments, which should be replaced only as they need to be. They should be worn to death. As for fabrics, I prefer to use leather, chiffon, drill/canvas, and also Lycra, tweed/wool, power mesh, skin variations – salmon, stingray, clear vinyl – and high visibility reflective fabrics. I like the colors nude, black, metallic silver, gold, rust, copper, bronze, powder blues, muted earthy tones and army drab.

POST-MIC
IF IN DOUBT,
SPRAYPAINT IT GOLD

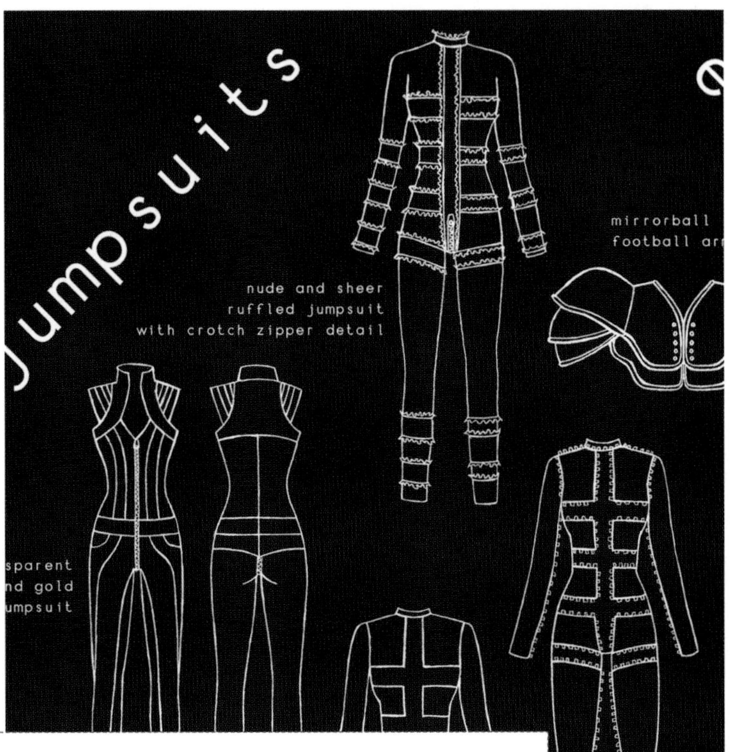

CREATION

The most fascinating thing to me are the pieces that can exist in a number of states at the same time. With this in mind, I create garments incorporating elements that trick the eye. This suit is made in its feminine form with ruffles to hide the panels of transparent mesh that would expose the wearer, and in contrast, a high visibility reflective fabric which illuminates when it is hit by direct light, transforming the wearer into a glowing silhouette and highlighting the curves of the body. Features are added with decadent practicality: the only contrasting element to the soft stretch fabrics is a heavy metal zipper, which sits in the crotch, like a piece of irreverent sexual jewelry. Worn in nude, it distorts the view of the figure. In black, it becomes sexy and cat-like, and as a reflective piece it has the feeling of a futuristic superhero. One version of the piece incorporates tiny loops in each seam to which any trailing material can be attached, creating a flowing undulating vision of chaos around a very tightly structural garment.

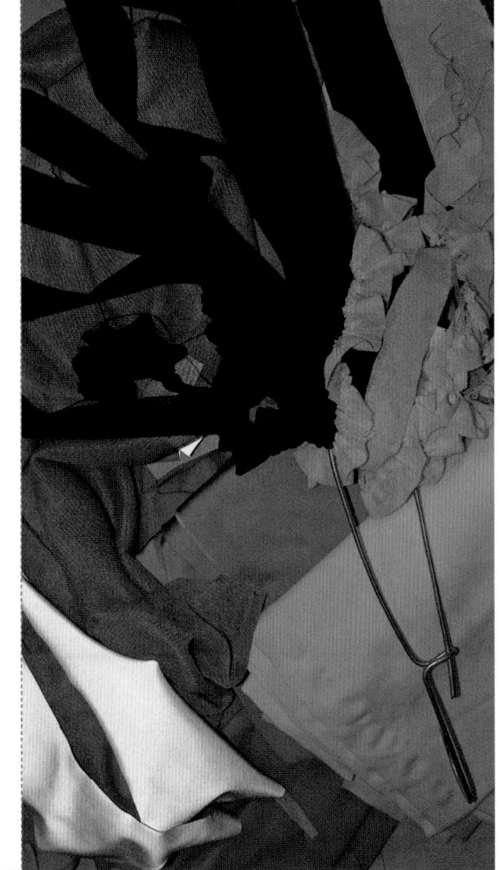

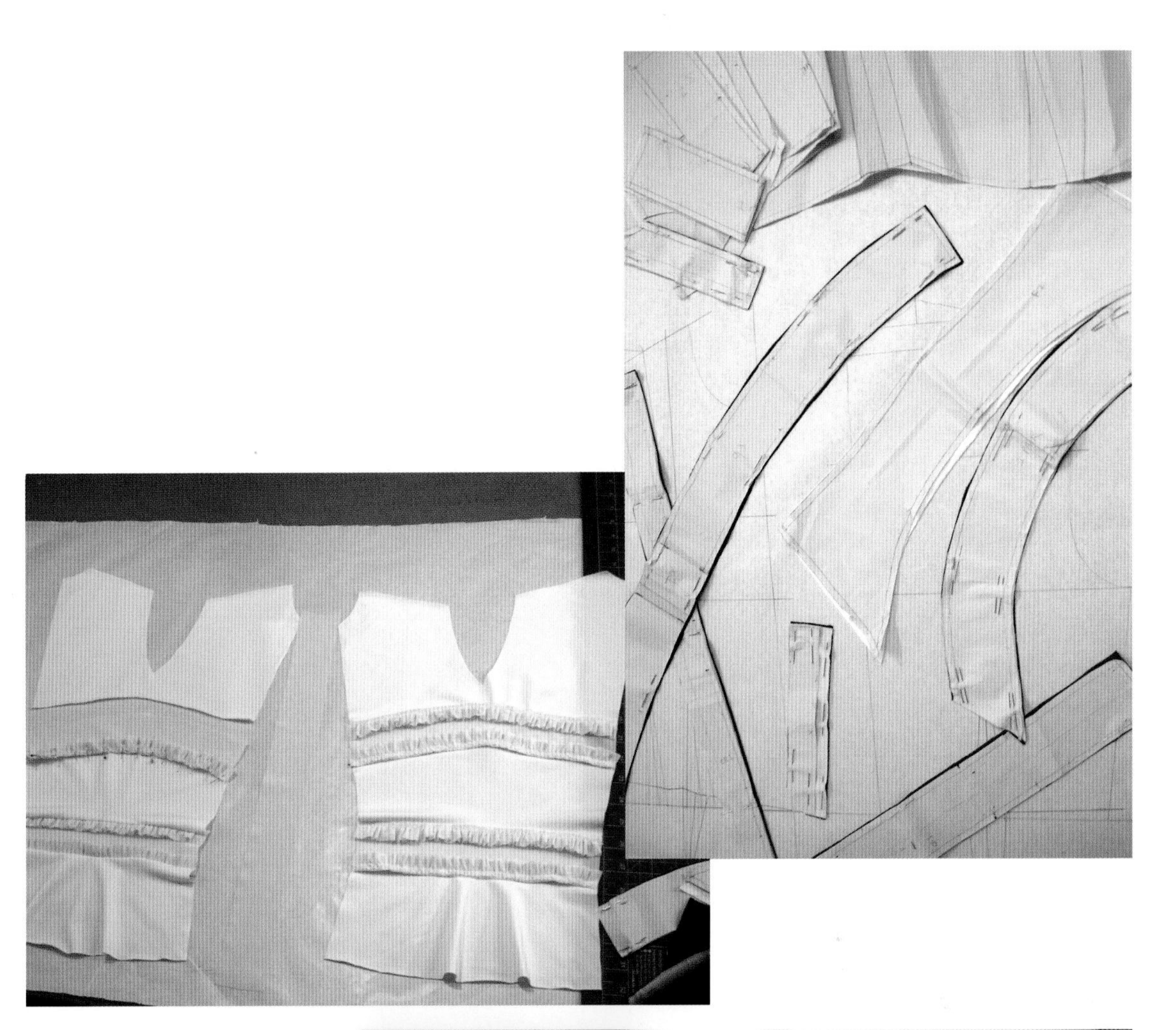

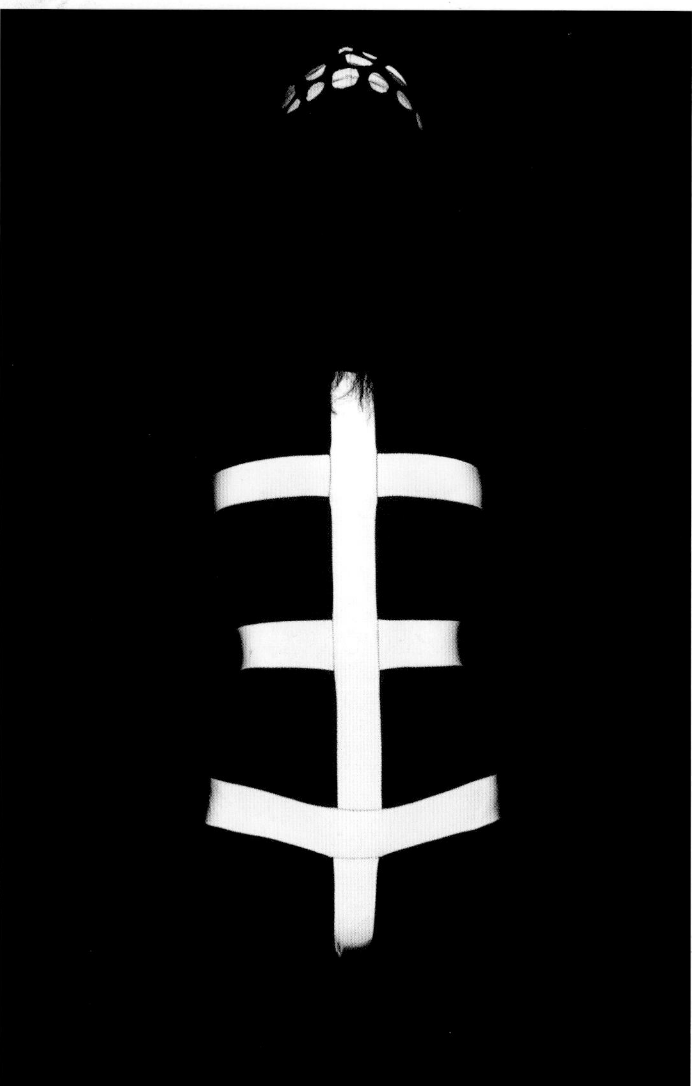

LOOK

This garment is echoed in various ways throughout the Rachel's fall/winter 2010/11 collection. It is designed to be completely body-con so as to allow the wearer complete freedom of movement, yet being incredibly intricate and embellished. It can be a piece which stands alone or worn as a base garment, and it embodies the look and feel of Rachel Freire. These three photos show three different versions of the catsuit: black, nude and reflective.

RAPHAEL HAUBER

www.raphaelhauber.com

In 2010 the German designer Raphael Hauber launched his eponymous label, bringing a radical change to the career he began in 2003 with the founding of Postweiler Hauber. He studied textile and clothing technology at the Hochschule Niederrhein University of Applied Sciences and graduated in fashion design at the Pforzheim University, both in Germany. Since that time he has taken part in trade and fashion shows such as Dune in Tokyo; Projekt Galerie, Bread & Butter, and Ideal in Berlin; and Rendez-Vous in Paris. For Hauber, fashion mainly means changes – the perception and filtration of the vibrations that have never previously been mentioned and described, and which finally end up as part of a product, a collection, and its presentation. His belief is that presentation, whether in a fashion show, performance, or video, is as important as the garment itself, because it helps him to experiment with the collection. He also considers common trends less significant, although this does not mean that he does not take notice of them. He does not invent new pants or new shirts as if by magic; rather, like a DJ, he makes new compositions, samples, and mixtures. Raphael Hauber creates fashion that can be worn by both men and women.

MY IT

My *Its* are modern, curious and creative. Women and men with an individual lifestyle and with a dry sense of humor, who are open-minded and who recognize what zeitgeist is. People who have similar feelings for the environment we choose to live in, people who discern the whole work.

INSPIRATION

We currently live in a society in constant change, in which many people are in continuous movement, knowing where they are and what their space is now, but not what tomorrow holds. This kind of mobile people with temporary lifestyles, like twenty-first-century nomads, "roomers," is my main influence, the source of my inspiration. The rug will be the piece symbolizing this concept, as it represents an easy way to mark out space, of limiting territory. I will be using printed denim, herringbone pattern linen, silk, and cotton. I've chosen black to contrast with the brightly colored prints that recall those of rag rugs.

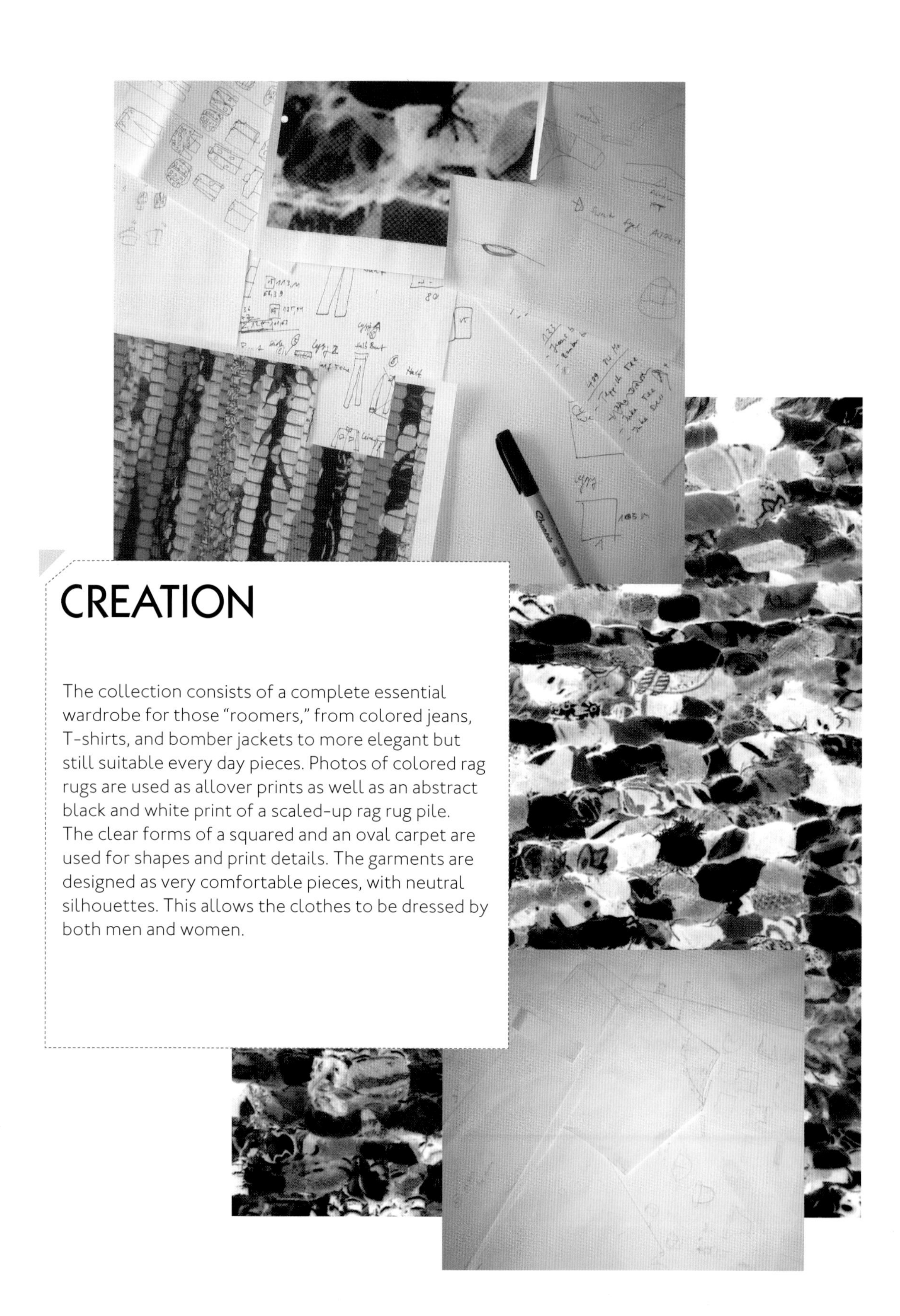

CREATION

The collection consists of a complete essential wardrobe for those "roomers," from colored jeans, T-shirts, and bomber jackets to more elegant but still suitable every day pieces. Photos of colored rag rugs are used as allover prints as well as an abstract black and white print of a scaled-up rag rug pile. The clear forms of a squared and an oval carpet are used for shapes and print details. The garments are designed as very comfortable pieces, with neutral silhouettes. This allows the clothes to be dressed by both men and women.

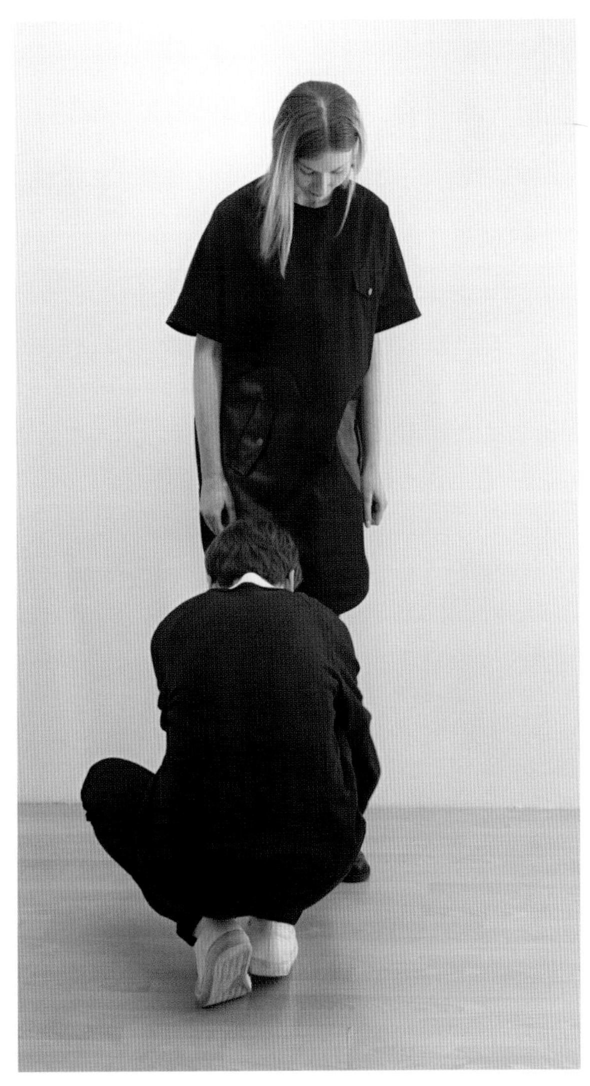

LOOK

While developing this interesting "roomers" concept, the result we achieved showed several possibilities. The image on this page shows the pants mixing the rag-rug prints, both in color and black and white, and combined with an oversized black T-shirt. On the right, the image shows a man's outfit (jacket and pants) with the same colorful rag-rug print and a woman's outfit (leggings and bomber jacket) with the enlarged or graded print in black and white. This work represents Raphael Hauber's mastery and technique in the use of prints. These casual and highly original looks are for contemporary people who live for the moment.

ROBERTO ZAMARRIPA

www.myspace.com/caballosazules

Artist Roberto Zamarripa was born in Mexico in 1984 and graduated with distinction from a degree course in design for graphic communication. He has developed multidisciplinary skills and professional experience in fields such as fashion design, photography, and contemporary dance. He specialized in publishing as the art and design director of a local fashion magazine. All the while he was carrying out independent projects of art creation and dissemination, together with works involving visual arts, performing arts, and collaborations for different Mexican magazines. His work has appeared in publications and books including the *Índice de Artistas Plásticos de Jalisco*. He has shared his experiences by teaching fashion design, graphic design, and advertising degree courses. In fashion, Roberto is the creator of the brand of fashion basics, Caballos Azules y Zamarripa, Prêt-à-Porter, collections of which he as presented at important events in his country like Mexico Fashion Week, International Designers México, and Minerva Fashion. He has been acknowledged in recent years with awards including Nuevo Talento in 2008 and Talento Textil from the Mexican National Textile Industry Chamber. Some of his designs have appeared on trend prediction websites such as WGSN.

MY IT

Unity, integrity, an honest and intelligent woman or man, coherent in their way of thinking and acting, a lover of aesthetics and of things with substance. It's a person who goes beyond genre, who is beautiful whatever they wear, since they communicate what they hold inside.

INSPIRATION

I start with inspirational propositions: modernity, redefinition, genre, nature, search, the canon of current beauty, of thought and imagination, or its transformation. The construction of a concept that reflects exterior beauty as a consequence of its expressive content. By merging the objectual values of some with the content of others, I select the expressive material that best communicates it. I remake the colors and shapes, expressing them as contrasts, ambiguously. I mix fabrics, colors, and textile process. In other words, the selection of these things isn't so much the material of inspiration for developing the design. Instead, they are entirely the result of the selection of the best expressive material in order to communicate the concept. I therefore move away in a dangerous way from trends in shapes and marked color schemes so that I can create an honest and individual design.

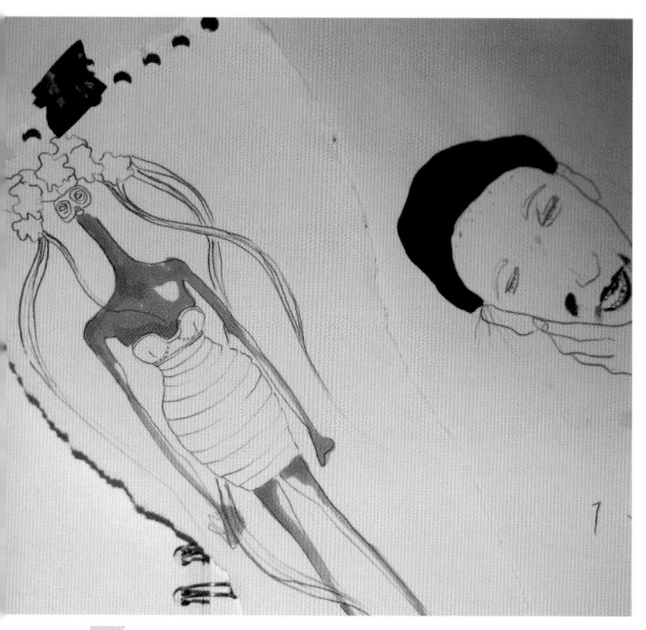

CREATION

The most important part of the design is the generation of a concept, the fusion that is the result of the research and of the discourse that the concept will support for its creation, in this case the dematerialization of the being. The concept is based on sound and other multidisciplinary materials, the generation of shapes, stories, colors, textures, etc. It's important that the result not only has weight and be aesthetically appealing. It should be the natural result of the actual expression of the design. What is important is to construct it as something that communicates, something that is produced for me in a creative moment. Here I've designed pieces that will work with this language. The images show some sketches reflecting much more than the actual garments. I like them to transmit my intention, as if they were illustrations. First I've designed a sleeveless T-shirt with braided strips in the same fabric that will sit around from the shoulder and will have tresses of hair hanging from them. The second choice is a floral print pencil skirt with a top. The lines are simple because the details have to be the focus of attention on this occasion so that the essence of the collection – the human being – comes through at first sight.

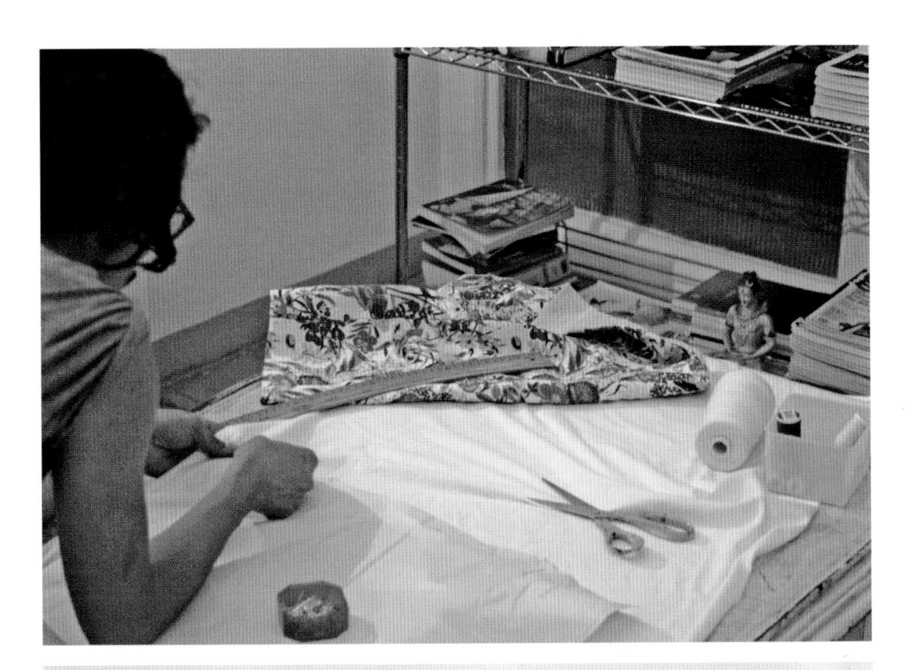

LOOK

The result reflects the dematerialization of the being by means of two options. The images show part of the disappearing, dematerialized body. The hair, hidden under stockings covering the models' heads, appears represented on the clothes, alluding to the same concept. The look on the right comprises two pieces, a high-cut floral tube skirt and a black top with volume on the sleeves and applications. The headpiece made of flowers is a strong reference to traditional Mexican costumes. On the left, the model is wearing a navy blue T-shirt with straps made from the same material on the shoulders and black shorts – an original outfit for boys with personality.

SIMON EKRELIUS

www.simonekrelius.com

Simon Ekrelius grew up in Stockholm, where he studied fashion design, art history, and illustration. He graduated from Stockholm's Tillskärar Akademi with a collection that was voted one of the best at the Swedish Sportswear International Fashion Awards (SIFA) of that year. He founded his own ready-to-wear label in 2006 after several years of making haute couture for advertising projects, private clients, and companies like BMG, British American Tobacco, and Wrigley's. Simon's fascination for modern and postmodern architecture has had a great influence on his collections. His pieces feature the use of strong prints, in contrast with delicate fabrics, asymmetric cuts, and a touch of ironic humor. His ready-to-wear line was presented for the first time in 2008 at Paris Fashion Week, and since that time it has been presented during London Fashion Week at the famous independent On|Off show. Some of Simon Ekrelius' designs were selected to form a part of the Fashion Cares event for HIV/AIDS awareness, sponsored by MAC Cosmetics. The Ekrelius label is a favorite with such celebrities as Alison Goldfrapp, Lady Gaga, Love Inc., The Plastiscines, Jessie J, and London's Fashion Stylist of the Year for 2009, Grace Woodward.

MY IT

My *It girl* in mind is independent, always on her own when it comes to style and look. She is not a follower. She is a girl aiming to set the trail and leading you to new ideas. She understands the future and the past. She is *It*.

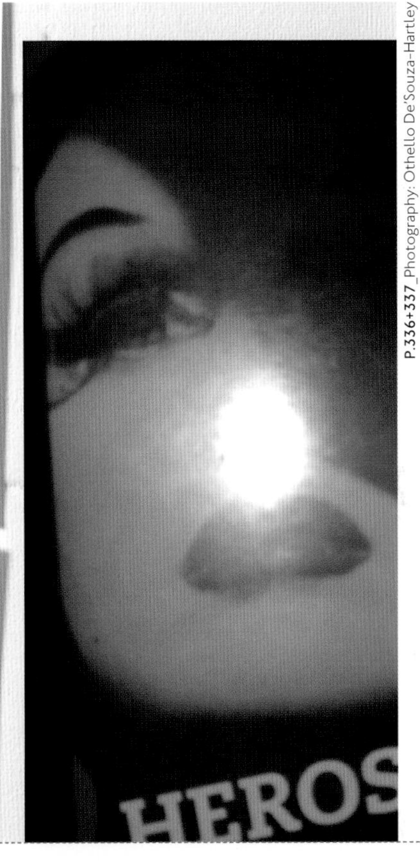

P.336+337_Photography: Othello De'Souza-Hartley

INSPIRATION

This jumpsuit is part of the fall/winter 2010/11 collection, inspired by Le Corbusier's Philips Pavilion at the 1958 World Fair in Brussels, of which I made use of the shape and attitude. It led me upwards and reminded me about the universe. I felt intrigued by the early way of looking at space. My *It girl* is a part of the whole story with early technology. The cover image of the film *Herostratus* became the inspiration for the attitude. The color palette included light silver, dark silver, gunpowder black, and bold black.

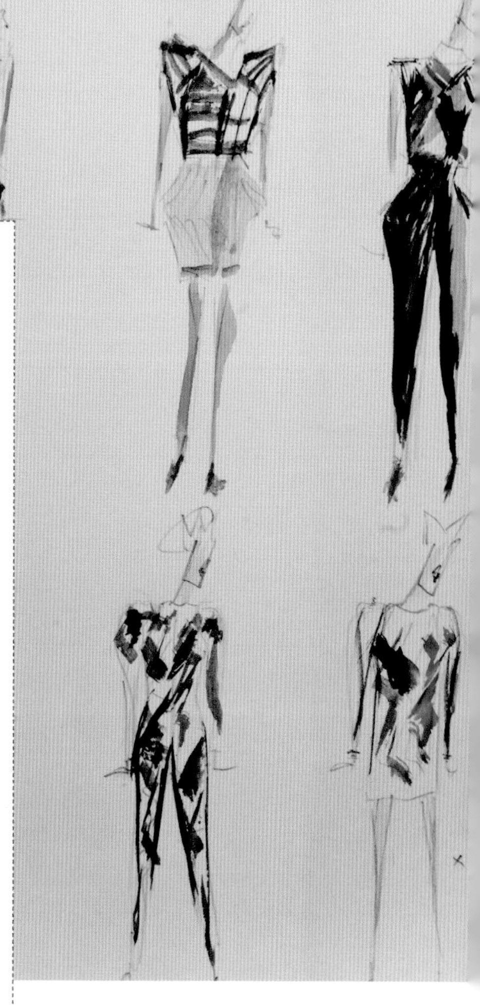

CREATION

The most important part of the process is my thinking period, which can start at any moment and goes on until the moment I'm about to start working on the new collection. It begins with a small thought and then I build ideas around it until the concept is firm enough to start the drawing process. I then lock myself alone in my studio, and I usually need one and half months to complete the collection. My work is based on my inspiration, so most important is my way of finding the best technical solution to express the feelings of the story. The fabrics come when I decide the color palette. I have a tendency to do too many toiles before I cut in the real material, but the precision and balance has to be right. Regarding this jumpsuit, I chose to use silk jersey to achieve a sort of slinky effect, while not being too tight. I wanted there to be just the right distance from skin to material, with obviously placed shoulder pads. The print and the cut reflect my inspiration completely: the speed in space, the energy, and the feeling of being before something unknown.

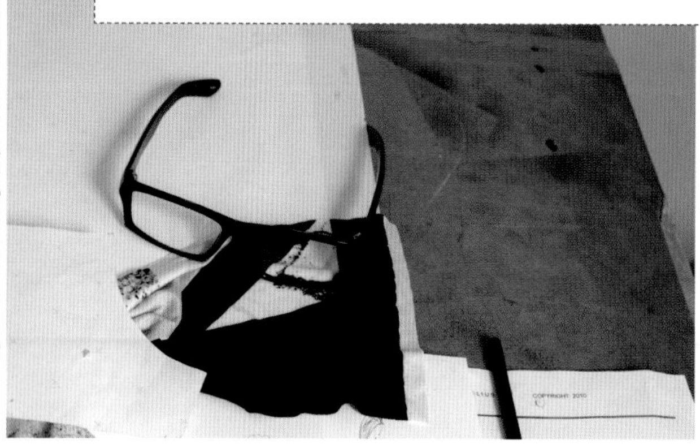

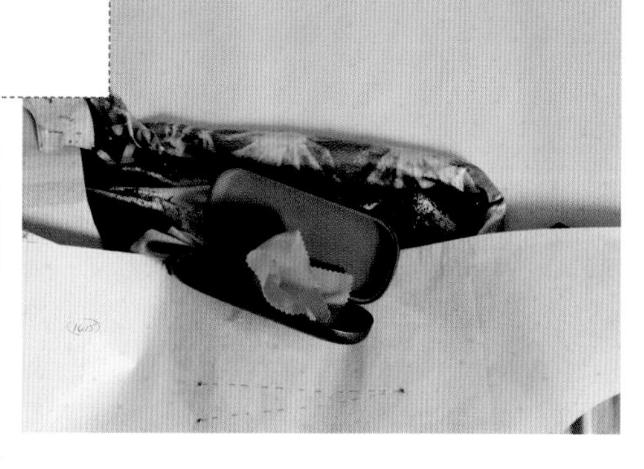

Pages 338+339 Photography: Othello De'Souza-Hartley

Was Jesus
Heterosexual?
2006
WHITE CUBE LONDON

Page 340 Photography: Othello De'Souza-Hartley. **Page 341** Photography: Jenni Porkka. Styling: Sasha Rainbow. Make-up: Afton R

LOOK

Simon Ekrelius loves the "over the top" sense of style. It is a big part of his way of looking at fashion. His *It girl* really knows how to style herself with his prints and the jumpsuit. She is well aware of her own look and she is the one who takes center stage. This is a piece that can be layered or worn on its own. It can be mixed with other prints or be kept with plain colored pieces.

Photography: Arjan Mak

SJAAK HULLEKES

sjaakhullekes.blogspot.com

Menswear designer Sjaak Hullekes was born in the little Dutch town of Zierikzee in 1981. He moved to Arnhem to study fashion design at the ArtEZ Institute of the Arts. Hullekes graduated in 2005, during the first Arnhem Fashion Biennale, from the school that was renowned for previously having produced such high profile designers as Alexander van Slobbe, Lucas Ossendrijver (Lanvin), and Viktor & Rolf. After graduating, he founded his company, Arnheim Fashion, together with his partner and former classmate Sebastiaan Kramer. Starting in January 2006, both worked independently for several fashion companies as they tried to gain a foothold in the sector. A year after setting up Arnheim Fashion, Sjaak Hullekes presented his eponymous menswear label at Amsterdam Fashion Week. Hullekes is the company's creative director and designer while Kramer is in charge of the business, sales, and PR side. In 2008 they presented themselves to the international market by showing their collection at the Paris and Milan Menswear Fashion Weeks. The quality of their designs has led to acknowledgements, such as the Mercedes Benz Dutch Fashion Award, which they received in November 2009.

MY IT

He is a dandyish yet sensible man, who takes the time to escape from daily cares and isn't afraid to romanticize his life. He is a hard-working man, and finds his peace by appreciating refined workmanship in everything he sees: art, architecture, fashion, and other gadgets. He lives in a metropolitan city, but knows there is a world beyond, a world he remembers from his childhood, which makes him a fragile gentleman who enjoys life.

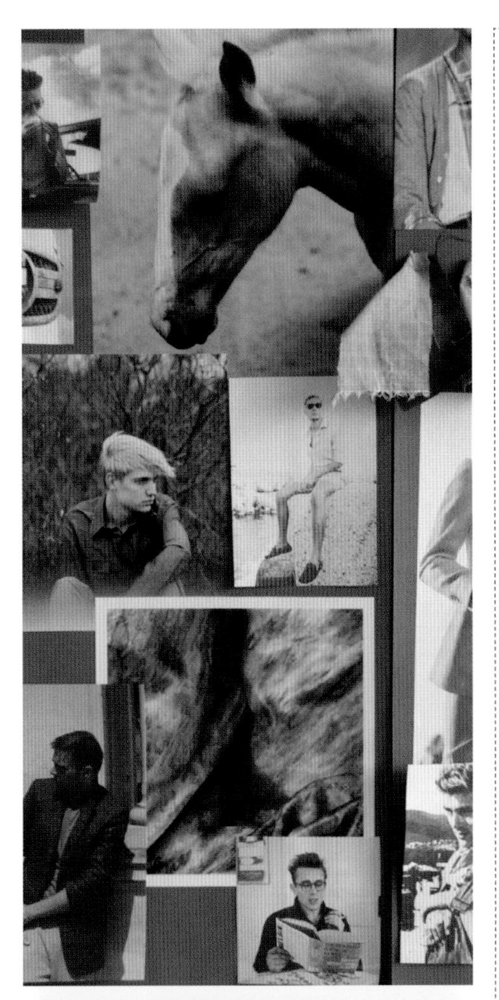

INSPIRATION

Nostalgia for a warm aesthetic, for handmade exclusiveness and sophisticated balance. Think 1970s automobiles, haystacks, forests, the Riviera of days gone by, antiques, Bauhaus, and so on. The fabrics used for the outfit are for a summer wardrobe. The pants, shirt and shawl have very fine yarn dyed stripes or checks. As I like to play with the fragility of a man, I often use transparent fabrics, like I did for my *It boy* too. Since this *It boy* feels confident with himself, he likes to wear more outspoken fabrics, such as the heavy mesh I used for his jacket. In combination with the mesh I choose to use a fine linen/cotton fabric in a contrasting color. All the fabrics I used are from a high-quality cotton or linen. Natural colors are a continue base in my collections. The natural colors used in this outfit will underline the character of the *It boy* even more, and make his outfit wearable for every occasion. Because of the use of cottons and linens, the colors automatically turn out to be duller, which brings a nostalgic feeling to the clothes and, at the same time, remind him of the country-life he used to live in the past.

CREATION

The most important thing for me before I start designing is to know what fabrics I will be using. By touching the fabrics I get inspired in creating garments, and I start sketching and drawing. In this case I draw the total look to get a feeling of what it is going to look like. The shirt for him is a bit oversized. Sensibility has been given to the shirt by the blind placket and the thin-striped cotton. The country-life comes back in the refined but slightly bigger chest pocket. The straight hem, the hand-stitched collar and cuffs, and my version of an "American" cuff-placket make this shirt not just an ordinary oversized shirt. The trousers have pick stitching made by hand at the fly and pockets, the inside of the pants' waistband has got box pleats, and all the pockets are taped. For trousers, a good fit in combination with good (inside) detailing is a must and will remind one of the 1970s. In combination with the heavy knitted cotton mesh the look of this jacket will become new. The mesh is combined with a brown fabric to give the jacket more "body," and to accentuate its transparency. To finish the jacket, it is taped on the inside with a brown cotton tape that matches the placket, cuffs, pocket flaps and collar. A small shawl adds the final touch to the outfit, because my *It boy* should not go out without a shawl. Then the designs are directly translated into patterns, and the fabrics are cut by the interns (together with me). While the seamstresses are making the items ready, I still like to have control of how things should be sewed, as I often come up with new ideas during the sewing process. I continuously fit the items on a tailor bust to see if everything is going as I would like it to be.

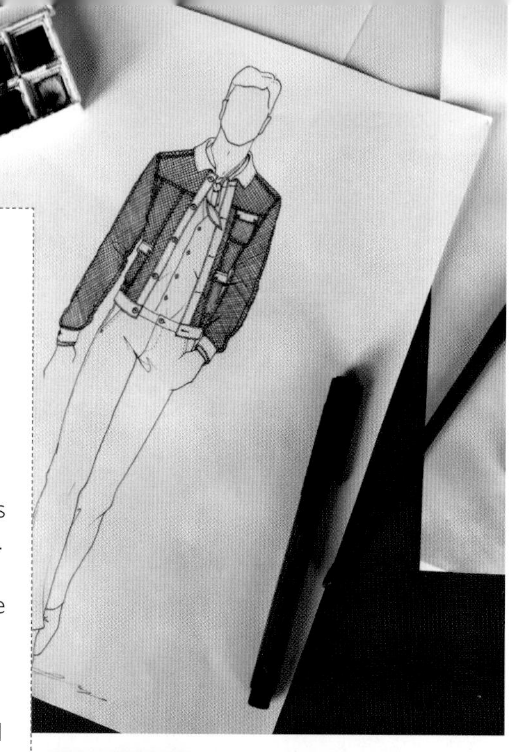

LOOK

The final look has got the sensibility of what Sjaak Hullekes is about, represented in an outfit consisting of three items and a small shawl. The model, Sander, is a perfect example of a Sjaak Hullekes *It boy*. He is a kind, fresh and gentle person, but masculine and self-aware at the same time. He is able to wear this outfit the way a dandy should wear it.

TARO HORIUCHI

www.tarohoriuchi.com

The Japanese designer Taro Horiuchi was born in Tokyo in 1982. The son of antique dealers, he spent his childhood surrounded by works of art from different periods: antique, modern, and contemporary. He studied at Kingston University in the UK, and later graduated with a fashion design degree from the Royal Academy of Fine Arts in Antwerp at the top of his class. He worked as an assistant to Raf Simons between 2004 and 2007, before doing an internship at the Nina Ricci fashion house. He has shown his collections in cities such as Paris and Tokyo, and in Italy. Taro Horiuchi created a magnificent collection for Diesel after having participated in the 2007 Diesel Award, which he won. In 2009 he founded his own label, characterized by the influence of art and architecture, and of nature, a major source of his inspiration. Horiuchi defines his designs as new expressions of beauty, and they are remarkable for their simple, elegant, and enveloping lines. The designer aspires to produce not only fashion in the future, but also everyday objects.

MY IT

I create for both males and females. However, I prefer to incorporate male details in my creations, enabling both men and women to wear the clothes if the size is suitable. They are people who are living calm and rich lives of minimalism. They can find even the simplest aspect of beauty in something in their daily lives. They are people who don't like to stand out, but have clear thoughts about art, construction and society as well as the ability to judge beauty and tenderness. At the same time, with their flexible and intelligent minds, they have no fear of accepting something new.

INSPIRATION

I have been deeply inspired by artistic works from both ancient eras – I grew up in artistic surroundings – through to futuristic things. Additionally, I have been affected by artistic works and structures that reflect a certain time period as well as by the social situation. My goal is to digest these things in order to be able to express them in my own way through my choice of fabric, product silhouette, jewelry and installation. Based on my concepts, all is designed to express beauty. I choose any necessary material, including the fabric. I try to express people's spirits and lifestyles through the filter of fashion. I aim to express "rich minimalism," a mixture of organic and inorganic texture and its balance. I have been inspired to design these ideas by artists such as Anish Kapoor and Isamu Noguchi, as well as the architect Peter Zumtor.

CREATION

When I design a collection, I first design the world that I believe to be the most beautiful. Then, I imagine the people in the world: their characters, lives and backgrounds as well as their favorite textures. These steps are very important for me to design my collections. When I create a product, I consider not only the percentage of each material to be used for making the desired fabric, but also the kind and the size of paper to be used for producing the brochures, for instance, as I believe that each item, no matter how slight the difference in feature or form, is important to create a beautiful product. Many products are sewn in a factory in Japan using beautiful silk and wool from Japan. For the fall/winter collection, under the theme of void, I collaborated with the artist Hisham Akira Bharoocha, who works in New York. I printed his photos on the lining and shirts. I thought that utilizing sensitive colors on black would highlight the contrast and would have a strong effect on the products. I have organically incorporated geometric lines, which express birds and a deer antler in the cut of the jackets, blousons and other items. I have also placed invisible pockets in the lines of the clothes.

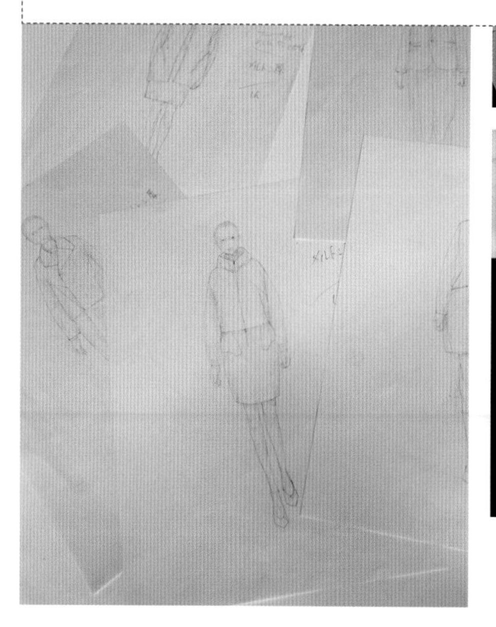

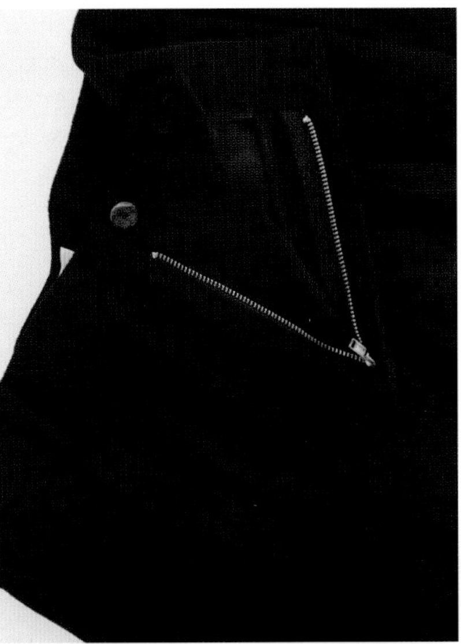

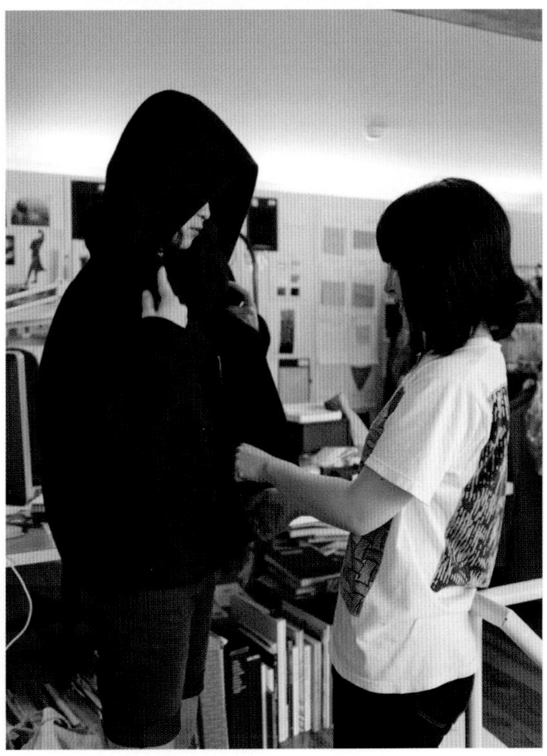

LOOK

The result is an outfit made up of two austere, minimalist pieces with a sculpted feel provided by Melton, a fabric the designer Taro Horiuchi had wanted to use for some time. It also features subtle padding in parts to give volume and to soften the strong image conveyed by black clothes. Sunglasses, black shoes, and a gold bracelet complete the look of this sophisticated, feminine, and cosmopolitan girl.

THE INDIVIDUALIST(S)

www.luiseandfranck.com

Luise was born in 1983 in Halle, Germany, to a family that instilled in her an interest in the arts and culture. She moved to Paris at the age of nineteen, where she first studied economics and, later, men's tailoring at ESMOD. Franck was born in Paris in 1979 and soon developed a good feel for aesthetics. After graduating from a leading French business school, he worked as a sales manager at the Franck & Fils department store, but his passion for design led him to study at ESMOD. He worked as a designer and patternmaker for Bill Tornade and Eymèle Burgaud, and, later with Luise at the Parisian 0044 label. Working together with the same outlook on fashion was the driving force that led them to create their first collection in 2007 under the label Luise&Franck. Their work was rewarded with international fashion awards, such as those given in France at the Dinard Festival for Young Designers in 2008, or in Japan by the Shinmai Creator's Project in 2009. The latter enabled them to show their 2010 fall/winter collection, Crying Light, at Tokyo Fashion Week. Their collections are now presented under the name of The Individualist(s), a label by Luise&Franck. It is the same label but with a new name, a reflection of the dual nature of their work.

MY IT

"Au commencement était l'emotion…" (Louis-Ferdinand Céline). Feelings and emotions are the source of everything we do. Therefore, it is obvious that our *It* is the incarnation of this idea: he is someone emotional and expressive who wants to share his feelings through the way he dresses. *It* is the image of a modern, strong and open-minded man who is not afraid anymore to show his fears and vulnerability, contrasting with the traditional image of men. Emotions are also the source of creativity. Our *It* is a dreamer, nostalgic and poetic, with lots of fantasy and imagination. He has fine, elegant taste, and appreciates and understands the beauty and aesthetic.

INSPIRATION

Inspiration is something almost unexplainable for us, all the more as we would say – using the words of French poet Charles Baudelaire – that its origin could be "anywhere out of the world." Our inspiration is often more conceptual than pragmatic and comes from the emotion that we share everyday together: while having a walk in the streets of Tokyo (a city that we love), watching a movie by David Lynch, listening to Antony Hegarty's music, or being hypnotized by one of Ikko Narahara's photographs. Our universe has been nourished from the beginning by all these references, always sharing a certain sense of poetry, nostalgia and idealism. That is probably what we are looking for in life itself and what we try to express in our garments. Out of this creative mood, our free interpretation leads us to design contemporary looks, both fitted and loose, oversized and tight garments, sometimes fun, other times serious, in order to express a beautiful duality just like human nature itself. The search and the work of the fabrics is really a central element of our creative process. At the moment, our studio is full of Japanese fabrics, as Japan is for us at the moment the leader in the combination of natural fibers and innovative finishes. Our color palette is sober, vanished and intimate, from deep blacks to lights grays and pastel beiges. It reminds us the hue of an old photograph, vanished by the time, presenting contrasted and irregular tones, and sometimes the memory of a color that once has been there and that has not completely disappeared yet.

CREATION

It is important we do research on the volume balance and general details for our future outfits leading to the creation of complementary elements. Tailored jackets are revisited to become modern and personal by the attention given to the collars and pockets or by reinventing traditional shapes. Coats are very structured or extremely loose while pants remain tight and fitted, sometimes low-crotched and with vertical cut-outs lengthening the silhouette. The range of pants is completed in an opposite way by very wide pieces with large superimposed pleats reminding one of the Charlie Chaplin style associated with thinner tops, therefore reversing the balance. Other important essentials are the asymmetrical shapes on vests or knitted tops, the contrast of colors on unique pieces, and the superposition of layers. The knitted tops are very long, sometimes presenting pleats on the upper part of the back and cutouts that could be reinforced by the use of transparency. A significant detail on these sketches is the use of square-patched pockets on pants, coats or trousers. As well as very high collars for jackets and coats, creating a protective hull. And the "fringe factor" of accessories such as scarves or belts finally brings some kind of a grunge touch to the outfits.

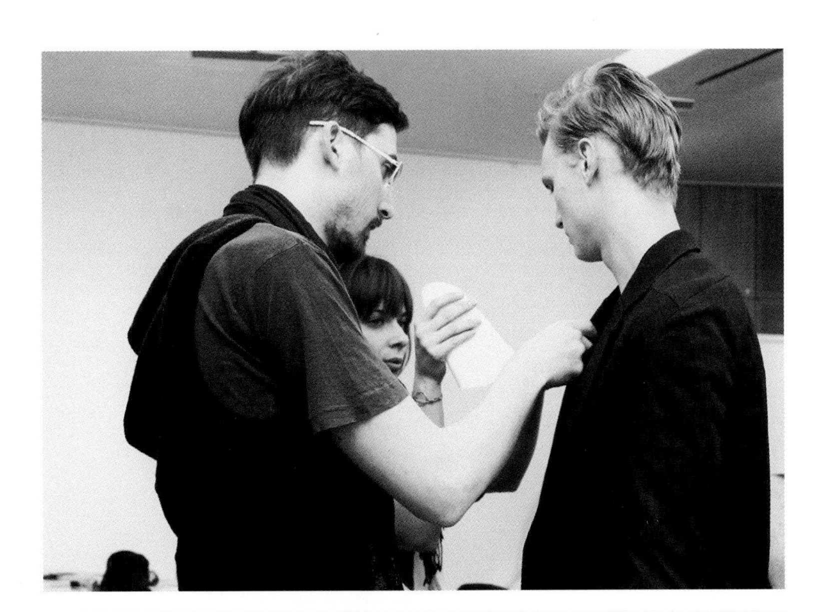

LOOK

The silhouette, reflecting a sophisticated simplicity, is made out of five garments. The ample coat, made out of a black silk-wool mixed fabric illustrates a smooth fluidity, with its large and deep revisited tailored collar in the front. Under the coat appears a dark gray, woolen, soft-knitted shirt, with a draped upper back curved towards the front. The oversized scarf adds an underground and trashy touch to this outfit; anyhow, the general aspect doesn't lose its elegance. This handmade piece is made out of ripped stripes laced up in a geometrical order. The upper part of the look is now contrasted by the structure and rigor of the slim-fitted pants made out of a rough heavy cotton-linen fabric. With their vertical cutouts, the trousers refine the silhouette and assure a strong rigorous shape, also reinforced by the military vintage boots, which bring back a lost but still memorable discipline into this apparent chaos. The subtle mix of those elements makes the look at the same time fragile, poetical and dramatic.

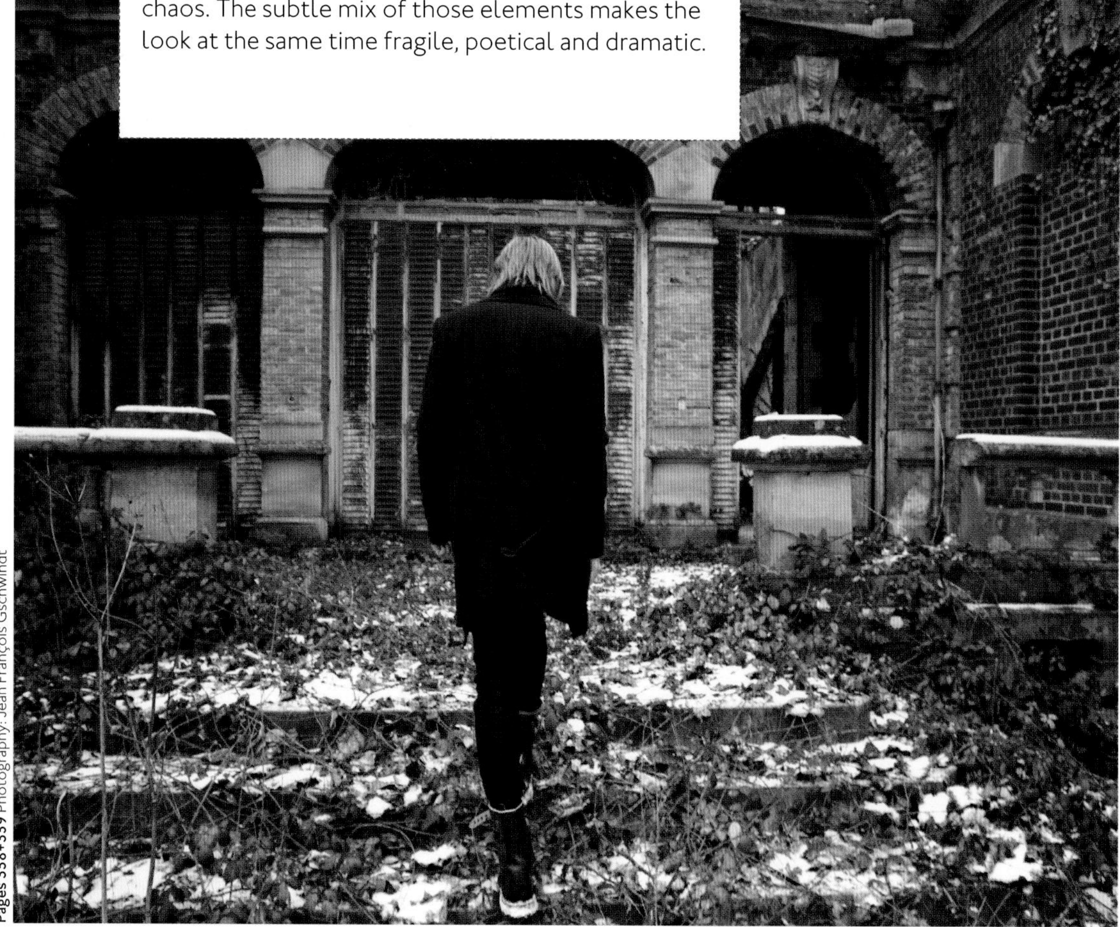

Pages 358+359 Photography: Jean François Gschwindt

THOMAS ENGEL HART

www.thomasengelhart.com

Thomas Engel Hart is a rebel's collage of traditional and innovative patternmaking techniques, rock references, and sophistication. Born in Manhattan, he studied at the Fashion Institute of Technology and played a major part in the New York arts scene of the 1990s. He moved to Paris in 1997 to broaden his knowledge at the Studio Berçot Fashion Design School. In 2001 he set up his eponymous menswear label, and his first collection soon graced the pages of magazines like *Dazed & Confused*, *Another Magazine*, *V*, and *Self Service*, among others. A leading force in the menswear revolution, Thomas Engel Hart received the ANDAM Fashion Award in 2002. He worked hard during the three following years to consolidate his label while designing for Martine Sitbon at the same time. In 2005 he put his label on hold to focus on the relaunch of Thierry Mugler Homme as creative director, drawing a new generation to the brand. However, his longing for the creative satisfaction that only his personal collections could provide led him to relaunch TEH in 2008, once again to great critical acclaim.

MY IT

A creative, intelligent and cultured guy who's not afraid to take risks. He's cool and sexy, with a strong personality. He wants to say something about himself.

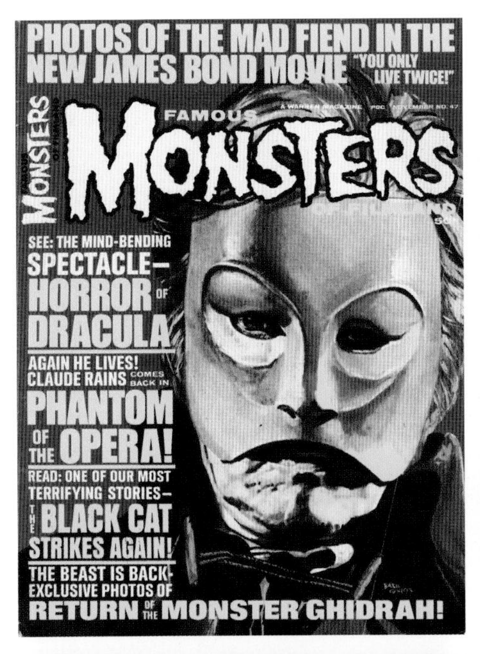

INSPIRATION

My fall/winter 2010 collection is about continuing a stylistic trip around the US. Last season focused on the costume-like punk scene found in L.A. This time it's about focusing on the early 1970s in New York, which was a mish mash of punk, as well as Victorian influences. Think about Joel-Peter Witkin, The New York Dolls dressed as Frankensteins, The Stiffs...
As far as the fabrics are concerned, we used denim, light Japanese cottons, heavy Teflon and moleskin cottons, wool and linen blends, wool and cashmere blends, stretch wool solids. The intense palette of blacks and grays, highlighted with reds yellows and blues, complements the moody personality of the Thomas Engel Hart man. With dark rich colors and bold striking prints, it's impossible not to pay attention when he enters the room.

CREATION

Our collage print, called Famous Monsters, alludes to the influences of the New York punk scene. Created by Thomas by cutting up old 1960s monster magazines, it was one of the real starting points of the collection. Meanwhile, the cuts are subtle, and oftentimes very odd, while remaining flattering and novel on the body.

VAMP
MIDNIGHT
DÉMONS.
LA FÊTE
AUX URNES
PHANTASME
THOMAS ENGEL HART
DE
nouveaux
dandies
TALK
THE
Mad
EERIE
REVENGE
OF
RETURN
FEAR
YOUR
MAKE-UP
THE
UNDEAD
MILITANT
Punks
les témoins
DISQUIETING
CELEBRATIONS
NEW
YORK
THE
FAN
THE
UNBELIEVABLE
gamut of gore
A
CIVIL
Anarchy
ON AIME
OU
ON N'AIME PAS
UNDEAD
ON THE
BRAIN
REVENGE
EERIE
Darkness
Prince
FANG
HORROR
MASK
THE CREATURE
CABINET
THOMAS ENGEL HART

LOOK

The final look typifies the Thomas Engel Hart man represented with the famous monsters print in a sharp angular and tailored fit. They paired the jacket with one of their finely tailored shirts and a bleached and destroyed Japanese denim jean to further anchor the look in the tattered elegance of Lower East Side New York circa 1972.

EERIE
HORROR
MASK
THE
FAN
THE
SAVAGE
MADNESS
MIDNIGHT

VICTORIO & LUCCHINO

www.victorioylucchino.com

At the end of the 70s in Seville, artist José Luis Medina del Corral, and José Víctor Rodríguez from Cordoba embarked on the Victorio & Lucchino project. Their idea was to make true their dream of a life where design ruled their work. Since their beginnings, six elements have defined their unmistakable and representative style: color, lace as the quintessential fabric, ornamentation marked by highly symbolic fringing, the ruffle, wedding gowns, and fusion with movement, which combine the craft traditions typical of southern Spain with contemporary design. Their prêt-à-porter designs for men and women are presented each season at Madrid Fashion Week, and they have shown their collections at fairs and fashion events in New York, Milan, Barcelona, Germany, and Japan, to name but a few. Their love of the arts has led them to collaborate on set designs for stage and screen productions, among others. The work of Vittorio & Lucchino has been acknowledged through dozens of awards, an example of which is the Gold Medal for Merit in Fine Arts, awarded by the Spanish Ministry of Culture in 2003.

MY IT

Her: a woman who appreciates technique and studied lines, contrasted with femininity and sensuality. Him: a restless, non-conforming, and elegant man who enjoys moments of comfort.

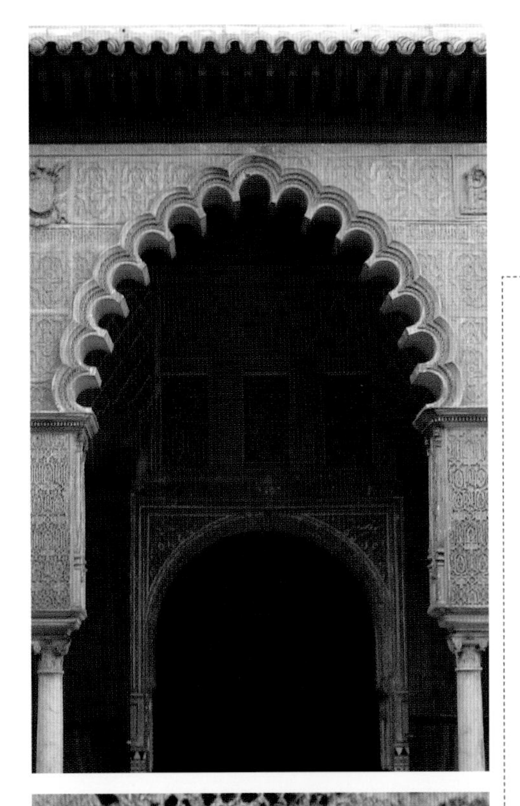

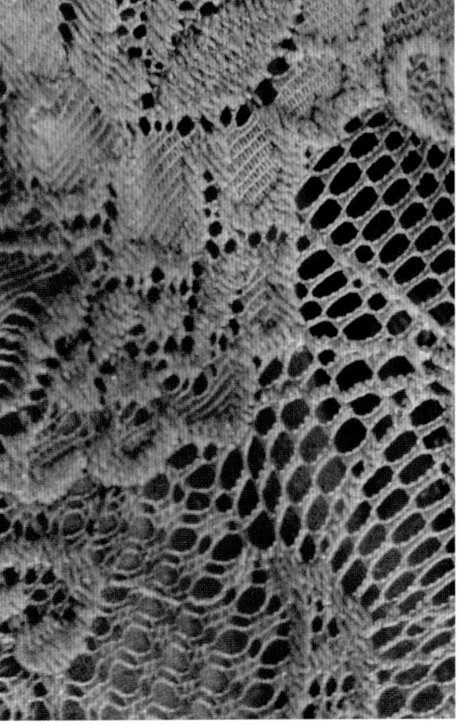

INSPIRATION

The spirit embodied in the collections represents the true soul of Andalusia, a cradle of co-existence between Arab, Christian, and Jewish cultures, which is the symbol of a genuine way of life. The forms, art, architecture, and character of Andalusia have always been present in our collections. We also think about subjects, feelings, and emotions to show what exists inside ourselves. We think of an ideal woman or man, and little by little we dress them with the look and philosophy we feel at the time. Here we show two looks for men and women from the fall/winter 2010/11 Conceptual collection. The inspiration comes from a body where creativity and materialization together play with a shape that is sometimes seductive and sometimes causes volumes and designs to arise and excite with their conceptual message. We envision women in subtle and restful colors, while for men we see darker neutral colors such as black, gray, and charcoal.

CREATION

Once the sketches have been completed, work begins with the fabrics and shapes. We do a lot of draping for women's pieces. We use a model whom we feel very comfortable with. With menswear, we tend to work more on the drawings. Women's dresses constantly feature draping and pleating as part of the volume. Small details, such as vanilla-colored ribbons, mark the waist and bust, creating an empire line and giving greater movement to the pleats that open from the bust to the feet. For men, elegant tailoring has become a hallmark of our collections, where impeccable lines join forces with the highest quality wool fabrics. The use of more casual fabrics and technical touches achieve a more urban and contemporary look.

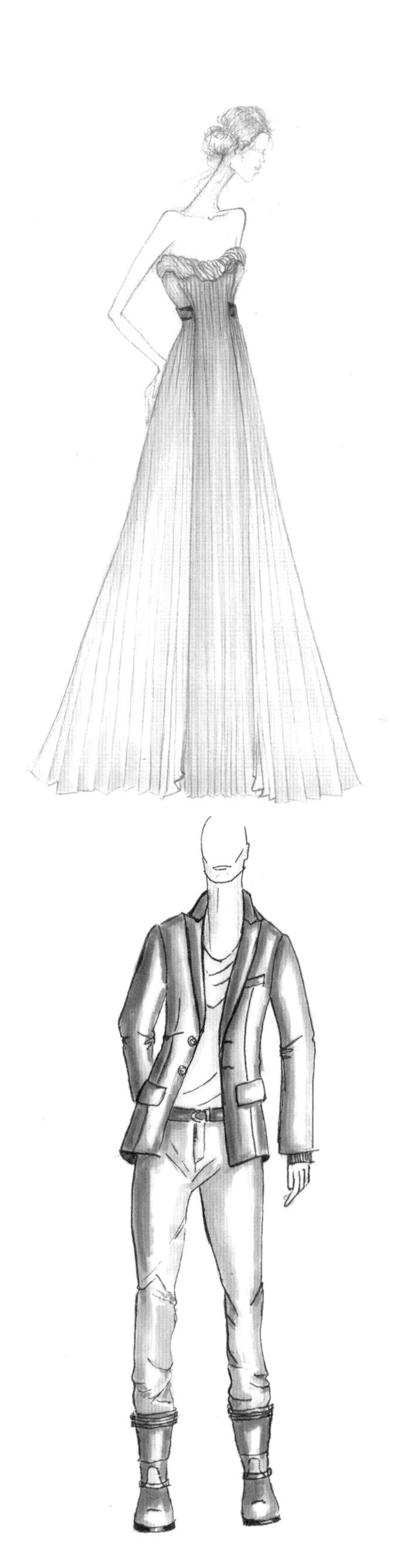

LOOK

These images show both looks, created with the mastery that typifies the Spanish designers Victorio & Lucchino. She wears a spectacular strapless empire-line gown in pastel pink silk, in which she appears to be dressed as a Greek goddess. The pleating and draping create a feeling of romantic lightness and elegance. The V-seam on the bust and the vanilla ribbons narrow the waist, stretching the figure to seem longer.

LOOK

The design for him consists of ribbed-knit tight-fitting pants in dark gray wool, a crew collar poplin shirt, a tailored vest in black velvet, and a charcoal gray velvet blazer. The look is completed with black military-style boots and matching woolen gloves.

YIORGOS ELEFTHERIADES

www.yiorgoseleftheriades.gr

A native of Greece, Yiorgos Eleftheriades has produced forty women's and twenty-two men's collections, which he has presented in different cities including Athens, Paris, London, Milan, Berlin, and Barcelona. In addition, he was also the creative director for the Greek company Grecotel, creating the uniforms that are still being used there, and has been collaborating with some of his country's most important screen and stage directors and actors. His love for classic forms and the search for contemporary elegance are behind his desire to create an urban style incorporating very interesting alternative forms, references to tailoring, and experimental combinations of fabrics and textures. He loves to play with contrasts in materials, between matte and shiny, high tech and retro, masculine and feminine, and combining luxury with the utilitary. He has always been committed to the environment, which is why he has been using natural and ecological fabrics since his beginnings as a designer. In each collection he uses a palette of neutral colors, followed by a mixture of intense colors. The result is usually striking and somewhat unconventional. The main quality in his way of perceiving fashion is that is designs are timeless and glamorous but with a fresh focus that enables them to be worn from morning until night.

MY IT

She is Efi Lioli, who during almost two decades has been my alter ego and my *It girl*. She was fashion editor at *Elle* magazine and one of the most stylish women in our country.

Photography: Nikos Vardakastanis

INSPIRATION

My inspiration is an independent and strongly opinionated woman. She has surely drawn her own path. She is a multi-tasker, who transforms herself at will from a professional to a hedonist, but always with ease and a sense of comfort. The textiles are organza, muslin and gabardine, all silk. The color is black, because of its trans-seasonal use, during all year.

Pages 374+375 Photography: Nikos Vardakastanis

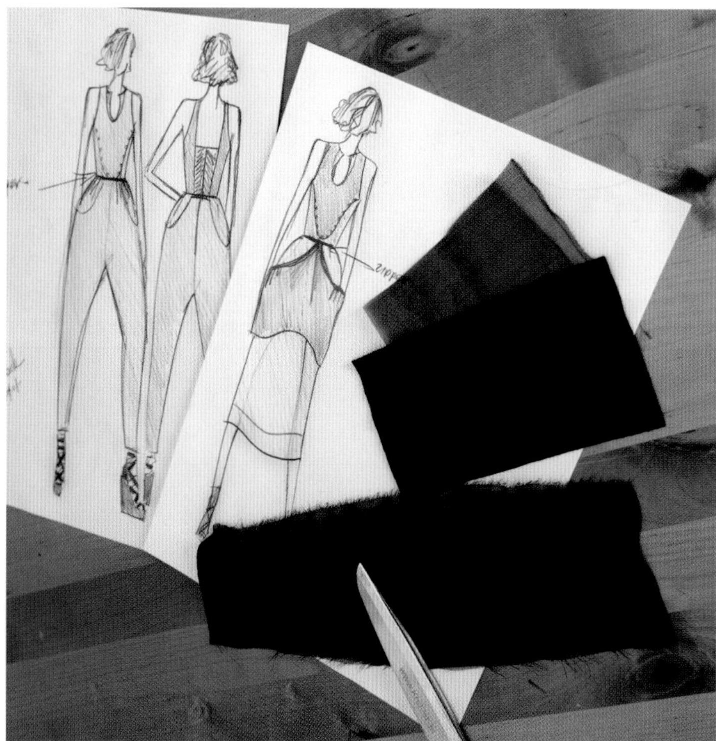

CREATION

When designing for Efi, first I offered her some suggestions I thought might match her personality perfectly. We then went over the idea together and looked at different alternatives until we came to a single idea that combined her style and personality with the label's identity. The outcome was a very versatile piece: a top with an invisible zipper at the waist, which can be used to join two different pieces (pants or skirt) to turn it into a dress or a jumpsuit. This outfit fits with the identity of the label and Efi's requirements, since she can use it from morning to night without having to change from daywear to eveningwear. The photos here show the complete process, including the final tryouts.

LOOK

Efi Lioli poses with the two alternative looks. The first option is the jumpsuit, combined with a frock coat, platform sandals, and a bracelet. In the second photo, the outfit becomes a dress, with subtle sheer inserts at the waist and the knees. This look is matched with elegant earrings and ankle-wrap platform sandals. Both looks represent an elegant and sophisticated woman who knows how to take advantage of her wardrobe, always well dressed for the time of day or night by playing with versatile pieces.

Pages 376+377 Photography: Nikos Vardakastanis

ZAZO & BRULL

www.zazobrull.com

Xavier Zazo and Clara Brull's work is characterized by their telling of stories through their collections. They believe that clothes are not only clothes, but also a means of expressing feelings, and that they have created an imaginary world through their personal experiences where they can depict a new leading character every season for either an already-existing story or one invented for the occasion. Since the label was created in 2003, they have presented their collections at local Spanish fashion events such as Pasarela Gaudí, 080 Barcelona Fashion, or the Madrid International Fashion Fair, and at such prestigious international trade shows as the International Fashion Fair in Tokyo or Rendez-Vous Femme in Paris. Their latest collections have attracted great interest owing to the strength of their inspiration. Titles such as Berenice, Diario de un Loco (Madman's Diary), La Novia Mutante (Mutant Girlfriend), and Heroínas Olvidadas (Forgotten Heroines) are suggestive enough for one to imagine there is no happy ending, only blood and broken hearts. Their distinguishing feature is their romantic silhouettes with dark nuances. Their most recent collection, Frágil, was presented at the Arts Santa Mònica Center in Barcelona, combining art and fashion by means of an installation.

MY IT

A sensitive, feminine, profound and elegant woman. She is romantic, beyond the clichéd melancholic states, infatuation or the wild daydreaming. It is a creative and innovative modern romantic, in which individuality, feelings, passion, idealism, love and liberty all reign to break established norms. A maverick woman who seeks to be independent in a dominating environment, without being pretentious or artificial. We found the sequence of four photos (opposite page) interesting, as we can only see her outline but subtly it tells us all we need to know about our *It girl*.

INSPIRATION

Each of our collections has a leading starlet, a heroine who helps us to express our inspiration. In the fall/winter 2008/09 collection Miss Serotonina was a woman who did not have the happiness hormone and on a daily basis she battled to overcome her constant mundane life. In the X-S09 collection, based on the novel *The Last Man* by Mary Shelley, she was the last survivor on earth. The look chosen for our *It* is from the Bushido spring/summer 2010 collection and is inspired by Samurai warriors. The colors are normally dark shades. Black prevails, and natural colors and gray tones are used frequently. On occasions red appears, as well as other colors, depending on the collection.

CREATION

The creative process is multifaceted. As this is a two-person job, the inspiration for the design comes from two different angles that gradually unify. Then we study the pattern of the garment to recreate the design as accurately as possible. In the case of the dress for our *It girl*, the most difficult parts are the embellishments. On the front part of the garment – from the neck to below the hip – we have added a lot of fringing with embedded metallic pieces. It is a long and painstaking process that we carry out by hand with precision so that the pieces are well attached and in the perfect place.

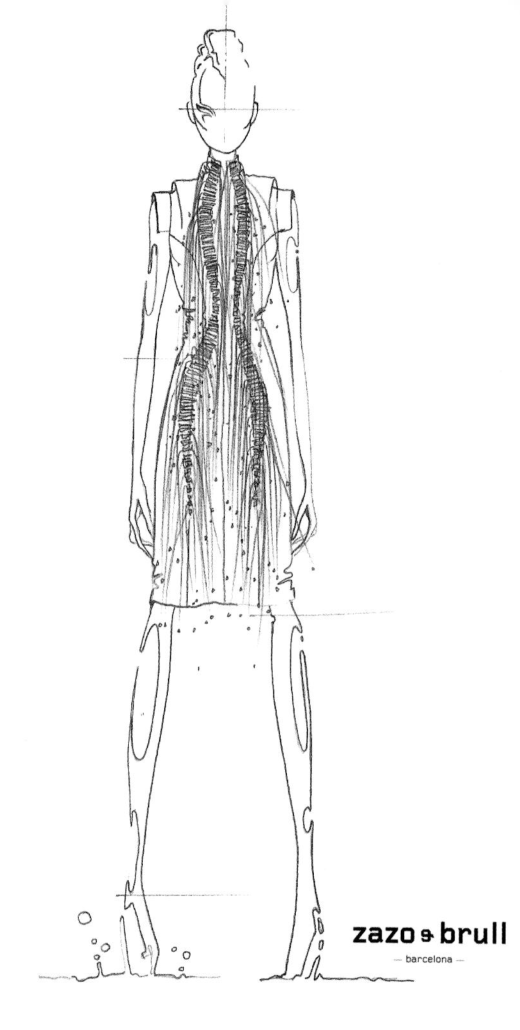

Page 383 Photography: Biel Sol

LOOK

The result is a black total look, with metallic embellishments that comprises of a fitted dress and bolero with the same spirit. It is an elegant look but with a hint of rebellion. The fringing helps to play with the flexibility of the dress and gives it a range of different interpretations. In the photo on the left, the *It girl* poses in an entertaining manner with the dress and the bolero. On the right, the dress as seen on the runway.

ACKNOWLEDGMENTS

I would like to thank each of the fashion designers who have taken part in this book for their special interest and assistance, and also their teams and the agencies representing them. This book would have been impossible without them.

My thanks also go to all of the people who have offered their views as fashion experts, El Delgado Buil, Iñaki Blanco, Anna María López López, Ramón Fano from *Neo2*, Fittings Division, Nelly Rodi, Pronovias, *Vogue*, CIFF, Freddy Gaviria, Mike Madrid, Jorge Herrera, and to our charming *It boy*, Pelayo Díaz.

To the team at **maomao** Publications, especially Anja Llorella (editorial coordinator), Emma Termes (art direction) and Esperanza Escudero (design and layout), for their special care with this book and for teaching me so much.

To my father Natalio, and to Rosa for supporting me and putting up with me; to my brother J. Pedro (the best) for listening to me when I talk about fashion; and to Blanca for taking care of him for me. To my friends for showing me every day that they are just that. To love for letting me work with a smile every day.

To Barcelona for making me welcome, to Córdoba that I miss so much. And, above all, to my mother Pilar for making me what I am. I dedicate this book to her memory.